W9-ACY-000

THE AESTHETICS OF ARCHITECTURE

PRINCETON ESSAYS ON THE ARTS

1. Guy Sircello, A NEW THEORY OF BEAUTY
2. Rab Hatfield, BOTTICELLI'S UFFIZI "ADORATION": *A Study in Pictorial Content*
3. Rensselaer W. Lee, NAMES ON TREES: *Ariosto Into Art*
4. Alfred Brendel, MUSICAL THOUGHTS AND AFTERTHOUGHTS
5. Robert Fagles, I, VINCENT: *Poems from the Pictures of Van Gogh*
6. Jonathan Brown, IMAGES AND IDEAS IN SEVENTEENTH-CENTURY SPANISH PAINTING
7. Walter Cahn, MASTERPIECES: *Chapters on the History of an Idea*
8. Roger Scruton, THE AESTHETICS OF ARCHITECTURE

THE AESTHETICS OF ARCHITECTURE

ROGER SCRUTON

PRINCETON UNIVERSITY PRESS
PRINCETON, NEW JERSEY

Published by Princeton University Press, Princeton, New Jersey

Library of Congress Cataloging in Publication Data will be found on the last printed page of this book

Clothbound editions of Princeton University Press books are printed on acid-free paper, and binding materials are chosen for strength and durability

Printed in the United States of America by Princeton University Press, Princeton, New Jersey

Die Menschheit hat ihre Würde verloren, aber die Kunst hat sie gerettet und aufbewahrt in bedeutenden Steinen.

SCHILLER

(Mankind has lost its dignity, but Art has recovered it and conserved it in significant stones.)

CONTENTS

Acknowledgments *viii*
Preface *ix*
1 Introduction: The problem of architecture 1

PART I

2 Architecture and design 23
3 Has architecture an essence? 37
4 Experiencing architecture 71
5 Judging architecture 104

PART II

6 Freud, Marx and meaning 137
7 The language of architecture 158
8 Expression and abstraction 179
9 The sense of detail 206
10 Conclusion: Architecture and morality 237

PART III

Summary 259
Notes 265
Bibliography 291
Index of names 293
Index of subjects 298

ACKNOWLEDGMENTS

THE AUTHOR and publisher would like to thank the following for permission to reproduce copyright photographs and drawings:

Anthony Jones: 37, 38, 39, 51, 54, 88; Bernard Brown: 9, 13, 14, 15, 22, 29, 30, 31, 33, 36, 40, 47, 61, 64, 71, 73, 76, 77, 78, 79, 80, 81, 87, 90; Bibliotheque Nationale: 4; Boudot Lamotte: 2; Cinegate: 67; Clare Jarrett: 17, 18, 19, 28, 63a and b, 82; Country Life: 59; Courtauld Institute of Art: 58, 66; Deutsche Fotothek Dresden: 52; The Master and Fellows of Downing College: 74; Instituto Editoriale Electa: 41, 42, 43; Instituto Italiano Edizioni Atlas: 68; Jean Roubier: 10; John Procopé: 53; The Mansell Collection: 5, 12, 23, 25, 26, 28, 32, 33, 34, 35, 55, 56, 65, 69, 70, 83; Marty Cobin: 85; MAS: 1, 72; National Gallery of Art, Washington: 60; National Monuments Record: 6; Pepi Mensio: 20; Royal Institute of British Architects: 75; Studio Chevojon: 16; University College London: 11, 24; V. K. Rothschild: 46.

PREFACE

WHAT IS architecture? Why is it important? How should one build? These questions have never been more urgent, but architects and theorists now seem hesitant to answer them in a serious and systematic way. As Hans Sedlmayr wrote, in *Verlust der Mitte*, 'the new type of architect has become hopelessly uncertain of himself. He glances over his shoulder at the engineer, he fancies himself in the role of inventor and even in that of a reformer of men's lives, but he has forgotten to be an architect.' In the present work I approach the subject *ab initio*, making as few assumptions as I can. Although the book is in the first place an application of philosophical aesthetics, the confusion of architectural theory seems to me so great that no philosophical enquiry can refrain from engaging with its arguments. I hope to show that the urgent questions which confront the architect are indeed philosophical questions, and that they can be clarified, and sometimes even solved.

The book has both a theme and a thesis. It is designed, first, to introduce the subject of aesthetics to those who have an interest in architecture, second, to explain the nature and value of aesthetic taste. In taking examples exclusively from architectural thought and practice, I hope to cast light both on the nature of architecture and on the nature of aesthetic judgement. The argument will benefit, not only because aesthetics stands in need of a systematic application, but also because the thesis that I wish to present – a thesis which relates aesthetic judgement to practical understanding – is most vividly illustrated by those enterprises, known collectively as the 'useful' and the 'decorative' arts, of which architecture is the most important.

The thesis is more elusive than the theme, and will require me to steer a middle course between two separate disciplines in a way that might at times prove offensive to the practitioners of both. My thoughts may prove insufficiently abstract for the philosopher, and insufficiently concrete for the arrchitectural critic and historian. But my hope is that the kind of systematic application of aesthetics which I envisage will be of value, not only as a clarification of critical theories, and not only as an intelligible introduction to aesthetics, but also as a valid form of philosophical speculation. In order that the theme should be as clear as possible I have attempted to provide illustrations wherever these are appropriate. Architectural critics and historians may disagree with some of my interpretations, but this should not matter. My purpose throughout is to illustrate the application of certain concepts to the discussion of buildings, and to derive an overall conception of the nature and value of critical argument. It would take me too far afield to pursue any particular interpretation to its conclusion.

Again in the interests of clarity, I have removed from the text almost all reference to the technicalities of modern philosophy. This is not because these are irrelevant to aesthetics, but because it has seemed to me important to try to convey a sense of the subject without their aid. However, specific arguments are elaborated or referred to in footnotes, and the interested reader is provided with material in the bibliography to pursue the philosophical discussions that occur in the text. Despite all these trappings of scholarship, however, I hope that the book can be read with pleasure by someone who prefers to ignore them. The footnotes in particular contain nothing that is essential to the continuity of the argument, and I have therefore placed them all at the end of the book so as not to discourage those for whom footnotes are a waste of time. I have also provided a summary, and those unused to the circumspect style of modern philosophy may prefer to begin with this; but I hope that the argument of the initial chapters moves gently enough to enable them to dispense with it.

I have benefited greatly from discussions with friends and colleagues, and previous drafts of this work have been improved and criticized by many of them. I owe a great debt to all of the following: Miss Ruby Meager, Dr John Casey, Miss Moira Archer, Dr David Watkin, Miss Victoria Rothschild, and the late Dr David Pole. Many of the illustrations were provided by friends, and I am particularly grateful to Mr Bernard Brown and Mr Anthony Jones for their photographic work. I am also indebted to Maria-Teresa Brown for her enthusiastic encouragement, to Howard Burns for his original scepticism, and to Sir Denys Lasdun for drawing my attention to matters that I had preferred to ignore.

THE AESTHETICS OF ARCHITECTURE

1
INTRODUCTION: THE PROBLEM OF ARCHITECTURE

THE SUBJECT of aesthetics is as old as philosophy; nevertheless, it takes its modern form from Kant, who was the first philosopher to suggest that the sense of beauty is a distinct and autonomous employment of the human mind comparable to moral and scientific understanding. Kant's division of the mental faculties, into theoretical, practical and aesthetic (or, as he put it, understanding, practical reason and judgement[1]), provided the starting point for all later investigations, and gave to aesthetics the central position in philosophy which it occupied through much of the nineteenth century and would, but for established scholasticism, occupy even now. What I say in this book will show the influence of Kant; but I shall try to demonstrate that the division between practical reason and aesthetic understanding is in fact untenable, and that until the relation between the two is re-established they must both remain impoverished.

The first task of aesthetics must lie in the correct understanding of certain mental capacities – capacities for experience and judgement. I shall therefore be discussing questions in the philosophy of mind, and my concern will be to understand the nature and value of our interest in architecture. Now it is necessary to distinguish the philosophy of mind from empirical psychology. A philosopher's prime concern is with the *nature* of our interest in architecture, and if he sometimes talks, as a psychologist would, of its causes, then this is only because he thinks of these causes as casting light on the aesthetic experience.

For the philosopher the question is not what causes us to prefer Lincoln cathedral to the minster of York, but rather, what *is* aesthetic preference – what *is* it, to prefer one cathedral to another? And what significance does such a preference have for us? The philosopher wishes to describe aesthetic experience in its most general terms, so as to discover its precise location in the human mind, its relation, for example, to sensation, to emotion and to judgement. This task he conceives of as a necessary preliminary to any discussion of the significance and value of art. Suppose, for example, that it were shown that people prefer smooth stone to rough, straight lines to squiggles, symmetrical to irregular forms. Those are psychological observations of no relevance to aesthetics. Nor are the explanations of those preferences relevant to our enquiry. It does not matter that the preference for smooth against rough can be 'explained' in terms of Kleinian psychology,[2] or the preference for symmetrical forms in terms of the organization of the optic nerves. Those facts are, no doubt, of some interest in themselves; but they presuppose, for their proper understanding, the kind of study that I shall be engaged in. If I refer to psychological hypotheses in the ensuing chapters, it will therefore only be because some of them have been thought to be specially relevant to the nature and validity of aesthetic argument.

But now, it will be said, psychology too is concerned with the nature of experience, and not only with its causes. How then is it to be distinguished from the 'philosophy of mind' that I shall be engaged in? A simple answer is this: psychology investigates facts, while philosophy studies concepts. But, as recent philosophers have shown,[3] that answer is far too simple. Philosophy does not merely *describe* the concepts of the common understanding, nor does it deal only with concepts, if that is meant to imply that its conclusions are innocent of matters of fact. Indeed, there is no more troublesome question for philosophy than the question of its own nature, and the reader must necessarily rest content with a partial answer. Philosophy, as exemplified in these pages, attempts to give the most general description possible of the phenomena to which it is applied. Such a description tells us, quite simply, what we are talking about when we refer to something. If we do not know what we are talking about, then all scientific enquiry is pointless. Usually the knowledge of what we are talking about is tacit and unarticulated; the task of philosophy is to make it explicit. And that is not a simple task. As we shall see, many writers on the topic of architecture have either failed to make explicit, or failed even to possess a knowledge of the thing which they purport to be discussing.

Furthermore, philosophy is not interested in any particular person's 'concept' of architecture, or of the aesthetic, or whatever. It is interested only in the concept to which it can ascribe a general significance. For philosophy also aims at the discovery of value. The only interesting philosophical account of aesthetic experience is the account which shows its importance, and this is the account that I wish to present.

I shall be concerned with such questions as the following: what is it to enjoy a building? What kind of experience is derived from the contemplation of architecture? What is taste? Are there rules which govern the exercise of taste? And so on. While those questions concern mental phenomena – understanding, experience, taste – they also impute to them a certain characteristic kind of object. Now it is impossible to describe or understand a mental state in isolation from its object: it might be said that the object, or at least a certain conception of the object, is of the essence of a mental state.[4] Consider, for example, the emotion of jealousy. It would be impossible to describe the nature of jealousy without exploring the nature of its characteristic object. A man feels jealousy not as he would a fleeting sensation in his toe; if he is jealous, he is jealous *of* or *about* something – his jealousy is 'directed', it has an object and not just a cause. Jealousy, therefore, will involve some characteristic conception of its object, and to describe jealousy is to describe this conception (the conception, as one might put it, of a *rival*). In just such a way, a theory of architectural appreciation cannot stop short of giving a theory of its proper object. We shall then be led, at every juncture, into an enquiry into the nature and significance of architecture.

In the light of that, it is not surprising that theories of architectural appreciation have tended to concentrate not so much on its form as on its object. They attempt to say what architectural appreciation is by describing what we respond to in buildings. Functionalism, in one of its many forms, asserts that we appreciate the aptness of form to function. Other theories argue that we appreciate symmetry and harmony, ornament and execution, or mass. There is also the popular view, assocated with the works of Frankl and his followers, that the object of appreciation is space, or the play of interlocking spaces. Now clearly, if we are to think of the analysis of the object of architectural interest as casting light on the nature of appreciation, then we must consider the object only under its widest possible description. As I shall show, none of the theories that I have mentioned provides a satisfactory description, since each ignores some feature of architecture that is both intentional and of the greatest architectural significance. Their claim to give *a priori* grounds for critical judgement is therefore unconvincing. In place of such theories, I shall try to approach the question more formally, concentrating on appreciation in itself, in abstraction from its object. I shall then try to say how that object must be, if appreciation is to have the significance we demand of it.[5]

It is essential to distinguish architectural aesthetics, as I conceive it, from something else that sometimes goes by the same name, but which one might call, for clarity's sake, architectural theory. Architectural theory consists in the attempt to formulate the maxims, rules and precepts which govern, or ought to govern, the practice of the builder. For example, the classical theory of the Orders, as it is found in the great treatises of Vitruvius, Alberti, Serlio and Vignola, which lays down rules for the systematic combination and ornamentation of the parts of a building, belongs to architectural theory; so too do most of the precepts contained in Ruskin's *The Stones of Venice* and *Seven Lamps*. Such precepts assume that we already know what we are seeking to achieve: the *nature* of architectural success is not at issue; the question is, rather, how best to achieve it. A theory of architecture impinges on aesthetics only if it claims a *universal* validity, for then it must aim to capture the essence, and not the accidents, of architectural beauty. But such a theory is implicitly philosophical, and must be judged accordingly; we will wish to know whether it succeeds in establishing its claims *a priori*, by a consideration of the phenomena in their most abstract and universal guise. As a matter of fact it has been characteristic of architectural theorists, from Vitruvius to Le Corbusier, to claim this universal validity for their laws. And no architectural aesthetics can leave such claims untouched. Vitruvius, Alberti, Ruskin and Le Corbusier cannot all be right in believing that their favoured form of architecture is uniquely authorized by the rational understanding. As we shall see, they are all wrong.

It may still be thought that there is no real subject of *architectural*, as opposed to general, aesthetics. If philosophy is to be as abstract as I claim it is, ought it not to consider the aesthetic experience in its full generality, in isolation from the accidental constraints imposed by particular art forms and particular conceptions of success? Why is there any special need for a philosophy of architecture, other than the purely ephemeral one, that architecture is misunderstood by so many of its present practitioners? Is there not one and the same concept of beauty employed in the discussion of poetry, music, painting and building, and is there not one single faculty involved in the appreciation of all those arts? Once we have made the distinction between architectural aesthetics and architectural theory it may seem that little remains to the former other than the delineation of abstractions that have no special application to the practice of the architect. And it is certainly true that philosophers have approached the subject of aesthetics as though it could find expression only in such comprehensive abstractions, and could make none but passing and inessential references to the individual forms of art.[6]

Now as a matter of fact architecture presents an immediate problem for any such general philosophical theory of aesthetic interest. Through its impersonal and at the same time functional qualities architecture stands apart from the other arts, seeming to require quite peculiar attitudes, not only for its creation, but also for its enjoyment. Generalized theories of aesthetic interest, such as those of Kant and Schopenhauer,[7] tend to give rather odd accounts of architecture, and those philosophers who have treated the problem seriously – among whom Hegel is perhaps the most prominent[8] – have often described the appreciation of architecture in terms inappropriate to the other forms of art. For Hegel, for example, architecture was a medium only half articulate, unable to give full expression to the Idea, and hence relegated to the level of pure symbolism, from which it must be redeemed by statuary and ornament.

It is not difficult to see why Hegel should have thought that. It is natural to suppose that representational arts, such as painting, drama, poetry and sculpture, give rise to an interest unlike the interest aroused by such abstract arts as music and architecture. But it is also natural to suppose that music has expressive, sensuous and dramatic powers in common with the representational arts. Only architecture seems to stand wholly apart from them, being distinguished from the other arts by certain features that cannot fail to determine our attitude towards it. I shall begin by discussing these features, since a grasp of them will be essential to understanding later arguments, and since they will show what a frail and fragmentary thing is this concept of 'art' that we have inherited.

First among these distinguishing features is utility or function. Buildings are places where human beings live, work and worship, and a certain form is imposed from the outset by the needs and desires that a building is designed to fulfil. While it is not possible to compose a piece of music without intending that it should be listened to and hence appreciated, it is certainly possible to design a building without intending that it should be looked at – without intending, that is, to create an object of aesthetic interest. Even when there is an attempt to apply 'aesthetic' standards in architecture, we still find a strong asymmetry with other forms of art. For no work of music or literature can have features of which we may say that, because of the function of music, or because of the function of literature, such features are unavoidable. Of course a work of music or literature may *have* a function, as do waltzes, marches and Pindaric odes. But these functions do not stem from the essence of literary or musical art. A Pindaric ode is poetry *put* to a use; and poetry in itself is connected only accidentally with such uses.

'Functionalism' has many forms. Its most popular form is the aesthetic theory, that true beauty in architecture consists in the adapting of form to function. For the sake of argument, however, we might envisage a functionalist theory of exemplary crudeness, which argues that, since architecture is essentially a means to an end, we appreciate buildings as *means*. Hence the value of a building is determined by the extent to which it fulfils its function and not by any purely 'aesthetic' considerations. This theory might naturally seem to have the consequence that the appreciation of architecture is wholly unlike the appreciation of other forms of art, these being valued not as means, but for their own sakes, as ends. However, to put the point in that way is to risk obscurity – for what is the distinction between valuing something as a means and as an end? Even if we feel confident about one term of that distinction (about what is it to value something as a means), we must surely feel considerable doubt about the term with which it is contrasted. What is it to value something as an end? Consider one celebrated attempt to clarify the concept – that of the English philosopher R. G. Collingwood.[9] Collingwood began his exploration of art and the aesthetic from a distinction between art and craft. Initially it seems quite reasonable to distinguish the attitude of the craftsman – who aims at a certain result and does what he can to achieve it – from that of the artist, who knows what he is doing, as it were, only when it is done. But it is precisely the case of architecture which casts doubt on that distinction. For whatever else it is, architecture is certainly, in Collingwood's sense, a craft. The utility of a building is not an accidental property; it defines the architect's endeavour. To maintain this sharp distinction between art and craft is simply to ignore the reality of architecture – not because architecture is a *mixture* of art and craft (for, as Collingwood recognized, that is true of all aesthetic activity) but because architecture represents an almost indescribable *synthesis* of the two. The functional qualities of a building are of its essence, and qualify every task to which the architect addresses himself. It is impossible to understand the element of art and the element of craft independently, and in the light of this difficulty the two concepts seem suddenly to possess a formlessness that their application to the 'fine' arts serves generally to obscure.

Moreover, the attempt to treat architecture as a form of 'art' in Collingwood's sense involves taking a step towards expressionism, towards seeing architecture in the way that one might see sculpture or painting, as an expressive activity, deriving its nature and value from a peculiarly artistic aim. For Collingwood 'expression' was the primary aim of art precisely because there could be no *craft* of expression. In the case of expression, there can be no rule or procedure, such as might be followed by a craftsman, with a clear end in view and a clear means to its fulfilment; it was therefore through the concept of 'expression' that he tried to clarify the distinction between art and craft. Collingwood put the point in the following way: expression is not so much a matter of finding the symbol for a subjective feeling, as of coming to know, through the act of expression, just what the feeling is. Expression is part of the realization of the inner life, the making intelligible what is otherwise ineffable and confused. An artist who could already identify the feeling which he sought to express might indeed approach his work in the spirit of a craftsman, applying some body of techniques which tell him what he must do to express that particular feeling. But then he would not need those techniques, for if he can identify the feeling it is because he has already expressed it. Expression is not, therefore, an activity whose goal can be defined prior to its achievement; it is not an activity that can be described in terms of end and means. So if art is expression, it *cannot* be craft (although its realization may also involve the mastery of many subsidiary crafts).

Those thoughts are complex, and we shall have cause to return to them. But clearly, it would be a gross distortion to assume that architecture is an 'expressive' medium in just the way that sculpture might be, or that the distinction between art and craft applies to architecture with the neatness which such a view supposes. Despite the absurdities of our crude functionalism (a theory which, as Théophile Gautier once pointed out, has the consequence that the perfection of the water closet is the perfection to which all architecture aspires) it is wrong to see architecture in such a way. The value of a building simply cannot be understood independently of its utility. It is of course *possible* to take a merely 'sculptural' view of architecture; but that is to treat buildings as forms whose aesthetic nature is conjoined only accidentally to a certain function. Texture, surface, form, representation and expression now begin to take precedence over those aesthetic aims which we would normally consider to be specifically architectural. The 'decorative' aspect of architecture assumes an unwonted autonomy, and at the same time becomes something more personal than any act of mere decoration would be. Consider, for example, the Chapel of the Colonia Guëll, Santa Coloma de Cervelló, by Gaudì (Plate 1). Such a building tries to represent itself as something other than architecture, as a form of tree-like growth rather than balanced engineering. The strangeness here comes from the attempt to translate a decorative tradition into a structural principle. In the sixteenth-century Portuguese window by J. de Castilho (Plate 2) the nature of that tradition is apparent. Structurally and architecturally the window is *not* an organic growth; its charm lies in its being decked

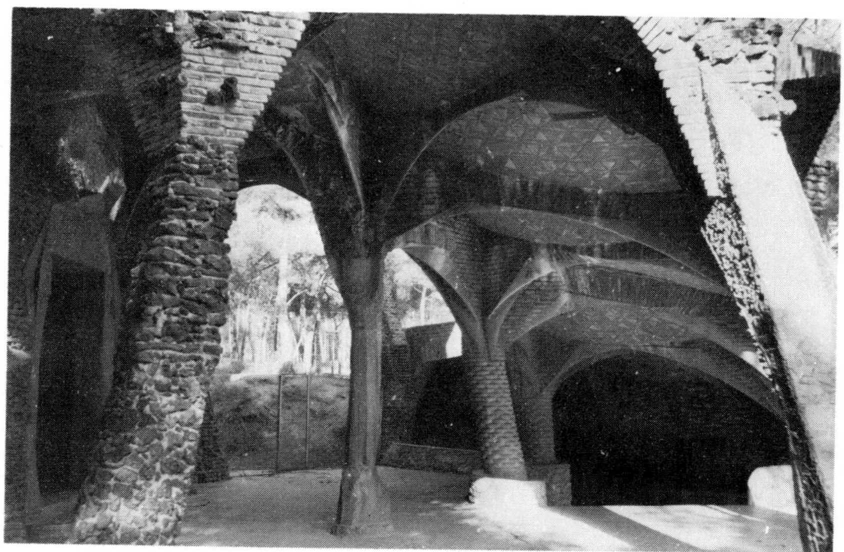

PLATE 1 A. Gaudì: Santa Coloma de Cervelló, Church of the Colonia Guëll

out like that. In Gaudì, however, the accidental has become the essential, and what purports to be architecture can no longer be understood as such, but only as a piece of elaborate expressionist sculpture seen from within. It is perhaps the same sculptural view of architecture which finds an architectural significance in the polished geometry of an Egyptian pyramid. It was indeed the pyramid which Hegel regarded as the paradigm of architecture, since its monumental quality, its solidity, and what he took to be its utter uselessness enabled him to see its sole function as a symbolic one, divorced from any actual or possible employment.

Now there have been attempts other than the spectacular one by Gaudì to break down the distinction between architecture and sculpture. André Bloc, for example, has built certain 'inhabitable sculptures', designed to answer to traditional uses while obeying only 'sculptural' principles of organization. But such an enterprise is marked by a singular confusion of thought. If the building is really to be understood as sculpture, then its excellence and beauty must depend upon such factors as the balance and expressiveness of the forms employed. Success can bear no significant relation either to the effectiveness of the sculpture as a place of habitation, or to the feelings which are the natural consequence of living, eating and working in it, rather than strolling through it as one might through a private

PLATE 2 Jean de Castilho: Window Convento de Cristo, Thomar

museum. In other words, the standard of success will not be architectural at all, and the fact of the structure's being inhabitable will be a curious but irrelevant feature, like the fact that Nelson's column provides a convenient roosting place for birds. Alternatively, we may judge the 'sculpture' successful only, or primarily, by reference to the feelings which arise from inhabiting it, or from thinking of it as a place of habitation. If that is so, then clearly our response to the 'sculpture' will be quite unlike our response to the works of art which normally go by that name, and we shall expect an obedience to aesthetic constraints which cannot be reduced to the sculptural canons of beauty. We are likely to find ourselves dissatisfied, for example, with the rough and undulating walls of Bloc's *habitacle*, just as with the strange root-like quality of Gaudì's chapel. The sculptural view of architecture involves the mistaken idea than one can somehow judge the beauty of a thing *in abstracto*, without knowing what *kind* of thing it is; as though I could present you with an object that might be a stone, a sculpture, a box, a fruit or even an animal, and expect you to tell me whether it is beautiful before knowing what it is. In general we might say – in partial opposition to a certain tradition in aesthetics (the tradition which finds expression in eighteenth-century empiricism, and more emphatically in Kant[10]) – that our sense of the beauty of an object is always dependent on a conception of that object, just as our sense of the beauty of a human figure is dependent on a conception of that figure. Features that we would regard as beautiful in a horse – developed haunches, a curved back, and so on – we would regard as ugly in a man, and this aesthetic judgement would be determined by our conception of what men are, how they move, and what they achieve through their movements. In a similar way, our sense of the beauty in architectural forms cannot be divorced from our conception of buildings and of the functions that they fulfil.

Functionalism can be seen, then, as part of an attempt to reassert architectural against sculptural values. As such it has sought to extend its explanatory powers through more subtle, and more vague, presuppositions. We are told that in architecture form 'follows', 'expresses' or 'embodies' function, ideas associated with Viollet-le-Duc, with the American pragmatism of Sullivan, and with certain aspects of the modern movement.[11] There is also the more subtle functionalism of Pugin and the mediaevalists; according to this view the reference to function is necessary as a standard of taste, a means of distinguishing genuine ornament from idle excrescence.[12] In such diluted forms, functionalism no longer has the ring of necessary truth. Indeed, until we know a little more about the essential features of architectural appreciation we will not even know how the theory of functionalism should be formulated, let alone how it might be proved.

A further distinguishing feature of architecture is its highly localized quality. Works of literature, music and pictorial art can be realized in an infinite number of locations, either through being performed or moved, or even, in the limiting case, reproduced. With certain rare exceptions – frescoes, for example, and monumental sculpture – this change of place need involve no change in aesthetic character. The same cannot be true of architecture. Buildings constitute important features of their own environment, as their environment is an important feature of them; they cannot be reproduced at will without absurd and disastrous consequences. Buildings are also affected to an incalculable extent by changes in their surroundings. Thus the architectural *coup de théâtre* planned by Bernini for the piazza of St Peter's has been partially destroyed by the opening up of the Via Della Conciliazione,[13] as the effect of the spire of St Bride's from the Thames bridges has been destroyed by the saw-like edges of the Barbican. We know of buildings whose effect depends in part on their location, either because they are ingenious solutions to problems of space – such as Borromini's church of S. Carlo alle Quattro Fontane – or because they are built in some striking or commanding position that is essential to their impact – such as the temple at Agrigento in Sicily – or because they involve a grandeur of conception that embraces a whole environment, in the manner of Versailles, where the architectural influence of Le Nôtre's garden is infinite in ambition. This is not to say that buildings cannot be reproduced – there are several neo-classical examples to the contrary, such as the composite souvenir of Athens known as St Pancras' church.[14] However, it must be acknowledged that the point of reproducing buildings is not generally comparable to the point of reproducing or copying paintings, and is certainly unlike the point of performing the same piece of music again. It is a scholarly exercise, playing no part in the natural distribution and enjoyment of a work of art. Indeed, we often feel a certain hostility towards the attempt to translate buildings, in this way, from one part of the world to another. We expect an architect to build in accordance with a sense of place, and not to design his building – as many a modern building is designed – so that it could be placed just anywhere. It is true that the architectural instinct can show itself even in the dwellings of nomadic tribes, but the impulse to which we owe most of the fine architecture that we have inherited is an impulse founded in the sense of place – the desire to mark a sacred spot or place of martyrdom, to build a monument, church or landmark, to claim possession and dominion of the land. This impulse is to be found in all serious architecture, from the antique temple and the martyrium, to the Chapel at Ronchamp and the Sydney Opera House, and it is an impulse which leads us to separate architecture from nature only with a certain considered reluctance.

This sense of place, and the consequent impression of the immovability of architecture, constrains the work of the builder in innumerable ways. Architecture becomes an art of the ensemble. It is intrinsic to architecture that it should be infinitely vulnerable to changes in its surroundings. This is a feature that architecture shares with such pursuits as interior decoration, dress, and the many quasi-moral, quasi-aesthetic activities that fall under the notion of taste. The interest in *ensembles* is partly responsible for the attention paid in architectural theory to style, and to repeatable form. All serious architecture aims at an effect of unity, and it is indeed tempting to think, with Schopenhauer,[15] that this unity is nothing more than an effect of style. For the particular notion of harmony that informs our interest in buildings cannot be understood independently of our sense of style. On the other hand it is clearly untrue to suggest that harmony amounts to nothing but stylistic unity. If this were so, then the harmoniousness of St Mark's square would be inexplicable, as would the particular structural unity of St Eustache in Paris, with its astonishing combination of classical and Gothic parts (see Plate 3).[16] But at least we see one further way in which architecture is constrained by external influences. Things have to fit together, and often the ambition of the architect resides not in individuality of form, but rather in the preservation of an order that pre-exists his own activity. Indeed, it does not

PLATE 3 Church of St Eustache, Paris

seem to me that we should talk of architecture as though it were a self-dependent art-form, divorced from town planning, gardening, decoration and furniture. Once again we seem to have discovered a factor which leads away from the manner in which we are commonly held to appreciate art, imposing limits on our attitude to buildings.

A further feature of architecture should here be mentioned – the feature of technique. What is possible in architecture is determined by the extent of human competence. In architecture there are changes initiated quite independently of any change in artistic consciousness; the natural evolution of styles is cast aside, interrupted or sent off at a tangent by discoveries that have no aesthetic origin and no aesthetic aim. Consider, for example, the discovery of reinforced concrete, and Maillart's use of it in his well-known bridges, which curve through the air across ravines where no straight path would be apt or possible.[17] The aesthetic consequences of that technical discovery have been enormous, and nobody could have envisaged them, still less intended them, in advance. In music, literature and painting evolution has followed more nearly a changing *attitude* to art, and hence a shifting spirit of artistic creation. And while it is true that here, too, there can be technical discoveries, such as that of the piano, which actually interrupt the flow of aesthetic consciousness (as well as others, such as those of the violin, the clarinet, the saxophone and the Wagner tuba, which are more naturally seen as *consequences* of a change in taste); and while there are also engineering achievements (like that of Brunelleschi's dome), which result from aesthetic aspiration, these passing similarities only serve to underline the real distinction between architecture and the other arts. One must greet with a certain scepticism, therefore, those critics[18] who hail the modern movement as a creation of architectural forms more in keeping with the 'spirit of the age', as though the change in these forms were a product only of artistic enterprise, and not of engineering skill.

A more important distinguishing feature of architecture is provided by its character as a public object. A work of architecture imposes itself come what may, and removes from every member of the public the free choice as to whether he is to observe or ignore it. Hence there is no real sense in which an architect creates his public; the case is wholly unlike those of music, literature and painting, which are, or have become, objects of free critical choice. Poetry and music, for example, have become selfconsciously 'modern' precisely because they have been able to create for themselves audiences attuned to novelty and active in the pursuit of it. Clearly, the architect may change public taste, but he can do so only by addressing himself to the whole public and not merely to some educated or half-educated part of it. 'Modernism' in architecture therefore raises a special problem which is not raised by modernism in the other forms of art.

It is pertinent to return at this point to the elusive but fundamental idea of 'expression' as a characteristic, or even principal, aim of art. Whatever this term means (and I shall later attempt to say more precisely what it does mean) expression cannot have the significance in such public arts as architecture as it may have in the private arts of poetry, painting and music. The private arts acquire much of their expressive character from the 'personal' manner in which we may approach them, from the ability of such arts to address themselves to a specific, and perhaps highly specialized, audience. Suppose it were said that 'Lycidas' expresses a tender grief, or the overture to *The Flying Dutchman* a demonic yearning; the reference here is to acts of *communication*. Of course we do not necessarily attribute the emotions to Milton or to Wagner; nevertheless, we hear their works as though these were the direct expression of personal feeling, as we might hear a piece of dramatic poetry. The expressive features of architecture are not, and cannot be, of this private kind. They consist rather in the objective representation of style and manner, in impersonal and unspecific meanings that speak to us as though from far away and with a public voice. It is the restlessness of the vestibule to the Laurentian Library that we notice, not the personal feeling which might be thought to underly it. And if we are also struck by the building's relation to some state of mind, it will be a general, impersonal state, such as the 'spirit of the age' that has so invaded contemporary criticism of the decorative arts.

As I remarked, modernism in architecture raises questions that are not raised by the 'private' forms of art. For modernism in these other arts has depended upon a certain subjectivity of outlook. By which I mean that modernism has been both self-conscious in its pursuit of an audience, and determinedly individualistic in its expressive aims. Consider the remarkable art of Schoenberg, who argued that he had provided canons of form and structure which were from the auditory point of view equivalent to those of the classical tradition.[19] To the educated ear, the Schoenbergian theme was to be as intelligible and as imbued with musical implications as a melody of Mozart. One can of course doubt that even the most melodious of Schoenberg's themes (for example, the opening theme of the piano concerto) achieves the immediate intelligibility of Mozart, and one might even doubt that one *ought* to hear a Schoenbergian theme as inflected in the manner of a classical melody (that is to say, as *progressing* towards a conclusion). Be that as it may, it certainly cannot be doubted that the transformation of musical experience which Schoenberg envisaged was a self-conscious affair, in a way that the experience of architecture cannot normally be. Music, for Schoenberg, achieves continuity with its own tradition – the tradition against which the modern style defines itself and without which no 'modernism' could be properly meaningful – by a self-conscious transformation of traditional procedures. This remains true, even if no *intellectual* understanding of the rules of the twelve-note system is presupposed in the listener. In some sense the listener has not merely to immerse himself in the music but also at the same time imaginatively to reconstruct the tradition which underlies it. Tradition was for Schoenberg what it was for T. S. Eliot, an ideal to be rediscovered by the modern consciousness, not a datum available to every man, whatever the state of his imaginative understanding.[20] Moreover, I doubt that Schoenberg's particular ideal of a genuinely 'modern' music can be fully understood without recourse to the subjective notion of expression. For consider how one might formulate the thought – vital to the very conception of modern music – that the classical style is no longer *available* to the modern consciousness, that it is no longer *possible* to compose like Beethoven or like Brahms (despite Sir Donald Tovey's noble efforts in the latter direction). Surely this thought requires one to represent the existing musical forms and methods as somehow exhausted. They have fallen into desuetude, not because we are bored by them (for we will never be bored by Mozart), but because they do not allow the modern composer to express what he wishes. They are not adapted to the full complexity of the modern consciousness, and do not lend themselves to expressing the true feelings of a modern man. It is because music, poetry and painting are seen at least partly in this expressionistic way that their self-conscious reconstruction becomes intelligible. The artist's ability to create his audience, to demand of them a permanent sense of their own modernity, is a necessary precondition not only of the success of such an enterprise but also of its attempt. It is in this way that music, painting and literature continue to survive, even in a state of cultural chaos, through the invention of what are at first (before the successful adoption of a style) arbitrary choices and arbitrary constraints.

Now I doubt that we could freely take up such an attitude to architecture as the one I have sketched. For I doubt that we could consistently view architecture either as a form of personal expression, or as a self-conscious gesture designed for the 'modern consciousness' alone. Architecture is public; it imposes itself whatever our desires and whatever our self-image. Moreover, it takes up space: either it crushes out of existence what has gone before, or else it attempts to blend and harmonize. Architecture, as Ruskin emphasized,[21] is the most political of the arts, in that it imposes a vision of man and his aims independently of any personal agreement on the part of those who live with it. Of course, all the arts have served, and continue to serve, political purposes. But it is only lovers of literature who are exposed to the vision of Shakespeare's histories or to that of *Illusions Perdues*, while every man, whatever his tastes and aptitudes, is forced to confront the buildings which surround him, and to absorb from them whatever they contain of political significance. A building may stand as the visible symbol of historical continuity, or equally as the enforced announcement of newfangled demands. As we have seen, architecture cannot, in abandoning its traditional forms, simply take refuge, as music has taken refuge, in a kind of complicitous subjectivity. Architecture can become new, but it cannot be 'modern' in the peculiar sense of that term which has been applied to recent Western music. Architecture becomes new by creating new expectations, and in general this requires the modification of some pre-existing style (as happened in the case of the Gothic, however inventive was the achievement of Abbot Suger at St Denis), or else through the imitation of some previously successful manner. It is true, of course, that every form of art has its revivals, and looked at in one way the rise of the 'Gothick' style in the eighteenth century can be seen as part of a single impetus of romantic mediaevalism, which swept simultaneously through many of the arts. Moreover literature, like architecture, has had its periodic 'classical revivals': in the French theatre, for example, and in Augustan satire. But the proneness of architecture to revivals runs deeper than this. A 'revival' in literature is a species of imitation, in which thought, feeling and diction remain entirely modern. Indeed, one cannot envisage in either literature or music a total return to some previous style that is not in some way ironical, in the manner of Stravinsky's neo-classicism, or else precious, in the manner of Morris's cult of the Middle Ages. In architecture, on the other hand, one encounters throughout history comparable revivals that have been not only total in their intention, but which have entirely changed the course of building. In fact, the continuousness of these revivals has been such as to make the word 'revival' seem almost inappropriate. It is surely not unwarranted to suggest that there is, in our attitude to building, a character of respect for the past that allows such returns while remaining innocent of irony. For the serious architect the past exists not as a legacy to be possessed through a self-conscious act of the 'modern' will, but as an enduring fact, an ineliminable part of an extended present. From Vitruvius through the Renaissance to the Gothic revival, responses to architecture have been at one and the same time practical and backward-looking. Even the architecture of the future envisaged by Ledoux[22] was based on conceptions of architectural symbolism, and of architectural detail, that are profoundly classicist in their inclinations. And the pervasiveness of this respect for the past is only confirmed by the hysterical nature of recent attempts to break with it.

But perhaps the most important feature of architecture, the feature which serves most of all to give it a peculiar status and significance in our lives, is its continuity with the decorative arts, and the corresponding multiplicity of its aims. Even when architects have a definite 'aesthetic' purpose, it may not be more than a desire that their work should 'look right' in just the way that tables and chairs, the lay of places at a table, the folds in a napkin, an arrangement of books, may 'look right' to the casual observer. Architecture is primarily a vernacular art: it exists first and foremost as a process of arrangement in which every normal man may participate, and indeed does participate, to the extent that he builds, decorates or arranges his rooms. It does not normally aim at those 'meanings' ascribed to it by the practitioners of

Kunstgeschichte, nor does it present itself self-consciously as art. It is a natural extension of common human activities, obeying no forced constraints, and no burden of an 'artistic conception', of anything that might correspond to the romantic's *Kunstwollen*, or to the Hegelian 'Idea'.

The architectural vernacular is exemplified everywhere, and we are never surprised to find a Doric column supporting a wine table, an egg and dart moulding on a wardrobe, a Gothic hat-stand, a Bauhaus corner-cupboard, or a tea-caddy obedient to the law of the Golden Section. In using the term 'vernacular' I offer no *explanation* of the endurance of these popular forms; nor do I suggest that there is a vernacular style which might be proposed as a definite objective for the builder. (As Sir John Summerson has persuasively argued, conceived as an objective rather than as a summary of existing practices, the vernacular is a mere chimera.[23]) But I do mean to suggest that the existence and predominance of an architectural vernacular is an inevitable consequence of the distance that separates architecture from the other arts, of the relative absence from the art of building of any true artistic autonomy, of the fact that, for the most part, a builder has to fit his work into some pre-existing arrangement of unchangeable forms, being constrained at every point by influences which forbid him the luxury of a selfconsciously 'artistic' aim. Architecture is simply one application of that sense of what 'fits' which governs every aspect of daily existence. One might say that, in proposing an aesthetics of architecture, the least one must be proposing is an aesthetics of everyday life. One has moved away from the realm of high art towards that of common practical wisdom. And here one might begin to see just how inappropriate is our post-romantic conception of art to the description of the normal aesthetic judgements of the normal man, and how obscure are all the concepts, such as the concept of expression, which have been used to elucidate it.

Against the background of these differences, we must recognize the immense difficulty that exists in giving any articulate criticism of architecture. Set beside the achievements of literary and even musical criticism, the standard works of architectural criticism look shallow indeed. On the rare occasions when critics have been prepared to make discriminations, to assert, for example, that a certain building or a certain style is ugly or unsuccessful, they have done so, like Pugin, Ruskin and the functionalists, with a peculiar dogmatism, and with an unargued generality that has often served to discredit their conclusions. Judgement has often masked an uncritical moralism, and has rarely founded itself on individual understanding of individual buildings. That ideal of criticism recently upheld so forcefully by I. A. Richards and F. R. Leavis – the ideal of criticism as an articulation and justification of the individual response, not as an isolated 'aesthetic' impulse but as an expression of emotions that connect with the very centre of individual life – that ideal has had few advocates in the criticism of architecture. Questions of value are often introduced either extraneously, through a peculiar species of moralism which we will have cause to analyse in a later chapter, or else through vague and generalized notions of 'meaning' which could be applied indifferently to almost any building in a particular style. And for the most part, it is almost impossible for someone without a specialized education to express in words the beauties of architecture; if terms like 'proportion', 'harmony', 'space', and 'atmosphere' spring to mind, it is not as a rule because any very clear general idea is associated with them. The spectator is forced to that level of breathlessness recorded by Sir Henry Wotton, when he described Santa Giustina in Padua as 'in truth a sound piece of good Art, where the Materials being but ordinary stone, without any garnishment of sculpture, doe yet ravish the Beholder, (and he knowes not how), by a secret Harmony in the Proportions.'[24]

I have described these features of architecture in an extreme and somewhat uncompromising way, for it is necessary to remember a difficulty that might otherwise be overlooked. Aesthetics begins with a notion of art, and of aesthetic interest, often without pausing to examine whether there is any significant unity in either notion. The considerations I have raised are in fact very much in need of interpretation. It is clear that features analogous to those I have mentioned can sometimes be found in the other arts. *Tafelmusik* has a dominant function, as does occasional verse; frescoes cannot always be moved without loss of character, nor in a more subtle way, can early Church music preserve its spirituality in a modern concert hall. And painting, being continuous with so many of the decorative arts, must necessarily show a tendency towards that publicity of aspect which I have discerned in architecture. Besides, it will always be possible to find respects in which the several art forms differ: simply to mention the publicity and utility of architecture is to give no proof of its distinctiveness. On the other hand, we must remember that philosophers often write as though it were possible to treat just anything aesthetically, whether it be a philosophical essay, a mathematical proof, or an *objet trouvé*. Hence, although we may have reason to think that we sometimes treat buildings as aesthetic objects, it does not follow that in appreciating them as *buildings* we are appreciating them aesthetically. When we regard a proof from the aesthetic point of view we do not consider it only as mathematics, and we can fully understand its mathematical validity without being concerned with its aesthetic power. The aesthetic attitude may, then, be connected only peripherally with the art of building; it may be that aesthetic requirements are a minor irritation in the practice of the architect, and in no sense fundamental to his aim.

Of course, we do not yet know quite what these 'aesthetic' requirements are. But we can perhaps gain some negative understanding of them if we consider the view just adumbrated, the view that a building is to be understood primarily in terms of its utility, and that aesthetic constraints, while they are possible, are by no means necessary, in the builder's enterprise.

PART I

2

ARCHITECTURE AND DESIGN

ARCHITECTURE, someone might say, is identical to building – a special case of the activity of design. That was the view of Alberti, and other thinkers of the early Renaissance, for whom the idea that there should be architecture on the one hand, conforming to aesthetic standards and setting itself the highest aims, and building on the other, a mere craftsman's activity of no aesthetic consequence, designed only to satisfy a function, was inimicable to their thought. The idea of a fundamental separation between building as art and building as craft was wholly inconceivable. For example, Alberti describes the joining of lines and angles as being the most important and difficult of the architect's tasks, and it is clear that he is referring to a problem that is at once one of construction and of aesthetics.[1] No true understanding of what he means can be gained until it is seen how closely the two aspects of the problem constrain each other, and how the true solution will be intelligible only as a synthesis (and not a mere concatenation) of its component parts. It was left to the practitioners of the late Gothic revival to make the distinction between architecture and building vivid in the popular mind, and it was Ruskin who gave final expression to it, in the first chapter of *Seven Lamps of Architecture*, where he expressly confined the name 'architecture' to whatever is useless, unnecessary, or mere incrustation.[2] Alberti, by contrast, wrote of a single universal art of building, which 'consists in the design and the structure'. 'The whole force and reason of the design', he continued, 'consist in finding an exact and correct way of adapting and joining together the lines and angles which serve to define the aspect of the building. It is the property and business of design to appoint to the edifice and all its parts an appropriate place, exact proportion, suitable disposition and harmonious order, in such a way that the form of the building should be entirely implicit in the conception.'[3] Ideas of what is 'right', 'appropriate', 'proper' and 'proportionable' determine from the beginning the direction of his thought. I have quoted from the first page of his treatise. On the next page he writes of the function of walls and apertures, the intricacies of roof construction, the effects of climate, sun and rain. He passes unhesitatingly from the abstractions of the philosopher to the realities of the working engineer. And yet the ideas of what is 'appropriate', 'proportionable' and 'decorous' never cease to dominate his argument. According to Alberti it is as much the business of the common builder as of the architect to know what is appropriate,[4] and to build in the light of that knowledge.

Now it is fair to say that the idea of 'aesthetic' as opposed to, say, 'functional' considerations is largely a philosophical invention.[5] We are dealing with a technicality, introduced to name something which we would normally be reluctant to define. Even our vague intuition suffices, however, to suggest that Alberti, in his repeated emphasis on what is appropriate, fitting, ordered and proportionable, is placing aesthetic considerations at the heart of the builder's activity. Moreover, it is also apparent that, for Alberti, the pursuit of aesthetic excellence is not properly speaking detachable from the other elements of architectural interest. The constraints implicit in these notions of the appropriate and the proportionable permeate the entire practice of the architect or engineer, so that he cannot consider some problem of structure, say, and then solve the problem of 'appropriateness' independently. He cannot, that is, fragment his task into a set of connected 'problems' among which the requirements of aesthetics form only one. For it is within the framework provided by the notion of the 'appropriate' that all the architect's problems are envisaged.

A cultural historian might argue that the sense, implicit in all Renaissance thought, of the primacy of aesthetic values, is somehow inessential, a mere reflection of a particular social order, and neither more inevitable, nor more desirable, than the social order itself. If we take such arguments seriously, then we might find ourselves tempted to reject these ideas of what is apt, appropriate and proportionable, reject them, that is, as the ruling concepts in architectural thought and practice (some Marxists would think that it is mere 'false-consciousness' to retain them). And it might seem that, in doing so, we remove aesthetic considerations from the centre of architectural thought and banish them to the periphery. It is the possibility of that banishment that I wish to explore.

Contemporary architects often speak of 'design problems' and 'design solutions',[6] and in that notion of design is encapsulated, as a rule, precisely the attempt to which I have referred, the attempt either to banish aesthetic considerations entirely, or else to treat them simply as one among a set of problems to be solved, either wholly or partially, in the derivation of some ideal, or 'optimal', design. 'Design' is not what it was for Alberti, a process through which aesthetic values permeate the entire conception of the architectural task, but rather a complex, quasi-scientific mode of functional experiment. Aesthetic considerations are most often admitted not as part of the aim of design, but as its unpursuable by-product. As one distinguished architect has written:

> Beauty is a consequential thing, a product of solving problems correctly. It is unreal as a goal. Preoccupation with aesthetics leads to arbitrary design, to buildings which take a certain form because the designer 'likes the way it looks'. No successful architecture can be formulated on a generalized system of aesthetics.[7]

And certainly it seems arbitrary to require of architecture a pattern of thought and reasoning which would not be required in the design of a kettle, a spade or a motor car. In all these activities, it has been suggested, the aim is to achieve a 'clear' or 'rational' design – a specification or blueprint which will lead to the greatest satisfaction among those who use the finished object. The first task in design, therefore, is to understand the needs of a potential client; the architect must then study the interaction of those needs, and finally devise a mechanism which is as responsive to them as possible. Beauty may be a consequence of his activity, but it is no part of his aim.

In order to make the issue as clear as possible I have set up a man of straw. I shall therefore not give more than a cursory glance to the history of 'design methods' and I shall confine all detailed reference to footnotes. However, it is perhaps worth pointing out that this particular equation of architecture with problem-solving is already present in many of the modernist manifestos from the earlier years of this century,[8] and that some modern design theorists affirm (whether rightly or wrongly) that their aims are really those of the 'constructivist' architects in post-revolutionary Russia.[9] It is certainly true that constructivism aimed to discover an ideal of an architecture which, in expressing the complete economy of means to ends, would be appropriate to the revolutionary spirit in which it was conceived. This ideal would give to the works of architects a comprehensive utility that would be both satisfactory to the user and apparent, as a kind of abstract beauty, to the passer-by. In this pursuit of the 'reasonable' the architects of the Russian Revolution looked back to the theories of the French Enlightenment. But the Russian school – initially at least – attempted to find its ideal of the reasonable in the relation of means to end. By contrast, for the architects of the French Enlightenment – for Boullée and Ledoux[10] – Reason was an end in itself, made *manifest* in architecture and worshipped not only as a moral and aesthetic inspiration but as a quasi-religious ideal. It was not the *function* of Ledoux's house of love that necessitated its phallic ground plan (see Plate 4), but rather an overmastering aesthetic conception which sought to embellish and make intelligible the blasphemous rationalism of its architect. For the early constructivists Reason was not so much an aesthetic ideal as a means to the banishment of all merely aesthetic constraints in favour of some comprehensive social significance. Of course, the label 'constructivism' has meant many things, and has been applied to themselves by architects who would strongly reject the views of which I here seem to accuse them. To do justice to the constructivists and their progeny is no part of my purpose, and I hereby consign them to a footnote.[11] But I shall use the label 'constructivism' rather than 'design theory', since I do not wish to imply that there *is* any serious theory that goes by the latter name.

Suppose, then, that we were to follow this ideal of Reason and eliminate from the architect's brief everything that could be described as incorporating a purely 'aesthetic' aim. Does this supposition define a coherent and reasonable practice, something that a rational man might engage in and fully know what he is doing? I shall argue that it does not.

A problem is immediately presented by the multiplicity and intangibility of non-aesthetic aims. It has been recognized for some time that it is not enough for an architect to make his main aims explicit and then look for a method which will best fulfil them. For there may be other aims, as yet inexplicit, which are thwarted in the process. A familiar example is central heating, a device which answers perfectly to the limited aim of maintaining warmth throughout a house. It did not take long to discover that central heating dries the atmosphere, cracks certain types of plaster and wooden furniture, makes it impossible to keep a musical instrument, is in innumerable ways inconvenient and unhealthy. The remedy, it is thought, lies in the installation of a system to control humidity. That in its turn proves to be expensive, troublesome to maintain, unsightly and even noisy, and gives rise to many more elusive irritations consequent on maintaining human beings in a 'controlled environment' like pictures in a gallery or creatures in a zoo.

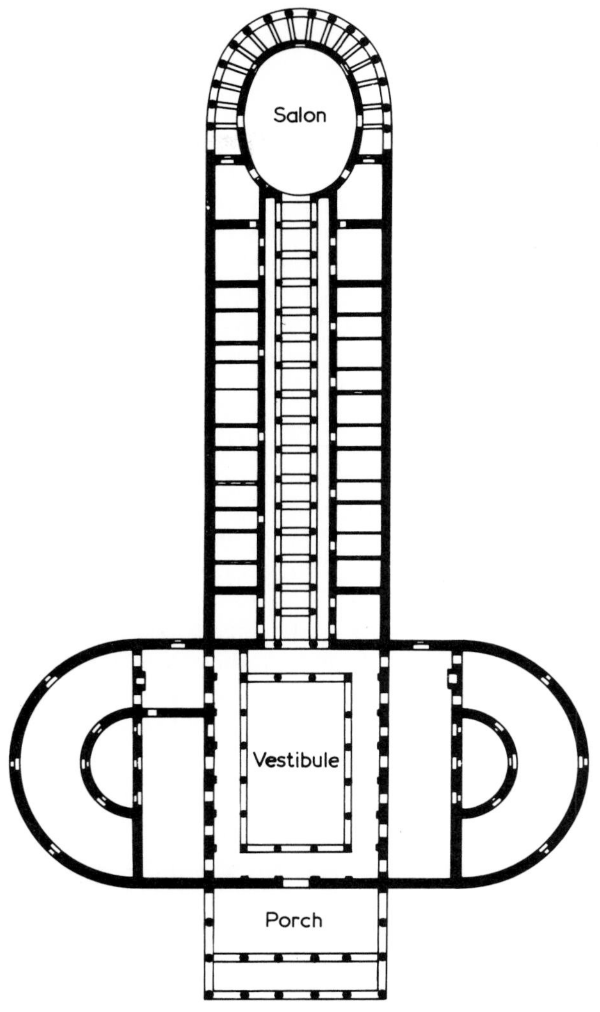

PLATE 4 Claude-Nicolas Ledoux: project for a house of love

So further measures must be taken, and the question now arises how this chain of 'improvements' might ever be brought to an end and whether it would not be better to start again. As one writer has suggested,[12] design is characterized precisely by the instability of the problem, which elusively changes during the course of its attempted solution. It is difficult to know, therefore, quite what 'method' the designer should pursue, or even whether 'method' is the best description of his need.

One response to these difficulties is that made familiar by Christopher Alexander,[13] who blames the inadequacy of many contemporary 'design solutions' upon their combination of self-conscious aims with inadequate concepts. He compares them unfavourably with the 'unselfconscious designs' exemplified in the grass huts of Polynesia, the Italian hilltop town, and our own architectural vernacular. The unselfconscious design is, one might say, a product of evolution: it evolved in response to an unformulated cluster of desires and needs, and achieved a realization unmediated by thought or reflection, like the hexagonal cells of wax which so perfectly house the bee. Our self-conscious procedures, by contrast, exist not because of their inherent good sense, but by design. They are the outcome of thought, and the thought is confused because it employs concepts that make only superficial contact with the designer's problem. The concepts we employ provide us with no practical mastery; for we classify on the basis of observed aims and functions, without understanding (as the unselfconscious architect intuitively understands) the underlying structure of their relationship. The study of design must therefore provide us with better concepts – concepts which locate the true nexus of influences in the architectural problem.

Now it is of great interest to see architecture in this way. For, at first sight, it could hardly be denied that architecture essentially involves a 'problem', and that the first task of the architect is to solve this problem as best he can. For example, an architect may be required to place rooms, each of certain minimum dimensions, within a given ground plan, and he might be required to find the maximum number of such rooms. But it may also be that a given arrangement proves to be far less effective for purposes of heating, for example, or for the purpose of communication between parts of the building. The designer must therefore synthesize the various problems and present a solution which satisfies each of them as well as possible, while allowing for the partial satisfaction of the rest.

Such aggregated problems might admit of solution – even mathematical solution – provided certain assumptions are made. It is necessary to assume, for example, that the relative importance of each component in the problem can be judged, and that degrees of satisfaction can be specified for each of them. Clearly, until one knows *how* important it is to achieve a large number of rooms in comparison to a certain ease of communication between them, it will be impossible to evaluate a plan which fully satisfies the first of these but only partially satisfies the second. In other words, the 'elements' of the architectural problem must be doubly quantifiable – both internally, with respect to themselves, and externally, with respect to their competitors. But (even supposing we are to ignore 'aesthetic considerations', whatever they may be) a difficulty again arises. In every serious task there are factors which, while of the greatest importance, cannot be assigned a relative value – not because their value is absolute, but because a man may not be able to judge in advance just when he is prepared to tolerate their remaining unsatisfied. Consider, for example, the problem of the position of the windows in a house. Most people would wish for their windows to open on to some lively, pleasant or interesting prospect. But how many would know just when they would be prepared to sacrifice that desire to some other requirement – say, of warmth, privacy or light? (In many Arts and Crafts houses – such as those of Voysey – the architects seem on the verge of dispensing with windows altogether, rather than depart from their aesthetic aims.) There is, indeed, something repugnant in the idea of a man whose desires in these matters exemplify some comprehensive order, so that he can specify the components of his 'architectural problem' in isolation from any knowledge or experience of the individual circumstances in which he has to choose. At least it can hardly be a necessary truth that the rational man or his architect is like that. As we shall see, to be like that is hardly to be rational at all.

Let us state the problem in its most abstract form. Suppose that the ideal of the 'design methods' school were realized. Suppose, that is, that there were to be developed a comprehensive theory of built forms, together with a biological, social and engineering science of such completeness that the true causal interdependence of the functions which a building must satisfy could be accurately delineated.[15] Even so, there would be no real answer to any architectural 'problem', for the reason that the 'solution' has to be understood not as a scientific optimum but as a basis for practical activity. Suppose, for example, that our 'optimal plan' were to produce the fastest, safest and most economical route between the rooms of a hypothetical office block. The ground plan is so designed that the applicant who enters the building can proceed as rapidly as possible to his final destination. It may be that the 'optimal solution', so calculated, defies our capacity to envisage it. The applicant is unable to retain a visual map of his progress, and wanders in bewilderment from one unwanted office to the next. If that is so, then the whole 'solution' is nugatory.

This difficulty may seem trivial. It might be argued that the applicant could learn from a map, or from experience, how to find his way about. But that reply misses the point. Of course, in so far as such difficulties as the one I have mentioned can be overcome, the building is successful. But the criterion of success lies not in any 'optimal solution', scientifically derived, but in the ability of rational beings to *understand* the solution that is proposed. A 'solution' to a design problem will be satisfactory only if it presents, to those who live and work with the product, a suitable basis for their own practical understanding. Therefore, the search for some ideal solution, which satisfies some given set of functions as well as circumstances permit, must take account of an intuitive understanding, not only of the 'problem', but of the 'solution' itself. Being constrained at both ends, as it were, by the limits of human intuition, it is hard to see that the process of design can hope to free itself from intuition, or that it ought seriously to try to do so.

But now, *is* this practical understanding at which the architect should aim? There have been many philosophical attempts, from Aristotle to Wittgenstein, to clarify the distinction between theoretical and practical knowledge, between rational belief and rational activity, and it is fair to say that none of these attempts has been wholly successful. But that there is a distinction between the theoretical and the practical, and that both realms exhibit reasoning, cannot be doubted. My attention in this work will be focused on only one part of practical understanding, the part which is affected and determined by the aesthetic sense. But I shall argue that this part, far from being insignificant, is utterly central to our knowledge of what to do.

Practical understanding pervades every sphere of active life, and is not reducible to rational action only. A man may be ignorant not just through being unskilful, or through acting in error, but also through feeling or wanting what it is inappropriate to feel or want. Activity includes all emotion and desire, and these are as susceptible to rational assessment as any act of will. Unless we acknowledge this pervasiveness of practical reason we shall not, I think, be able to understand the aesthetic sense.

There is one area, however, where the theoretical and the practical seem to merge, the area (which has so far concerned us in this chapter) of means. Here practical knowledge cannot be separated from the theoretical understanding of matters of fact. But in considering the questions raised by our hypothetical 'constructivism', we will see at once that it will never be enough to think of architecture in terms of the discovery of a means to an end. For we must consider too how an architect achieves an understanding of the *end* of his activity, and – as the example of the window shows – this end can seldom be reduced to a set of competing functions specifiable in advance. How, then, should we analyse the notion of an end of action? Contemporary architectural theory has possessed itself of a concept in terms of which to discuss these things, a concept which has proved of great rhetorical significance in the development of modern architecture, the concept of a human 'need'. It was this concept which guided Le Corbusier, not only in his plans for the destruction of all civilized cities in the interests of fresh air and football, but even in the most basic principles of his thought. According to Le Corbusier, the human being has a need for air, light, open space, movement, everything, in short, that is *not* architecture; the high glass tower raised on pilotis above a park seemed to follow almost as a matter of deduction from that statement of the human 'problem'.[16] This is not to say that Le Corbusier was in any sense affected by the anti-aesthetic ideology of our hypothetical constructivists. Nevertheless, the absurdity of his plans, and the manifest dissatisfaction which has ensued upon the use of his 'solution', serve to suggest that this concept of a need, in its standard architectural usage, is an impoverished one, and can be used to reduce architecture to a species of 'problem-solving' only by fundamentally misrepresenting the architect's purpose.

The concept of a need is connected with that of flourishing.[17] A plant needs water because without water it cannot flourish. A need is of the *essence* of whatever possesses it (and already one senses a muddle in the contemporary architect's talk of 'changing needs'); *x* needs *y* only if the *being* of *x* depends on *y*. But men may flourish in at least two ways; for men have a dual nature. They may flourish either as animals or as persons (as rational beings[18]), and what they need for the first of these – food and shelter – will not be sufficient (and not, according to the Stoics at least, even necessary) for the second. Clearly, it is man's needs as a rational being which must be catered for if the concept of a need is to lead us to some ideal of 'rational design'.

The fulfilment of a rational agent – what the Greeks called *eudaimonia* and we happiness – comes only when the agent has that which he values, as opposed to that which he merely desires. And perhaps the most striking feature of the 'architecture of human need' is that it seems so often to conceive the world as a world in which there *are* no values, but only animal needs – fresh air, health, exercise, food. Let us, then, try to separate the concept of value from that of animal need. The superficial difficulty in making the distinction stems in part from the fact that both needs and values express themselves through the activity of desire. Indeed, there is a temptation, again manifest among design theorists, to reduce both values and needs to 'preferences', to matters of 'subjective choice' of what people happen, for whatever cause or reason, to prefer.[19] The rational design can then still be conceived as the one which best satisfies the given preferences. The idea is that, if the architectural machines of the constructivists displease us, it is because their machines are *imperfect* – they do not permit the fulfilment of our many and varied preferences, and therefore we must return to the study of what we want, in search of a more satisfactory design. Thus arises the idea of 'correct construction' which construes 'correctness' as the answer to a social problem.[20] The machine, far from being the source of human alienation, is its principal remedy: the only thing which is needed for a humane architecture is a *complete* statement of the problem which the machine must solve.[21]

In fact there is a radical difference between values and mere desires, a difference which the philosophy of correct construction systematically disregards. It may be true that values are a species of preference. But not all our preferences are values. Some of our preferences (for example, in food and wine) we regard as reflections of our own personality or constitution; these we are content to regard as *mere* preferences, and we consider ourselves under no obligation (although we may have a desire) to justify them when challenged. Values are more significant, and have a kind of authority in practical reasoning that no mere preference could acquire. Not only do we feel called upon to justify them with reasons when necessary, we also learn to see and understand the world in terms of them. A value, unlike a mere preference, expresses itself in language such as that used by Alberti: it pursues what is right, fitting, appropriate and just. It is the outcome of thought and education, and can be supported, overthrown, or modified by reasoned argument. It does not manifest itself simply as an isolated preference in some fictitious 'choice situation'. A value is characterized not by its strength but by its depth, by the extent to which it brings order to experience. It is difficult to see how such a thing could be measured, or set against competing preferences as a single factor in some composite 'design problem'.

Now values, as I have described them, are one special case of *ends* of conduct; they define what we are aiming at, not just in the particular case, but generally. And it is partly through the acquisition of values that we are able to arrive, even in the particular case, at the conception of an end. For consider what it is, actually *to have an end in view*. To understand the end of one's conduct means not just to know, in a theoretical way, what one is aiming at: it is to be able to envisage what it would be like to *achieve* that aim. The phrase 'what it would be like' points to a question which cannot be reduced to one of utility or function. It is a question not about the efficiency but about the quality of something, the quality of an experience. The question is answered when the architect can predict the full effect of his completed building, and understand its relation to the experience of those who will use it. The understanding involved here is therefore partly imaginative – it involves envisaging a non-existent state of affairs and achieving some effective premonition of its quality. It is also evaluative, involving a sense, not just of present purposes, but of the appropriateness of one's action to purposes which it may not yet be possible to define.

In this connection it is important to see that the particular end of a course of conduct may not be given in advance of our engaging in it: it may have to be discovered, as it were, as we go along. This is, surprisingly, as true of those activities that have a professed 'aim in view' as it is of those which do not. For the 'aim' in question – if it relates to the lives of people and lays claim on their time and interest – will be essentially open to qualification in the light of the perceptions, values and desires of those who pursue it. Consider, for example, the use of clothes. It is natural to suggest that there are governing purposes in the wearing of clothes – the purposes of hiding one's body and keeping it warm. But a design that was *determined* by those purposes would never be recognized as acceptable, for all its superficial reasonableness. People live in their clothes and, therefore, see their clothes not in terms of any narrow sartorial function but in terms of the aims and accidents incidental to their lives. Their clothes come to represent them, in the sense of heralding the nature which they wish to claim as their own. Consider, for example, the 'functional' suit of blue denim, as this is envisaged by its more usual purchasers. This proclaims itself as an object of utility in defiance of ornament, pretension or style. That very proclamation constitutes its style; once again 'Reason' reveals itself, not as an adaptation of means to end, but as an end in itself, a value through which we perceive the world. What pretends to be 'functional' appeals precisely because it is something more than that, because functionality is *expressed* in its appearance. The case is as far from the constructivist ideal in building as is Ledoux's house of love. The 'functional suit' acquires its character not because of its utility (for it is not particularly useful), nor because of its cheapness (for it is far from cheap), but because it both expresses a certain outlook and, in the course of doing so, anticipates the experience of the man who wears it.

The aims which might actually be offered for the purchase of a denim suit are not, then, the full reason for its acquisition. They must remain subordinate to something else, which is not so much an aim in itself as a sense of the accommodation of the suit to all present and future aims, whatever they chance to be. And the possession of that sense involves the acquisition of values. The suit seems fitted to a certain style of life, and the aims of that style of life are not given in advance (how could they be?) but discovered by the agent as he engages in it. Nevertheless, he is able to know – as an intuitive certainty rather than a specific formula – that a particular object will be suitable to those aims, even before he is able to say what they are. In other words, he may form an opinion of the *appropriateness* of a particular dress in advance of any purpose for which he may wear it, and that opinion of appropriateness may properly take precedence over any partial or temporary aim. Indeed, it could be said of the man who approaches the purchase of clothes with this sense of what is appropriate that he tries to *understand* the aims which guide him – understand, that is, in advance of any apprehension of what they might concretely amount to, and before they can enter into his deliberations in any other way.

Here we begin to see one way in which something that we might wish to call 'aesthetic value' might be an essential ingredient in our understanding of what we are doing when we purchase clothes, decorate a room or build a house. All these acts have consequences which lie beyond the satisfaction of any desires that we could presently confess to. Nevertheless, we are still obliged to search for the forms and details that will be appropriate to our lives. That sense of the appropriate requires some kind of imaginative understanding; it requires us to reflect on the look and feel of something, and to imagine what it would be like to live with it. To gain that perception of 'what it would be like' is to leave aside any merely functional calculation, for it is to transcend the framework – the framework of desire and satisfaction – within which functional calculation makes sense. It is to create, through the present experience, a sense of the object's appropriateness not just to this or that desire, but to one's self, as an entity greater than the sum of its desires. The man who always acts in obedience to a ruling purpose is not necessarily, therefore, the most rational. Lacking that sense of the 'appropriate' which aesthetic values inculcate he may in fact be led always to choose irrationally – that is, to choose what will not satisfy him, or what will not satisfy him for long. He may have purchased certainty at the expense of knowledge.

Now the same is true of architecture.[22] Even with buildings like pumping works and power stations, which are in no sense designed to house people, it is impossible to arrive at a purely functional description of what they must do, a description that ignores the wider question of what it would be like for that function to be fulfilled in the suggested manner. (It is interesting in this respect to compare Battersea Power Station, with the much loved French baroque water pump that faces it from across the Thames.) So much the less can this question be ignored in the case of a building in which people have to live.

Many may still doubt, at this stage in our argument, that aesthetic values can be given the kind of central place in our experience that we are compelled, as rational beings, to accord to our morality. For what are aesthetic values? The constructivist may say that aesthetic values concern 'the way it looks', while for him the important thing is 'what it really means', or 'what it really does'. But our sartorial example shows that simple conception to be mistaken. There is no clear distinction between 'the way it looks', 'what it means' and 'what it does'. In the art of building, the study of 'how it looks' and the reasoned apprehension of one's true end of action, are inseparable. One of my contentions in this book will be, therefore, that the study of what is right and appropriate in matters of aesthetic judgement is vital to practical wisdom, being indispensable to a true intimation of future aims. Through the aesthetic understanding our future aims become vivid to us before we are able to formulate them as policies or plans. Through the cultivation of taste our ends of conduct become 'immanent' in the activities which lead up to them, and so may be rationally acknowledged even before they can be actively pursued.

Let us return again to the distinction between the theoretical and the practical. The study of what is right and appropriate does not lead to theoretical knowledge: since there is no fixed external aim it follows that there is no fixed and necessary body of rules which describe the means to it, rules which one might learn as one learns the axioms of a natural science. The aesthetic understanding is a form of practical reason, and involves education rather than learning. In aesthetic education one acquires the capacity to notice things, to make comparisons, to see architectural forms as meaningful and appropriate accompaniments to human life. That process of education has the same structure, the same discipline and the same reward, regardless of whether the rules of composition involved in it, and the particular comparisons made in it, can be laid down as universal laws. Through such education the architect acquires the sense of what it would be like to live and work in his completed building. In other words, he acquires knowledge of the end of his activity, and not just of the means to it. Without that knowledge, there is no way in which an architect can seriously know what he is doing when he begins to build.

If that is true – and I hope that I can show it to be so – then we have no difficulty in seeing what is wrong with our 'constructivist' programme, and with the conception of a building as a kind of machine. Since the outset of the Industrial Revolution there has been a suspicion that it is not the incompetence of existing machinery that makes it inappropriate as the principal background to our lives, but rather something about human life itself, something which reason demands, and which will always be left out of consideration in a world conceived wholly under the aspect of function. Man stands to the machine, say some, in an 'essentially alienated' relation, and the attempt to reduce architecture to a piece of machinery, even a piece of machinery fully adapted to all the needs and desires that can be presently formulated, will succeed only in alienating men from the ensuing product. As one melancholy Marxist has put it:

> Technology . . . expels from movements all hesitation, deliberation, civility. It subjects them to the implacable, as it were an historical demands of objects. Thus the ability is lost, for example, to close a door quietly and discreetly, yet firmly. Those of cars and refrigerators have to be slammed, others have the tendency to snap shut by themselves, imposing on those entering the bad manners of not looking behind them, not shielding the interior of the house which receives them. The new human type cannot be properly understood without awareness of what he is continuously exposed to from the world of things about him, even in his most secret innervations. What does it mean for the subject that there are no more casement windows to open, but only sliding frames to shove, no gentle latches but turnable handles, no forecourt, no doorstep before the street, no wall around the garden? . . . Not least to blame for the withering of experience is the fact that things under the law of pure functionality, assume a form that limits contact with them to mere operation, and tolerates no surplus, either in freedom of conduct or in autonomy of things, which would survive as the core of experience, because it is not consumed by the moment of action.[23]

We must then search for that core of experience, for that 'surplus' in which we find ourselves reflected, not as creatures of the moment, consumed in the present activity, but as rational beings, with a past, a present and a future. We must try to re-capture what is *central* in the experience of architecture. Like Alberti, Serlio and their followers, we will find that we can do that only if we reinstate aesthetic values at the heart of the builder's enterprise, and allow no question of function to be answered independently of the question of the appropriateness of a building, not just to its function, but to a style of life.

But I have not said enough about the concept of 'aesthetic value' for that suggestion to be persuasive, and it is necessary now to remedy this defect. Various influential theories have been proposed to account for the nature of our experience of architecture, and it is to these that we must first address ourselves, in order to acquire an understanding of the full complexity of the aesthetic attitude in building.

3
HAS ARCHITECTURE AN ESSENCE?

THERE are many ways of studying architecture – from the point of view of the engineer, of the historian, of the critic, of the client – and each way seems to propose its own favoured concepts, and seems to arrive at an organization of the subject which, if not at variance with its rivals, at least bears no clear relation to them. According to his preconceptions, therefore, a student of architecture may describe the nature of buildings, our experience of them, their meaning and their value, in many unrelated ways. And while this to some extent reflects a general vagueness in all discussions of anything that aspires to the honorific name of 'art', there seem to be particular obstacles in the case of architecture to a clear understanding of its aesthetic nature. In this chapter I propose to take some popular doctrines concerning the nature and experience of architecture, with a view to discovering, through their inadequacies, both the true complexity of our problem and the ground of its ultimate solution.

The doctrines that I shall consider speak sometimes of the nature of architecture, sometimes of its value, sometimes of the experience which we derive from it. Nonetheless, they have a certain rhetorical affinity which enables them to be used together, and to be combined into what has become a compelling critical standpoint. Their very vagueness has well adapted them to this end, and the reader might therefore consider that I misrepresent them in attributing to them a precision that they do not claim. But this attribution will be necessary, not because I wish to disparage the work of those who have espoused these doctrines, but because I wish to state and examine the intellectual basis of their thought. The doctrines I shall consider are functionalism, the 'space' theory, and the philosophies of *Kunstgeschichte* and proportion.

FUNCTIONALISM

It will not have escaped the reader's attention that the straw philosophy which I labelled 'constructivism' corresponds to little that has been practised by modern architects, and that many of the changes in form and style that our century has witnessed have been motivated by just that desire for an apt or appropriate appearance which I attributed to the theorists of the Renaissance. Despite the aesthetic parsimony of the modern movement, the popular 'functionalist' theories which have surrounded it have been used not to condemn but to articulate aesthetic values. In its most influential form, functionalism purports not to deny the priority of aesthetic values in architecture so much as to provide a comprehensive theory of their nature.[1] It argues that, in all true experience of architecture, form is inseparable from function. Aesthetic experience, according to some versions of the theory, is nothing more than an experience of function – not function as it is, but function as it appears. In the ideal building, therefore, the form must express, make clear, or – to use the word favoured by Sullivan – 'follow' the function.

As we have seen, there is a sound principle behind that theory, the principle that the utility of a building is one of its essential properties, so that there will be no true understanding of a building that ignores its functional side. Hence a feature that is apt or beautiful in a church may not be so in a house or factory. It is, indeed, impossible to abstract from our knowledge of a building's utility, and cast judgement on it in some pure 'aesthetic' void.

But, having made those remarks, it is difficult to see what follows from them. Certainly, functionalism, as it is normally stated, does not follow. Consider this, not too distant, analogy: it is an essential fact about a song that it consists in a setting of words to music. It does not follow that our experience of song is no more than an experience of words uttered in musical form, or that a song is perfect or beautiful just so long as it reveals or follows the verbal meaning. For one thing, the words may be foolish. Or the music, in following them, may lose all life and vigour of its own. There is no doubt that Wolff was a master at fitting words and music in an apt relation. But that does not suffice to raise him to the level of Schubert when, for all his genius, he lacked the melodic gift, drama, simplicity and naturalness which would deserve such praise. Nor is this analogy really misleading. For it shows that an essential property may not suffice to define the nature of the thing which possesses it. While it is true that a song is essentially a musical

PLATE 5 L. B. Alberti: façade to S. Maria Novella, Florence

setting of words, it is also more than that. For example, it involves a melody, and might be appreciated for its melody by someone who can neither hear nor understand the words. To say otherwise would be to affirm that there is no relation between the beauty of the song 'Death and the Maiden', and the beauty of the slow movement of the Quartet which bears that name: an absurd point of view. Likewise in architecture: function is not the only essential feature of a building; necessarily a building must display a form or pattern, and we may come to understand the pattern in contexts divorced from the given function. Consider, for example, Alberti's beautifully incrusted façade to the Florentine Church of S. Maria Novella (Plate 5). Many of the patterns there exhibited might have formed part of an ornamental cloth, and been found similarly beautiful. Moreover, to remove them from the façade – to present a bare face of serpentine or marble – would be to remove a major part of its charm, while preserving whatever deserves the name of an expression or revelation of its use.

But there is a more serious objection, and this is that the terms of the theory are fundamentally, and perhaps irremediably, obscure. What, for example, is meant by the term 'function'? Are we referring to the function of the building, or to the function of its parts? If only to the latter, does it suffice that a building should simply display all its functional details, like the tubes and wires which deck out the Centre Pompidou? If that is our ideal of aesthetic excellence, then clearly it would be better to discard aesthetics altogether. But it is only in a very superficial sense that such a building expresses or reveals its function, the function of the building being something quite different from the function of its parts. And the function of the whole building – in this case of the Centre Pompidou – is something indeterminate. In so far as the Centre is in competition with no. 4 Carlton House Terrace (which houses London's moral equivalent, but which was in fact designed as a private house), who can say which building best reveals the given use? And are we to think that the Round House Theatre, which presumably goes on 'revealing' or 'following' its past function as a railway shed, must for that reason be compromised in its present employment? Such examples show that the idea of 'the function' of a building is far from clear, nor is it clear how any particular 'function' is to be translated into architectural 'form'. All we can say – failing some more adequate aesthetic theory – is that buildings have uses, and should not be understood as though they did not.

Nor is the theory made more plausible by restricting our enquiry to the function of architectural parts, although, as later arguments will show, the theory, so restricted, contains valuable insights. For we find that now, far from providing a comprehensive aesthetic of architecture, functionalism must *depend* on some such aesthetic if it is to be understood. For example, it could be said that the function of a column is to support the entablature above it. But then, it could equally be said, that the function of the entablature is to lie on the column. Each of these functions is internal to the activity of architecture – which is to say, that we can understand them *as* functions only because we have some prior understanding of architecture, of why the parts of a building should be combined in *this* particular way. There is no way of using the idea of function to cast light on the nature of architecture, since it is only if we know what architecture is that we can understand the function. It follows that the theory, as an account of the nature of building, is simply vacuous.

Another difficulty for the theory is provided by such terms as 'follow' and 'express'. As we shall see, the only way of making sense of this concept of 'expression' is one that removes from functionalism any universal or *a priori* validity. That there is a difficulty presented by the notion should already be evident. Does the form of the strainer arch in Plate 6 follow or express its function more perfectly than would a

PLATE 6 St Mary Finedon, Northants, strainer arch

stretch of scaffolding? If so, why? And how does the functionalist explain the beautiful cresting and pierced quatrefoils in the Gothic example, the first adding nothing to the function, the second positively detracting from it? It is presumably because of the looseness of this concept of 'expression' that functionalism tends to be re-cast in ever-weaker forms. As a *weak* doctrine its pretensions are not philosophical but critical. That is, it claims not to capture the *essence* of architecture, but simply to denote one kind of architectural success. For example, there is a form of functionalism held up by Ruskin as the 'Lamp of Truth', a form which praises buildings for the structural honesty of their appearance. (On this view the Centre Pompidou deserves no praise, since what is revealed is structurally inessential, while the

Gothic cathedral has much to recommend it, even in an age when it has lost its principal use.) To elevate this principle into a dogma would have surprising consequences, for example, that St Paul's Cathedral, which hides functional buttresses behind screens of stone, is of less merit than the air terminal at Heathrow, or that the RAC Club in Pall Mall, which disguises steel and concrete behind a classical façade, some of the columns being mere hollow channels through which drains are conducted, is so debased as scarcely to deserve the name of architecture.

PLATE 7 (*above*) Karl Friedrich Schinkel: design for Werdersche Kirche, Berlin

PLATE 8 (*right*) Karl Friedrich Schinkel: design for Werdersche Kirche, Berlin

The mark of a critical doctrine, as opposed to a principle of aesthetics, is that it cannot be established *a priori*. If it lays claim to universal validity, then inevitably it must appear arbitrary and uncompelling, and to continue to reaffirm it in the face of these obvious counter-examples is indicative of nothing so much as a failure to observe what is there. As we shall see, a critical doctrine must be established case by case, by detailed exploration of the individual experience and the individual building. It will therefore be at best a generalization, at worst an unrepeatable observation of a single work of art. And even if it could be shown that the revelation of structure forms some part of our experience of every building, that would not have exhausted the resources of criticism. More than one form might 'follow' a single structure – as in the structurally equivalent plans for Schinkel's Werdersche Kirche in Berlin (see Plates 7 and 8). As such an example shows, the question of style – and therefore of meaning – might still arise, even when structural 'honesty' is not in doubt (for neither of Schinkel's plans is more 'honest' than the other). It follows that a large part of architectural experience will be simply ignored by the functionalist doctrine, and, until we have some independent understanding of the aesthetic problem, we shall not even know that the part which is ignored is not the part which is essential.

SPACE

Ever since the work of Wölfflin and Frankl the idea has been prevalent of a connection (variously described) between architecture and space. Once again the emphasis has been essentialist – this is what architecture essentially *is*, and therefore space, spatial relations and the play of interlocking voids are the true objects of architectural experience. 'Space', as one modern architect has written, 'is the most difficult aspect of architecture, but it is its essence and the ultimate destination to which architecture has to address itself.'[2] The doctrine represents an attempt to find the merit of architecture elsewhere than in its function, but like functionalism, which refers to houses, factories and railway stations, the space theory has fed itself upon a one-sided diet of examples – in this case, palaces, temples and churches, which are, among all buildings, the most emancipated from functional constraints, and the most given over to dramatic expression.

Taken literally, the theory that the experience of architecture is an experience of space is obviously indefensible. If space were all that interested us, then not only must a large part of the architect's activity seem like so much useless decoration, but it is even difficult to see why he should bother to build at all. If I stand in an open field then I can have a full experience of all the separate spaces that are enclosed in St Peter's in Rome. The only difference is that here the shell which Bramante and Michelangelo constructed around those spaces does not exist, and so does not interfere with the pure unmediated contemplation of the spaces as they are in themselves.

But it is clear that the theory should not be taken quite so literally; for what it means to say is that the essence of architecture is not space but the enclosure of space, or space as enclosed. In the words of Bruno Zevi:

> the essence of architecture . . . does not lie in the material limitation placed on spatial freedom, but in the way space is organized into meaningful form through this process of limitation . . . the obstructions which determine the perimeter of possible vision, rather than the 'void' in which this vision is given play.[3]

It is that conception of the essence of architecture which thinkers like Zevi, Giedion and their numerous following have applied with such enthusiasm to every type of building, and from which a certain critical orthodoxy has arisen. The first criticism to be made is that, whatever it strictly means (and it is not obvious, in fact, what it does mean), it must surely fail to provide an account of *all* that we appreciate in buildings. Zevi's description may seem to apply without strain to the foyer of the Stazione Termini in Rome, or to the treasury of Atreus at Mycenae, where the sense of 'moulded space' is prime among our perceptions, but it certainly does not capture all that is interesting in St Paul's, where, despite the 'spatial' grandeur, we have also deliberate and impressive effects of light and shade, of ornament, texture and mouldings.

One response of the critic given to the language of 'space' is to refer to all architectural details – light, ornament, carved and modelled forms – as expressing or 'articulating' the fundamental spatial relations, deriving their interest and value from the outlining, emphasizing and clarifying of volume, shape and space. Thus one might be led to think of an interior cornice as having an architectural (as opposed to a merely functional) interest because it brings the space of the wall to an effective conclusion, and defines thereby the hidden geometry of the roof cavity: as in the interior of St Peter's, which we come therefore to see as a rectangular box upon which rests a long half-cylinder of illuminated space – and here too the lights can be seen as enhancing that very same spatial division (see Plate 9). By contrast, the relatively unemphatic string courses which divide the wall-space of a northern Gothic cathedral serve only, as it were, to rest the eye on its upward movement, and do not truly divide the interior space, often breaking at the point of contact with the vertical shafts and leading to no sense of the roof cavity as a space separate from that defined by the upward movement of the walls (see Plate 10). And then, it might be said, it is precisely that opening out of space which provides the characteristic experience of the Gothic church.

Now this enterprise could succeed in establishing the primacy of space (or of the 'shaping' of space) in architectural interest only if it could show how each important feature of a building may be seen as a feature of the space which surrounds it, in the way that a wall may be seen as the enclosure of a space, and a door as an aperture into it. So that the theory falls to the ground as soon as we discover features which cannot be so translated: consider, for example, the nature of the builder's material. It is hard to think that the beauty of the colonnades at S. Spirito in Florence would be unaffected were they to be rebuilt in wood or granite, instead of the grey sandstone (the *pietra serena*) of the

PLATE 9 St Peter's, Rome, interior of nave

Florentines (see Plate 11). And it is odd to suggest that the beauty of the Lady Chapel at Ely has remained unaffected by the mutilation of its statuary, just because, at any point from which the spatial effect of the statuary (its ability, as the vague phrase goes, to 'articulate' the surrounding space) can be observed, the damage remains invisible. It might be said that we should accept that last proposition, on the grounds that statuary is not of the *essence* of architecture. But, if we are to extract this essence by such drastic strokes of elimination, then it is hard to see what will remain at the end. For there are important features of architecture which seem not to be detachable, in the way that statuary may be detachable, and which cannot be reduced to properties of architectural space. Consider the distinction between carved and modelled forms, as this is exemplified in building.[4] Clearly it is an immediately perceptible quality of a detail that it is carved into

Prospetto interno della Chiesa di S. Spirito dei R.R. P.P. Agostiniani. posta in Firenze

PLATE 11 Brunelleschi: S. Spirito, Florence

stone rather than modelled out of stucco or plaster. And while there are minute spatial properties which are responsible for the perceptible difference, it is not in terms of a *spatial* conception that the difference is seen. Consider, for example, the flank of Alberti's Tempio Malatestiana (S. Francesco) in Rimini (Plate 12). The beauty of this composition depends not only on the rhythm of the arcade, but also on the immediately perceptible quality of workmanship which can be seen in its finely sculpted lines. The same forms, moulded into concrete or stucco, would possess only the smallest remnant of their present emotional power. To reduce the effect to one of space is surely to misrepresent the entire nature of our experience.

Now it might still be argued that there is some architectural essence underlying all these examples which can be abstracted from the accidents of ornament and execution. But the suggestion begins to look less and tess plausible, as we recognize that 'spatial' effect may itself be dependent on significant detail. Consider, for example, the triumphant pouring of light from the cupola of S. Ivo in Rome (Plates 13 and 14). It is clearly quite reasonable to refer here to a spatial effect. But how could that effect be perceived unless one were also aware of the finely modelled mouldings of the cornice, which not only arrest the eye on its

PLATE 10 Nôtre Dame, Paris, interior of nave

PLATE 12 L. B. Alberti: flank of Tempio Malatestiana, Rimini

upward movement, but also define and re-define the stunning geometry of the church? What is seen is not just a dramatic space, but also a complex harmony of interrelated planes. And that harmony is observable only because of the finely worked details which principally attract our attention. And when one turns to the minutely worked interior of the same master's S. Carlino (Plate 15), where the boldness of 'spatial' organization depends at every point on yet bolder and yet more significant detail, the whole conception of a 'spatial' meaning falls into the background. Of course, the advocate of 'space' may not be driven to defeat by these examples; he may try to re-describe all these recalcitrant experiences as subtle variations of the one central experience which obsesses him. But the more he does so, the more one is inclined to suspect that, far from using the concept of space to illuminate the understanding of architecture, he is rather using that of architecture to illuminate what he means by an experience of space. His explanation of architectural experience becomes, like that of the functionalist, vacuous and circular.

It is for this reason that we will find that the concept of 'space' can be eliminated from most critical writings which make use of it without any

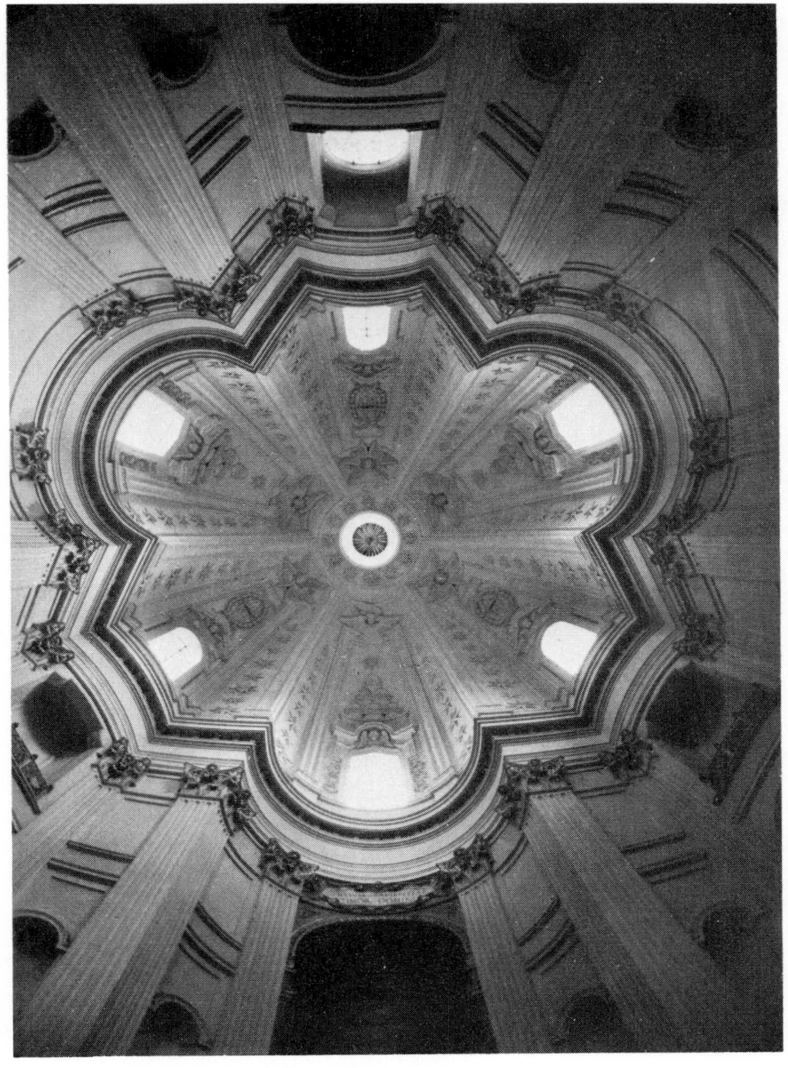

PLATE 13 Francesco Borromini: S. Ivo, Rome, cupola

real detriment to their meaning. Here is Frankl writing of the Jesuit churches of Posen and Breslau, and the Schlosskirche in Friedrichshafen:

> The relative height of the galleries has an important influence upon the spatial effect. If they are entirely below the spring of the nave

vault, they combine additively with the chapels below. If they extend *above* the spring, so that they break into the great vault like lunettes, then the higher they extend the more closely the total spatial effect approaches that of a hall.[5]

PLATE 14 Francesco Borromini: S. Ivo, Rome, cupola

Here the reference to a 'spatial effect' is in fact entirely redundant; the sense of the passage remains unchanged if one substitutes for the expression the simpler term 'shape', for clearly all that Frankl's examples show is that the higher the galleries extend the more closely does the *shape* of the church approach that of a hall. The reference to a distinct 'spatial effect' is brought in by a sleight of hand, as is the idea of an 'experience of space' in the following passage:

> Alberti wanted to add to S. Francesco in Rimini a circular building *wider* than the nave, and Michelozzo did add one to Sta Maria Annunziata in Florence. This space, similar to the Pantheon in Rome, is not related organically to the nave, although it does enhance our experience of the space.[6]

The grounds for this judgement are roughly the following: that the circular choir of the Annunziata is too large and ill-lit, and in consequence falls into no easy relation with the nave; that it continues no order established in the rest of the church and brings nothing to a climax or resolution. At the same time, it has a sombre grandeur of its own, and while it demands to be seen as a self-dependent addition to the nave, it is by no means wholly unconnected to it. I doubt that, in continuing such a commentary, it would ever be necessary to refer to an 'experience of the space' (which space?), or that a use could be found for that

PLATE 15 Francesco Borromini: S. Carlino, Rome, interior

notion which might make it into an indispensable critical tool. Nevertheless, the doctrine of space remains an influential one, and its fascination still needs explaining.

Perhaps some explanation can be gleaned from the works of Giedion, the doctrine's principal advocate, who has used what one might perhaps call the rhetoric of space to manufacture the critical orthodoxies of the modern movement, and formed thereby the consciences of a generation of architectural students.[7] Giedion's *Space, Time and Architecture*, perhaps the most influential systematic treatise on architecture to have been produced in recent years, exhibits all the faults to which I have referred, along with many others deriving from the author's journalistic acquaintance with modern physics. (Thus he is led to describe modern art and architecture as providing the 'artistic equivalent of space-time', a conception that falls apart as soon as it is applied, and which presupposes – what is false – that the dimension of time is treated by Einstein and Minkowski equivalently to the three dimensions of space.) But the interesting feature of his use of the doctrine of space is that he manages to combine it with a peculiar form of historical analysis, and that this combination to some extent explains the doctrine's appeal. Consider the following passage:

> There are three stages of architectural development. During the first stage – the first space conception – space was brought into being by the interplay between volumes. This stage encompassed the architecture of Egypt, Sumer and Greece. Interior space was disregarded. The second space conception began in the midst of the Roman period. . . . The third space conception set in at the beginning of this century with the optical revolution that abolished the single viewpoint of perspective.[8]

What does it mean to say that the 'space' of the Greek temple was 'brought into being' by the 'interplay between volumes' (which volumes?), or that the Greeks 'disregarded the interior space' of the building – which is not meant to imply that they never went inside or took pleasure in what they found there? (Odysseus, narrating his encounter with the souls of the dead, pauses at a certain point to survey the silent array of amazed and lamplit faces in the 'shadowy hall'; if there is such a thing as a 'sense of interior space', it is certainly there in Homer's description (Od. XI, 333–4).) It is clear that Giedion's peculiar theory has some other source than the doctrine of space, and that this source provides a new energy and compellingness. For the doctrine has here been conjoined to the process of reflection that would attempt to divide the history of the world into clear successive periods and to find the nature and meaning of art in its relation to the period from which it derives. This is the next major confusion that we must examine.

KUNSTGESCHICHTE

The philosophy of Hegel set out not only to explain the structure of the world and the scope of human knowledge, but also to provide a universal system of human society. It set out to derive *a priori* what at first seem to be the most arbitrary and contingent among all observable facts – the phenomena of history. Beneath the superficial chaos it claimed to see the workings of a spiritual necessity, a kind of permanent proof of one moment of history from the preceding, which moves from premise to conclusion with all the rigour and all the abstract clarity (for those able to understand it) of a mathematical theorem. The place occupied by this theory in contemporary thought is sufficiently explained by its consolatory value, if not by its truth. History tends to be viewed even now under the aspect of necessity, and the mere fact that two events are contemporaneous is often regarded as showing some real connection between them. Burckhardt, steeped in Hegelian metaphysics, began a famous examination of the Italian Renaissance, looking everywhere for its dominant urge and unifying conception. It seemed to him that every work of art of the period must derive its significance from the same underlying spirit or idea. Wölfflin, Burckhardt's pupil, applied the method to architecture, and Wölfflin's pupil Frankl passed it on to Giedion and to Pevsner. The result is that it has become an established orthodoxy of English and American architectural scholarship, and while the Hegelian philosophy of history has been frequently attacked, in particular by Popper, it is only very recently that its consequences for the history of art and architecture have been critically examined.[9]

Let us suppose, for the sake of argument, that some version of the Hegelian view of history is true. It is important to see that it cannot be transformed into a basis for aesthetics, nor can it lead us to the true significance of architecture. Of course it is rare that the practitioners of the Hegelian approach have explicitly claimed to provide such a basis, rare, for example, to find them writing with quite the daring and spirit of Wölfflin, that:

> [Architecture] is an expression of its time in so far as it reflects the corporeal essence of man and his particular habits of deportment and movement, it does not matter whether they are light and playful, or solemn and grave, or whether his attitude to life is agitated or calm; in a word, architecture expresses the *'Lebensgefühl'* of an epoch.[10]

Nevertheless, the Hegelian theory has been used as the sole basis for aesthetic judgement by many recent critics.[11] Its aesthetic implications, therefore, are largely taken for granted. Of course, no-one doubts that men understood and appreciated architecture long before they fell under the spell of Hegel, indeed, long before it was possible to take an 'historical' view of art. But it may still be that, whenever men have taken an 'aesthetic' interest in some building – whenever they have seen a building as something more than a functional device – this has been because they have sought for its 'spirit' or 'Lebensgefühl'. And it may be true that the best description of such a 'spirit' – and the description which makes it accessible to men who do not share in it – is an historical description, showing its relation to the entire form of life through which it was expressed.

Now it might be argued that such a theory is bound to provide an inadequate basis for aesthetics. For if one building manifests the spirit of its epoch, so do all the other buildings of its time: in which case, where lies the difference between the good and the bad examples? A theory of architecture which says nothing about its characteristic success cannot really be a theory of its essence; so we must find an answer to that question. It is normal for criticism in the art-historical tradition to concentrate only on the really great and compelling products of a period – consider, for example, the writings of Giedion and Norberg-Schulz.[12] This habit reflects a covert belief (rarely made explicit) that it is only the successful work that truly expresses its *Zeitgeist*, spirit, or 'ruling space conception';[13] the unsuccessful work is merely inexpressive. But to borrow this concept of expression is to lay oneself open to certain objections. Nothing now stands in the way of the suggestion that a work might succeed, just occasionally, in expressing something other than its historical reality, and derive its success from that. For example, it might succeed, like Westminster Cathedral, in expressing the spirit of a world to which it does not belong, or in expressing some outlook that has no historical determinacy whatsoever, like the rugged simplicity of the Italian hilltop town. Indeed, we find that, like functionalism, the art-historical thesis soon loses its claim to generality, once it has laid all emphasis on the disorderly concept of 'expression'. For that concept is no more than a critical device, a means for associating a work of architecture with a meaning, while giving no general principle as to how the meaning is derived.

In general, then, it is not surprising to find that the insights of 'historicism' (as it has been called[14]) are not hard-won; they come ready-made, along with the axioms of the theory. When Giedion describes Pascal as a 'baroque master in another medium' (meaning mathematics),[15] all he really intends is that the architectural style known for various reasons as the baroque happened to be contemporaneous with Pascal's work in mathematics. There is nothing further to the comparison that would enable it to illuminate either the nature of Pascal's celebrated theorem, or the meaning of the architecture of Mansart. The same is true of his description of the Villa Savoie as peculiarly appropriate to the age of Relativity, being 'quite literally . . . a construction in space-time'.[16] His evidence for this is the unremarkable fact that the villa may not be fully comprehended from any single point of view, a feature which it shares with such well-known expressions of the ethos of Relativity as Lincoln Cathedral and the Taj Mahal.

For the advocate of *Kunstgeschichte*, architecture is one among many cultural products, which has its own means of conveying a significance, but no unique or peculiar significance to convey. In so far as a building acquires a significance through its art-historical interpretation it is a significance that is in all probability external to its aims and nature, a significance that might have belonged to any other expressive product of its age, and which is siezed through an act of understanding that gives no precedence to what is essentially, rather than only accidentally, architectural. It may once again be true that, in particular cases, and for particular reasons, it might be valuable to see a building in this way. But as a foundation for aesthetics the theory is useless, for it denies itself even the ability to *ask* what is fundamental to our experience of architecture – what makes it into an experience of *architecture*. It is for this reason that historicism tends to lean as heavily on the doctrine of space as that doctrine itself leans on historical analysis. The doctrine of space provides the needed description of architectural experience; the historical analysis is then used in its criticism.

Like all critical doctrines, the method may be sensitively or crudely used. And it is worth remarking on one particular crudeness, deriving from the simplistic determinism sometimes associated with Hegelian theory. It is often thought that, since a building is necessarily an expression of the spirit of its age, the attempt to build in the style of another age must be an exercise in 'false consciousness', an attempt to deny what it is necessary to accept; and as David Watkin has shown,[17] that belief has been a received dogma among many modern critics, from Lethaby to Furneaux Jordan. Such critics have systematically assumed that the attempt to build in the style of some other age will be necessarily unsuccessful; even thoroughly immoral. This is the most widely held of all the critical judgements which the Hegelian vision has manufactured, appearing in Giedion's defence of the forms of the modern movement as uniquely adapted to the spiritual reality of modern man, and in Pevsner's influential attack on the desire (experienced as it happens by almost every serious architect from the Greeks to the Edwardians) to build in the style of some preceding age. But such spurious determinism loses its force, just as soon as we realize that the 'style of an age' is not a critical datum, not something that can be identified in advance of the individual intentions of individual architects. Historicism has no real method whereby to associate the works of a given period with its ruling spirit. All it can do is to reflect on their association *after* the event, and try to derive, from a critical understanding of individual buildings, a suitable formula with which to summarize their worth. It follows that it can say nothing in advance of observation, and can set no dogmatic limit either to the architect's choice of style or to his expressive aim. There is something truly absurd about the attempt to command obedience to a rule which can be formulated only when it is already obeyed. It was, for example, only in the wake of Perret, Maillart and the Bauhaus that Giedion could begin to say what the spirit of modern man demands in architecture. And in selecting just those architects for his praise he was at the same time legislating in defiance of his own critical method. On what grounds, for example, could he ignore that great classicist Lutyens, who was as much of his time, and as much in command of his materials, as any of the architects whom Giedion praised? One might legitimately feel sceptical of the attempt to describe *the* valid style of an age or culture, and sceptical too of the very narrow understanding of architectural tradition which the determinist analysis involves.

I remarked earlier upon the ease with which the doctrines of space and of *Kunstgeschichte* can be combined. It is common to find a critic writing, for example, of 'the baroque conception of space', as though the discovery of that conception were the main purpose of critical enquiry.[18] Once again, as a piece of *criticism*, such a combination of viewpoints may prove fruitful. It goes without saying that the emphasis on space in the criticism of baroque architecture is often jejune and cliché-ridden. But that does not mean that there is no truth in such views as that the baroque ideal of space is more dynamic than that of the Renaissance, or that the spatial organization of an English cathedral is more disjointed than that of a French. And these observations can sometimes be connected in an illuminating way with the beliefs and customs from which the particular buildings arise. It is perfectly reasonable to remark, not just on the detail and style of the late nineteenth-century department store, but also upon a 'conception of space' with which these are associated. It is not absurd, for example, to see the running staircases beneath the glass roof of the Paris Bon Marché as 'taking possession' of the space surrounding them (Plate 16).[19] And it is an apt critical reflection to connect this act of possession with the prevailing spirit of mass consumption which the building embodied and announced. The space of the stairwell – being used for the display of goods – holds out at every point a promise of possession; and the rushing movement, exuberant decoration and cascading light all contribute to that stunning effect of massed but ephemeral splendour which may be scrambled for by every woman or man.

But to use doctrines of this kind as critical instruments is also dangerous. The doctrine of 'space' can often simplify the description of architectural experience to a point of near vacuity, and that of *Kunstgeschichte* lends itself to the facile manufacture of significances. The critic can therefore use them to advance directly from a description of an experience to a description of its meaning without any serious understanding of the building which he purports to describe. This, in a nutshell, is the critical method of Giedìon and his followers, and if it is necessary to criticize it at such length it is on account of the astonishing influence of that school.

PLATE 16 L. C. Boileau: Bon Marché, Paris

KUNSTWOLLEN

There is another Teutonic concept which should be mentioned at this juncture – the concept of the *Kunstwollen*, of the prevailing artistic intention which each work of art or architecture is supposed to display. The particular brands of 'historicism' that we have considered are really most plausible when considered as special cases of a more general theory, the theory that works of art owe their unity and expressive power to some underlying artistic intention or idea, and that it is for the critic to lay bare that ruling *Kunstwollen*[20] and to display its emergence in the concrete forms of the individual work. Historical analysis is no more than a part of such critical discovery, though it may sometimes be a necessary part, as in Panofsky's association of the Gothic style with scholasticism, or in Ruskin's powerful description of the Doge's Palace.[21] This more general, and rather vague, Hegelianism contains so much truth, and so much that is dubious or false, that its analysis will be a constant proccupation during later chapters. But once again, we cannot regard it as providing any account of what is peculiar to architecture, or even a more generalized account of the aesthetic enterprise. This is not because, as some might argue, it commits the so-called 'intentional fallacy' – the fallacy of seeing and judging works of art not as they are in themselves, but only in relation to some prior 'intention' of the artist – for the idea of such a fallacy rests on a philosophical mistake, the 'Cartesian' mistake of construing an intention and its principal expression as two quite separate things.[22] It is rather that the theory is vacuous until we can provide some independent account of aesthetic interest. For the 'intention' which the critic lays bare is specifically an *artistic* intention, one which can be described only in terms of some theory or conception of art. So we shall require some account of art and architecture before we can make sense of that idea, and of the concept of 'expression' which is employed in it. As we shall see, words like 'intention' and 'idea', with their mentalistic, subjective, artist-oriented implications, are far from being forced on us as necessary instruments in the critical description of architecture.

PROPORTION

Until the three doctrines considered above came to dominate the discussion of architecture, theoretical concepts were far more nearly indicative of what we would intuitively describe as an 'aesthetic' point of view. The theorists of the Renaissance were, of course, well aware of the multiplicity of architectural standards, and were from the beginning concerned by Vitruvius's division of his aims into the *utilitas, firmitas* and *venustas* which Wotton was to translate as 'commodity, firmness and delight'.[23] But they were yet more impressed by Vitruvius's expansion of the third of these into six separate categories – the categories of *ordinatio, dispositio, eurythmia, symmetria, decor,* and *distributio,* to which he proceeded to subordinate most other architectural aims. The consequent delight in the multiplication of 'aesthetic' terms can be witnessed in all the theoretical writings of the time. Alberti referred to many aesthetic virtues, including those of *dispositio, numerus, finitio, collocatio, proportio,* of the *aptus, concinnatus, commodatus, proprius, decentus* and *decus,* all of which register subtle gradations of critical significance. Even the level-headed Vasari was unable to write of architecture without introducing, in his preface to the third part of the *Lives*, five separate Vitruvian standards, the standards of *regola, ordine, misura, disegno* and *maniera*.[24] But despite this seeming multiplicity of aesthetic aims, critics have been fairly obstinate in their conviction that behind Renaissance theories of architecture there lies a single dominant idea – the idea of proportion – and that all this multiplicity of aesthetic terms is to be understood as nothing more than a detailed elaboration of that concept.[25]

The classical theory of proportion consists in an attempt to transfer to architecture the quasi-musical notion of an 'harmonious order', by giving specific rules and principles for the proportionate combination of parts. And it might be thought that, if this attempt were to succeed, it would provide a clear analysis, both of the nature of architectural success, and of the value of the experience which we derive from it. Since the only conceivable rules of proportion must be geometrical, the essence of proportion (according to many Renaissance theorists) must lie in mathematical relationships. This outlook seems all the more plausible when combined with Pythagorean reflections upon the harmony of the universe, a harmony illustrated in the mathematical theory of musical consonance attributed to Pythagoras, and in the mathematical cosmology which neo-Platonists had refined and propagated throughout the Middle Ages.[26] There thus arose the ambition (an ambition which is still present in the writings of Le Corbusier) to use mathematics in describing architectural success. From both mathematics and architecture we obtain a like sense of fittingness: in contemplating the relations of numbers and the relations of architectural parts, we derive a similar satisfaction and a similar sense of the intrinsic order of things. The analogy between mathematical and architectural harmony therefore enables us to use the former to understand, envisage and manipulate the latter. Furthermore, our sense of what is fitting reflects a deeper demand for order. We can see architectural forms as 'fitting' because architecture reflects the desires and responses characteristic of our rational nature. Architecture helps us to see the world as familiar, as reflecting the order and harmony that we find in ourselves: and something similar is true, according to thinkers of a neo-Platonic or Pythagorean cast, of mathematics.

It is not my purpose to expound this process of thought completely, or to introduce the reader to its impressive history. Suffice it to say that the Pythagorean cosmology, and the view of architecture which it implies, were by no means the invention of the Renaissance. The cosmology had survived as a ruling element in Christian thought, taking heart from the admiration of St Augustine, Boethius and Macrobius for the arguments of the *Timaeus* and of the *Republic*, in particular for the versions of these which Cicero had transmitted. The full architectural expression of Christian neo-Platonism occurred not in Renaissance Italy but in 'Mediaeval' France, at Chartres, where it coincided in place and time with a renowned school of neo-Platonist philosophy.[27] It was not a peculiar property of Renaissance 'humanism' that it should look for a secret mathematical harmony behind every form of architectural beauty: on the contrary, this has been the most popular conception of architecture, from the Egyptians to Le Corbusier. The builders of the Gothic cathedrals were as anxious to illustrate the divine perfection of mathematical relations as were the builders of the Renaissance temples, and often, it now seems, used systems of proportion that perfectly correspond to the systems of their sucessors.[28] The surprising disparity in style, while it might seem to cast doubt on the universal validity of the rule of proportion, as the essence of architectural success, serves in a deeper way to confirm it. For we are led to suspect the existence of laws of proportion more basic than the stylistic accidents of any particular mode of building, laws which define some common principles of architectural practice to be followed by every successful style. The fundamental idea is indeed simple enough: certain arrangements of shapes and lines seem peculiarly fitting or harmonious, while others appear vague, disproportionate and unstable. For example, the circle and the square have a property of intrinsic harmony which makes them pleasurable both to construct and to see, while imperfect forms of either shape, when they appear as decoration or as architectural parts, are apt to transmit an impression of clumsiness or discord, like the ill-executed cartwheels in the crossing of S. Maria delle Grazie in Milan, which compare so unfavourably with the geometrical perfection of the Gothic rose. Now the architect, who needs to combine contiguous parts and sections, should therefore try to discover, from these simple harmonious shapes, the mathematical law of their harmony, and so predict all the derivative harmonies which indirectly reflect it. The delight in buildings constructed according to the resulting law will be akin to the delight in music or in mathematical proof. Mathematical relations can therefore be used to predict visual harmonies, and even in forms which are without obvious mathematical paradigm, we may still discern in them the *intimations* of the perfect mathematical relationships from which they derive. (Consider, for example, the door from Serlio, illustrated in Plate 17. One might seek to explain the harmonious effect of such a composition by the fact of its mysterious visual intimation of the perfect square involved in its construction.)

The immediate consequence of any mathematical theory of proportion is the availability of a *system* of proportion, a rule, or set of rules, for the creation and combination of parts. The architect may now take some basic measure – or module – from which to derive all the lengths and forms exhibited in a building; the parts of the building will then of necessity stand to each other in a direct and intelligible mathematical relationship. This idea appears in Vitruvius, was clearly used by the

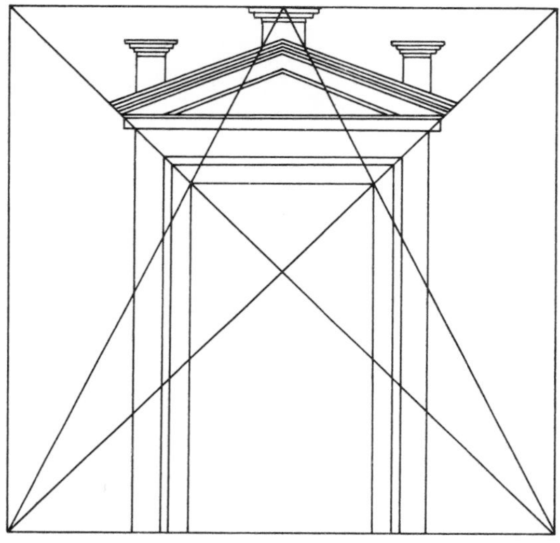

PLATE 17 Door from Serlio

mediaevals, and was re-expressed by most of the Renaissance theorists. The theory of the Orders, for example, is usually associated with a complete system for the measurement and combination of architectural parts, and can be seen as a device for the construction of precise mathematical relationships, which diffuse their harmony through the visual appearance of the building without ever being blatantly stated.[29] Nor is such a theory wholly dead; it is to be found in Le Corbusier's conception of the Modulor, which aims to create a comprehensive harmony from understanding the clear mathematical paradigms from which an architect must start.

Le Corbusier based his Vitruvian 'module' on the Golden Section (well known to the Greeks and the cornerstone of many Euclidean proofs), and derived his 'system' of measurement from the relation between the Golden Section and the Fibonacci Series, an old and familiar result of mathematics. It is likely that the Greeks derived their systems of proportion in some such way, and this renewed emphasis on the Golden Section must provide remarkable confirmation of the mathematical analogy.[30] For it has been remarked from the first that the rectangle formed by the Golden Section possesses a peculiar visual harmony – indeed it is the rectangle which, to the normal eye, shows the same visual stability as the square. This can be appreciated, I think, from the courtyard of the palace of Quetzalpapalotl, illustrated in Plate 18, in which a perfect square opening is flanked by two rectangular

PLATE 18 Courtyard, Quetzalpapalotl's palace, Mexico

openings constructed from the Golden Section. (Indeed the whole of this façade seems to be derived from the proportions exhibited by those openings. Such a use of the famous Greek measure, combined with a version of the well-known Greek composition of distyle in antis, exhibited in a civilization that knew nothing of the existence of Greece or Rome, must seem to provide yet more striking confirmation of the thought that there are *basic* laws of proportion in architecture, underlying all the accidents of manner and style.[31])

The Golden Section rectangle exhibits the ratio $(1 + \surd 5):2$ (Ø, for short). This is distinguished by the fact that $1 + Ø = Ø^2$; moreover, if one takes from the rectangle a square formed from its shortest side, the fragment which remains is itself a Golden Section rectangle. Such properties lend to the rectangle a mysterious mathematical affinity to the square, an affinity which, for the Pythagorean, would completely explain its visual harmony. And such rectangles, on account of this mathematical property, can be combined in ways that lead to the convenient generation of right-angles and the 'nesting' of corresponding parts: an example is provided by the bay from the Cancelleria in Rome, analysed in Plate 19.[32] It is of course immensely satisfying to observe these mathematical properties, and yet more satisfying to contemplate the visual harmony which results from them. Small wonder that the Golden Section should have provided such inspiration to the builders of the Greek temples, the Gothic cathedrals, the Renaissance palaces. Small wonder that Le Corbusier should have tried, in a moment of more than usual megalomania, to patent its architectural significance as a personal discovery.[33] For countless architects it has seemed to provide the one basic measure, the measure which, diffused throughout a building, gives harmony and humanity to the whole.

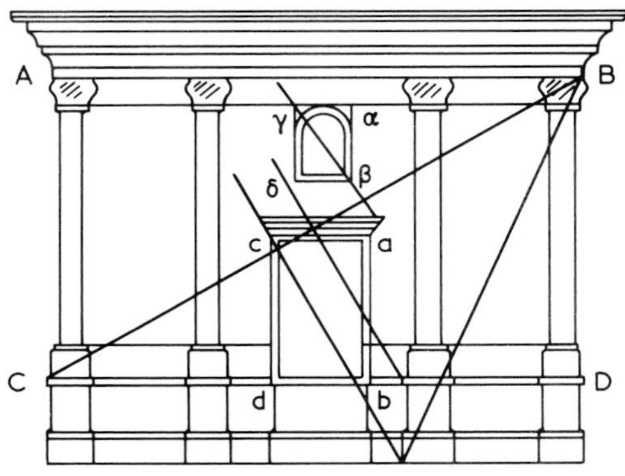

PLATE 19 Cancelleria, Rome, bay of upper storey
AB: AC = ab: ac = $\alpha\beta$: $\alpha\gamma$ = Ø

But despite this almost universal sense of an underlying mathematical paradigm of architecture, and the widespread confidence in a concept of proportion which derives from it, the theory provides no general aesthetic of construction. The first difficulty arises when we try to relate the abstractly calculated proportionality of a building to a concrete *experience* of proportion. It is true that this difficulty might not have worried the theorists of the Renaissance, many of whom were more concerned that their buildings should correspond to an *idea* of excellence, comprehensible to the mind of man, but not necessarily to his eye. But we cannot rest content with that. For the question that concerns us is a question about the appropriate *look* of things. A perfect geometry of architecture might well allow us to derive laws for what is 'fitting', in the sense of a mathematical canon for the combination of parts, but what guarantee is there that we will experience a building as the proper expression of that mathematical canon, or that we can always use it to predict the visual harmony of the result? It is true that in a façade, which can be comprehended immediately and from a single point of view, geometrical relations impose themselves with a certain immediacy and absoluteness. No-one has much difficulty in seeing the geometrical rhythms concealed, for example, in the façade to S. Maria Novella (Plate 5, p. 39). But once we move to the consideration of three-dimensional forms the difficulty of visual understanding may become insuperable. Consider, for example, one of the most influential of all 'mathematical' buildings, Brunelleschi's Old Sacristy in S. Lorenzo, Florence (Plate 20). Here the two perfect figures of cube and hemisphere are combined in a way that is immediately apparent

PLATE 20 Brunelleschi: Old Sacristy, S. Lorenzo, Florence

from a study of the cross-section and the plans. But nothing in the experience of the building need suggest that perfection: for the observer, the square might be only approximate, and the cupola short of a perfect hemisphere. Normally the squareness of a room can be gauged by standing in the centre, to observe the equidistance of the walls; that observation cannot be made at the Old Sacristy, since the entire centre of the room is taken up by a massive marble table that has been standing there since at least 1433 (four years after the building was completed). Nevertheless, the harmony of this building is apparent at once, long before we can be certain of its mathematical basis.

The true Pythagorean will not be disturbed by this objection. He will say that the perception of visual harmony is not in itself a knowledge of mathematical relations: the mathematics is unconscious, and can be used to predict that *soave armonia* at which Palladio aimed[34] but is no part of what is known to the beholder. As Francesco di Giorgio wrote, reflecting on Palladio: 'such harmonies usually please very much, without anyone knowing why, excepting the student of the causality of things (*le ragione delle cose*)'.[35] But the trouble with that is not only that the *ragione delle cose* cannot be described in Pythagorean terms (the mathematical cosmology of the humanists and their neo-Platonic predecessors being clearly false), but also that, construed in Palladio's sense, these 'reasons' are strictly independent of aesthetics. It becomes a mere *discovery* that visual proportion reflects a mathematical scheme, a discovery that might be upset by the first contrary experience.[36] And as soon as we place the experience of proportion first, giving it precedence over its mathematical 'explanation', we find, not only that the mathematical laws are inadequate to account for what we see, but also that the concept of 'proportion' is plunged once again into the darkness from which the Pythagorean theory seemed to raise it. The criticism was levelled again and again by the baroque theorists at their high-minded predecessors,[37] and much later by Hogarth, in his polemical *Analysis of Beauty*.[38] As the baroque architect Guarini noted,[39] what is harmonious from one angle is not necessarily harmonious from another, whereas in music and mathematics harmony is harmony from whatever point of view. How then can any purely mathematical theory be used to predict a 'harmony' that is in essence visual, dependent on the aspect of the building from many points of view in space? The difficulty is surely a serious one. For consider the beautiful library of St Mark's, by Sansovino (Plate 21). The immoderately high cornice of this building, out of line with the Classical Orders, and with the geometry established in the colonnade, is nonetheless required for the visual harmony. In fact the stretching of the cornice upwards is required precisely because there could be no sense of proportion unless this were done. The length of the library and its position on the piazetta entail that a proper frontal view of it – a frontal view in which the colonnade can be fully comprehended – is unobtainable. The only complete view of the building must be obtained by approaching it from the side; perspective therefore requires the cornice to be raised, lest the colonnade should seem to have nothing substantial to lie on it. Here the achieved harmony of the appearance is the sign of no mathematical order in the building. And, indeed, it is often precisely the pursuit of a mathematical order that leads to disproportion – which leads, for example, to the stretching of the drum of Ste Geneviève (the

Panthéon) in Paris, in order to enclose the composition within a triangle (see Plate 22). The result has none of the stability or calm proportionality of its model (St Paul's), and despite the many beauties of this church, it is difficult to view its dome from afar without an inexplicable feeling of unease.

PLATE 21 Jacopo Sansovino: library of St Mark's, Venice

These observations are scarcely unfamiliar to architects in the Serlian tradition, the tradition that puts perspective before everything, and which alters and amends quite freely in the interests of visual perfection.[40] But they serve to throw the whole concept of proportion into doubt. What does it mean to speak of one composition as 'proportionable', another as 'ill-proportioned', 'ill-fitting' or 'disjoint'? The mathematical theory fails precisely because it does not really capture the *meaning* of the concept which it purports to analyse, but at best only the hidden *ragione delle cose*. To provide a 'system of proportion' is not in itself to say what 'proportion' means, or why we should value it, not, that is, unless the system can really lay claim to the universal validity which we have refused it. What we have noticed is that the rules of proportion are *a posteriori*: they derive, not from the meaning of the term, but from some discovered criterion for its application. They do not tell us what proportion essentially *is*, but only give laws for its production, laws which hold at best only approximately and from certain points of view.

But what, then, *is* proportion? As we reflect on that question we come to see that, far from providing a general basis for architectural aesthetics, the concept of proportion requires such an aesthetics if it is to be understood. This can be illustrated by showing the dependence that exists between our sense of proportion and our recognition of aesthetically significant detail. We find that the sense of proportion

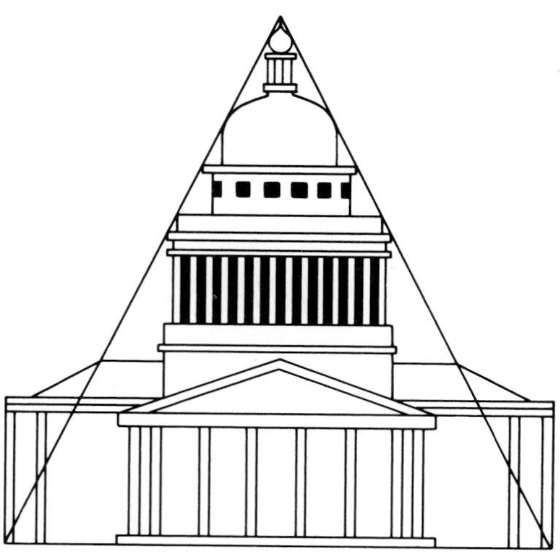

PLATE 22 Jacques-Germain Soufflot: Ste Genevieve (le Panthéon), Paris

and the sense of detail are in fact inseparable, and while the *theories* of the Palladian architect may seem to deny this fact,[41] his practice seldom does so. First of all, it is clear that we are prepared to overlook what are, from the geometrical point of view, manifest incongruities, provided only that our sense of detail be properly engaged: consider, for example, the two west towers of Chartres. More interestingly, we are even unable to appreciate the harmony of the majority of Gothic compositions until we can see the detailed correspondences, divergences and variations among their parts. Consider the harmonious but asymmetrical façade of the Ca d'Oro (Plate 23), a composition which represents the subtle rhythm of Venetian Gothic at its most delicate and refined. There is simply no way of beginning to describe the harmony of this building in mathematical terms; nothing that we could recognize as an account of its proportionality could really ignore the varied but answering details of the windows, the ambiguous rhythms of the tracery, the striking bareness of wall against which the round-arched portal is balanced. It seems absurd, in the face of such an example, to suggest that one might abstract from the knowledge of harmonious compositions some one set of rules of pure proportion, which can be applied

PLATE 23 Ca d'Oro, Venice, façade

irrespective of style, detail, and viewpoint. Of course, there are accepted patterns of composition which generally please us, such as the twin towers of a city gate, a composition imitated for symbolic reasons in the massive west towers of Gothic cathedrals, and the more fragile towers of the German and Italian baroque.[42] But there will be no universal law, no law to the effect that this composition must always be proportionable, whatever the quality of the detail, and whatever the style in which it is displayed. *Something*, after all, is wrong with the twin-towered façade of Ste Sulpice, and it is not a fault of material or workmanship. Is it not rather that the factitious Romanism of the style simply fails to give strength to the arrangement, so that the composition falls apart? One might also suggest, with one critic,[43] that the fault which we noted in the drum of Ste Geneviève would have been overcome by a more apt disposition of detail, by the insertion (as at St Paul's) of occasional niches between the columns, so that the dome ceases to 'spin' so disconcertingly on its uncertain legs.

Nor is it only the sense of detail that is necessary for this proper apprehension of proportionate forms. Every aspect of aesthetic interest seems already engaged in the judgement that an arrangement is well- or ill-proportioned, and the idea, that the meaning of 'proportion' can be captured by some mathematical paradigm must in the end seem little more than a naivety. Pugin even wrote that the use of large stones is in itself sufficient to destroy proportion,[44] a judgement which, while clearly of less than universal validity, rings true of many forms of Gothic masonry, and also, as one writer has noted,[45] of much unpretentious rural architecture. And to pass from what is most small in building, to what is most grand: how could one achieve a mathematical understanding of the visual harmony created by Bernini's piazza, with its sweep of columns imposing unity upon the contrasting façades of St Peter's and the Vatican; or of the harmony of the Spanish steps as they led up to and include the church of the Trinità dei Monti, or of the Piazza del Popolo, which unites the urbane façades of Rainaldi's churches,[46] the great gate of Rome, the church of S. Maria del Popolo, and the greenery of the Pincian hill, in one magnificent harmonious sweep? The meaning of these architectural achievements can be understood only in terms of the chance conglomeration of pre-existing forms. Their harmony is an effect of décor, and as such is the type of all true architectural proportion. For what builder can dispense with a concept of proportion, and yet how many builders may command a site where the demands of mathematics can be satisfied?

None of this is to deny the utility of 'proportion' as a critical concept, nor is it to refuse to that concept a fundamental place in aesthetic understanding. But it is precisely because proportion *is* so aesthetically fundamental that we should beware of tying it down to an explicit definition. As we shall see, Alberti was careful to separate the question of the meaning of 'proportion' from the mathematical theory of its realization; his actual *definition* can be understood only in conjunction with the whole accompanying gamut of aesthetic terms, some of which I mentioned at the beginning of this section. To understand proportion is to understand harmony, fittingness, appropriate detail and order. It is only in the framework of a complete aesthetics that the meaning of these terms can be described. It will be only at the end of our investigations that we shall be able to return to the problem of proportion, and by that time we will have left far behind us the mathematical analogy, and the intriguing speculations which derive from it. And we will find that there is little to be said about the aesthetic significance of proportion until we have descended from the level of abstraction that the mathematical theory requires. When we have so descended, we will find ourselves with a concept of proportion that not only is much altered from its Renaissance incarnation, but which can no longer occupy the soverign place in architectural criticism that it once possessed. Until then, however, we must put the concept to one side. It is neither clear enough to provide a basis for criticism, nor comprehensive enough to summarize our full experience of architecture.

CONCLUSION

The theories that I have considered in this chapter are premature. They try to arrive at abstract principles of architectural success before giving a proper description of the experience which it qualifies. Clearly, if we are to think of the analysis of the object as casting light on the nature of appreciation, then we must consider the object only under its widest possible description. In Scholastic language, we must define not the material but the formal object of architectural interest and appreciation: we must find the description under which an object *must* be seen and appreciated if it is to be appreciated as architecture.[47] Only in this way will we begin to characterize what is essential to our interest in building. None of the theories that I have discussed provides such a 'formal' description, for each ignores some feature of architecture that is both intentional and centrally significant. Moreover, each pretends to an *a priori* status that it cannot justify, pretends, that is, to characterize the essence of architecture and the core of our experience. We must now put these theories to one side, and see if we can approach that central core more directly.

4
EXPERIENCING ARCHITECTURE

WHY SHOULD it be difficult to describe the experience of architecture?[1] We see, touch and move among buildings, just as we see, touch and move among the other objects in our world. Surely then to describe architectural experience is to describe the basic processes of perception. Whatever difficulty that enterprise presents is not a difficulty for the aesthetics of architecture, but for the philosophy of perception, and nothing peculiar to architecture need be mentioned in such a philosophy. What is peculiar to architecture comes at the next stage, as it were: it is not the experience but the enjoyment that depends on it. Thus, someone might say that the fundamental form of architectural enjoyment is simply pleasure in the appearance of something, and that the architect's task is to construct something which is both pleasing to look at and at the same time functional. The actual *experience* is not in question; what is in question is the pleasure which it engenders.

That suggestion is too simple, for it fails to make clear what is meant by 'pleasure'. There are buildings from which we seem to derive a pleasure akin to the sensuous, buildings like Frank Lloyd Wright's celebrated wax factory, in which the effect is concentrated on an alternately crisp and silky exterior, the value of which seems almost tactile. But it is doubtful that such a building can represent the norm of architectural interest, or that it is in any case aptly described in sensuous terms. There is an important distinction between sensuous pleasures and those which have traditionally[2] been described as 'aesthetic'.

Aesthetic pleasure is not immediate in the manner of the pleasures of the senses, but is dependent upon, and affected by, processes of thought. As an example of the way in which the enjoyment of architecture might be so dependent, consider the sham façade. Our enjoyment of a façade is affected when we learn that, like the façade of the Old Schools in Cambridge, it is a piece of detached stage scenery. The change in enjoyment here is a response to thought: the thought that what we see has no real meaning as architecture. This dependence between the sense of beauty and intellectual understanding is exhibited by all the arts. The 'sensuous' pleasure induced by the sound of poetry is of a piece with our apprehension of its meaning, and even in music pleasure is wholly governed by the thought of what we hear. We take a different kind of pleasure in a Wagnerian *Leitmotiv* when we understand its full dramatic meaning, or in a Bach fugal subject when we follow its musical development: in each case the thought of the total composition affects the pleasure taken in its parts. In just the same way architectural pleasure is governed by a conception of its object. If that were not so, then the argument about the skilful sham would have no meaning. Whatever we think of this argument, we cannot simply deny that it is meaningful. There would be no place in a merely sensuous interpretation of architectural interest for Ruskin's view that an architect merits our attention only if he follows the 'Lamp of Truth'. For Ruskin a building can tell lies about its purpose, meaning and structure – it can even tell lies about the world – and this is a species of dishonesty as offensive as any that we might discover in a man.

In a similar way, we think of enjoyment in architectural matters as capable of evolution and transformation through knowledge: one has to *know* the Orders in order to take full pleasure in Roman buildings; one has to know the meaning of the sculptural details to take pleasure in the North Porch of Chartres; one has, simply, to know the use of a building if one is to enjoy it properly. There is no such thing as a pure, unmediated, sensuous pleasure in buildings.

It will be objected that the idea of such a 'pure' pleasure has no application in any case, there being no criterion whereby we might distinguish sensuous from intellectual pleasure. For a rational being, *every* pleasure may be absorbed into the workings of selfconsciousness; for such a being, all pleasure is influenced by reflection, being as vulnerable to puritanical hesitation as it is enhanced by selfconscious gourmandise. The meat loses its relish when we learn that it is the flesh of a favourite dog, reminiscences qualify the pleasure of wine, and sexual pleasures, even considered in isolation from their dependent human relations, vary with the thoughts and emotions through which we approach them. It is true that this last example has served as a parable of the distinction between sensuous and intellectual delight; at the same time, however, many have experienced the moral puzzle which derives from it. How can human love be an expression of our rational nature, when so many of the desires which determine it seek only animal gratification? How could Dante transform a transient, carnal and mortal appetite, into an exemplar of the intellectual love of God, while still believing that his two loves were essentially one and the same? It is the vividness of such examples which persuade us that there *is* a distinction between sensuous and intellectual pleasure; at the same time they seem only to add to the obscurity with which that distinction is enshrouded.

We should begin, I think, from the philosophical distinction between 'external' and 'internal' relations.[3] Specifically, we should distinguish the *causal* relations between pleasure and thought from those which are intrinsic or essential. A thought might extinguish my pleasure in what I eat or drink; however, I do not have to be thinking of what I eat or drink in order to experience the pleasure; in which case we must say that the relation between pleasure and thought is 'external'. And in so far as the pleasure is physical, this is true of any activity. That is part of what is *meant* by describing a pleasure as 'physical'. A pleasure is physical when its existence does not require thought or attention of any kind, even though it may, on occasion, result from, or be changed through, thought. A consequence is that, in the case of 'physical' pleasures, we do not speak as though pleasure had an object in addition to its cause. Indeed, one way of putting the moral puzzle about carnal love is this: how can sexual pleasure acquire a personal object, how can it be not just pleasure with someone but also pleasure at someone? Certain neo-Platonists and Christians, believing that it could not, have vigorously denied the part of sexual pleasure in true human love. Whatever the truth of their doctrine, it would be difficult to deny its application to the pleasures of eating and drinking. A man is not pleased *at* the wine he drinks just because he drinks it with pleasure.

In the case of architectural enjoyment some act of attention, some intellectual apprehension of the object, is a necessary part of the pleasure: the relation with thought is an internal one, and any change in the thought will automatically lead to a redescription of the pleasure. For it will change the *object* of the pleasure, pleasure here having an object in addition to its cause. It is my way of thinking of (attending to) a particular building that defines what pleases me: hence the building is not merely the cause of pleasurable sensations (as when I run my hand over a fine marble wall), but the object of pleasurable attention. When I point out to my companion, who is enjoying what he takes to be the fine finish of the marble columns in some Georgian vestibule, that the columns are in fact modelled in scagliola, his pleasure may promptly cease. If it does so this is not because I have brought some warring influence to bear on it, but because I have removed its object. My companion's enjoyment was founded on a mistake – indeed it *was* a form of mistake, just as my fear of a man whom I wrongly take to be carrying a gun is a mistake. Sensuous pleasures can never be *mistaken*, however wrong it might be, in a given case, to pursue them.

We may begin our enquiry then, from a distinction (as yet only partly characterized) between sensuous and intellectual pleasures. The pleasure in architecture belongs to the latter class, partly because the experience of architecture is dependent on a conception of its object. But in elucidating this relation of dependence we shall have to consider certain difficult questions in the philosophy of perception. I shall try to show that the experience of architecture is by no means the simple matter that it may appear to be. To see a building as architecture is not like seeing it as a mass of masonry. There is a distinction which I shall attempt to clarify between ordinary perception and 'imaginative' perception; I shall argue that the experience of architecture is essentially of the latter kind, and that this fact must determine our entire way of understanding and responding to buildings. We must begin, however, by attempting to dispel some of the obscurity involved in the assertion that the experience of a building depends upon a conception of its object.

A major source of this obscurity lies in the difficulty involved in separating the 'thought' or 'conception' involved in architectural understanding from the experience which accompanies or – more accurately, if less perspicuously – embodies it. It is not so much that I think of a building in a certain way – as fragile or solid, honest or deceitful; it is rather that I *see* it in that way. My experience of a building has an inherently interpreted character, and the 'interpretation' is inseparable from the way the building looks. To take an example: it is clear from Abbot Suger's account of the building of St Denis,[4] and from recent historical studies of the Gothic style, that the architects of the Gothic churches were motivated by a perceived relationship between the finished church and the Heavenly City of Christian speculation.[5] Sir John Summerson has further suggested that the Gothic style aims at a certain effect of accumulation.[6] Each great church can be considered as a concatenation of smaller structures, of aedicules, fitted together as arches, chapels, windows and spires, and so can be seen as an assembled city, rather than as a single entity minutely subdivided. And indeed, whether or not we *should* see a Gothic cathedral in this way (rather than in terms of the ever-aspiring upward movement that once seemed so remarkable), we certainly can so see it, as an accumulation of aedicules, formed into an harmonious city of contiguous parts. But the 'interpretation' here is not a 'thought' that is separable from the experience – it is there *in* the experience, as when I see the dots of a puzzle picture as a face, or the man in the moon.

Now there is a familiar point, made by both philosophers and psychologists (though in different terms, depending on the individual and on the school to which he belongs) that, in perception, experience and interpretation (or percept and concept) are inseparable. As a matter of fact the truth here does not seem to be merely empirical, a matter of psychology – not, at least, if that is meant to suggest that it was a scientific discovery which had to be confirmed through experiment.[7] In some sense there just could not *be* a perceptual experience that was not also the exercise of a conceptual capacity. There is, in the very idea of perceptual experience, a postulated unity and organization which cannot be removed from it, and to describe this unity one is obliged to employ concepts of an objective world and to apply them accordingly. To say how my experience is, I must say how the world seems to me. And that is to use the concept of an objective world. In which case, the view that concept and percept are inseparable begins to seem like a necessary truth, a logical consequence of the very attempt to describe our perceptions.

Kant, who was perhaps the first philosopher to place proper emphasis on this truth (an emphasis which changed the entire course of modern philosophy), characterized the relation between experience and concept as peculiarly intimate. Nevertheless, he felt that it could be in some sense laid bare, by postulating a faculty through which sensation and concept are united. To this faculty he gave the name 'imagination',[8] and he found precisely the same faculty at work in aesthetic judgement, the difference being that, in normal perception, the imagination is bound by the rules of the understanding, while in aesthetic taste it is 'free'. It is worth examining this theory of imagination in more detail; it will lead us to the second source of obscurity in the idea that the experience of architecture involves a thought or conception of its object.

Now in fact, since the eighteenth century, imagination has been the ruling concept in aesthetic theory. From Kant to Collingwood we find the same attempt to unite the aesthetic with the rest of our experience under a single mental capacity; and usually the word 'imagination' has been chosen to denote it. This is hardly surprising. From the beginning of the Enlightenment imagination was studied not only in aesthetics but also in metaphysics and the theory of knowledge. Neither Hume nor Kant considered that there was anything special about it, nor did they regard it as unequally distributed among men. For both of them it was imagination which knits together the scattered data of the senses into a patterned image of the world. It provides us with our beliefs about the past and future, and with that awareness of what is possible without which there can be no knowledge of what is.[9] While given to occasional flights, the imagination is more usually to be found perched in the cage of the common understanding, peaceably parroting its banal observations of the world.

Kant in particular gave the impetus to this 'general' theory of imagination. He saw it as a capacity exercised in every act of perception, a force active in the formation of every image and every cognitive state. But there is also a 'special' theory, associated with Sartre and Wittgenstein,[10] according to whom the imagination is manifest only in certain special forms of perception, imagery and thought. For example, it is an act of imagination to see a face in a picture (since that involves seeing what one knows not to be there), whereas it is not (as a rule) an imaginative act to see a face in something one knows to *be* a face. On this view too, memory, although it involves images, is not an exercise of imagination, for it does not involve that special element of creative thought which alone deserves the name.

Now the dispute between the two theories may appear to be a verbal one; in fact it is more serious. If we adopt the general theory then, like Coleridge (who was, in this, greatly under the influence of Kant), and like Hegel,[11] we find that the experience of art is no longer puzzling. Precisely the same capacities are exercised in imaginative experience as are revealed in ordinary perception. There is no problem, therefore, in showing how the first can illuminate the second, and the second give content to the first. If we adopt the special theory, however, then aesthetics, as we shall see, becomes more difficult.

It is in fact hard to accept the general theory. For what could it mean, to say that there is a single faculty exercised in seeing, remembering, and imagining, and that 'imagination' is the proper name for it? Surely, it can only mean that the process which is seen most clearly in the act of imagining is also a necessary ingredient in all perception. But what is that process? A characteristic feature of imagination is that it involves reflecting on an imaginary object, an object which is thought of as non-existent. In memory and perception, however, the object is thought of as *real*: seeing is believing. Argument is required if we are to find a similarity between imagination and perception that is more striking than so evident a difference.

Moreover, imagination shows itself in many ways: in imagery, in story-telling, in seeing such things as a face in a cloud, or action in a picture, where what is seen is also seen as non-existent. It can be shown[12] that there are important similarities between these processes, and that each is creative in a way that normal perception is not. The mental object here is not 'given', in the way that the object of belief is given, as a fact about the world, but rather 'posited'. In imagination the pressures of belief are in some way resisted, and thought attains to a freedom which it normally cannot possess. Thus, I can ask you to imagine that there is life on Mars, and you may freely obey me; but I could not ask you to believe it, perceive it, or remember it.

Now the argument for saying that there is a single process of imagination involved in all perception, imagery and remembering seems to consist only in the assertion (indubitably true) that in these mental processes thought and experience are inseparable. But to suppose, therefore, that there is some faculty ('The Imagination') involved in forging the connection between them is to fail to take seriously the fact that they *are* inseparable. There is no access to the experience, no way of classifying or describing it, except through the concept with which it is imbued. Just why that is so is not in question; for that it is so is agreed. It is not, as Hume thought,[13] that we first have perceptions and then imaginatively unite them, forming the concept of an object by a process of construction from fragmentary appearances. For an appearance is a knowledge of how things seem; it can be described only with the concept of the thing that seems. If we can speak of a 'synthesis' of appearance into the concept of an object, it is, in Kant's terminology, a 'transcendental' synthesis, that is to say, a synthesis which is presupposed in the very attempt to describe it. It is not, then, a genuine *process*, which begins from two separate items, and combines them to form a third.

Now, in considering this issue, of the relation between imagining and perceiving, it is tempting to propose a method of introspection. People are apt to feel that the memory image and the imaginative image, for example, are somehow similar, meaning that if you look at them sufficiently closely they will present the same appearance, or the same organization. But that way of conceiving the matter is highly contentious. It is very misleading to speak of facts which may be *discovered* by introspection. For what is this process of 'introspection'? And what guarantee is there that an image which I subject to introspection is similar to one which I do not? How do we know that introspection itself does not make some vital (and necessarily undiscoverable) difference to the contents of the mind? If we ignore introspection we are surely bound to conclude that the principal feature of an image, the feature which determines its nature as a mental act, is its relation to its object. An image is not an object of attention but rather a mode of attention to other things. It is not so much a thing with discoverable properties as a way of envisaging the properties of its object. The image, one might say, is wholly transparent.

Whether or not we accept the general theory of imagination will not be my principal concern in this chapter. But it will be my concern to distinguish what I shall call 'imaginative perception' – exemplified in the understanding of a picture, where the object of perception is seen as unreal – from 'literal' perception. But, it might be asked, if we reject the use of introspection, how is that distinction to be made? It is here that certain philosophers might have recourse to the method of 'phenomenology', a study proposed by Husserl, Sartre and Merleau-Ponty, though never clearly described by any of their following.[14] Phenomenology is held to be akin to, yet distinct from, introspection. It is akin to introspection in being a method whereby the subject determines the nature of *his* thoughts, and experiences. But it is distinct in that it records not accidental truths about experience, but the essential truths. Phenomenology is supposed to give us the essence of a mental state, and not its external relations.

Some ways of expressing the idea of a 'phenomenology' of perception are intolerably 'Cartesian'. That is to say, they imply that the results of phenomenology are results that I establish for myself alone, and which I cannot verify in the experience of others. A philosopher, however, ought to be wary of the suggestion that there are important results to be obtained through the observation of my experience, in abstraction from any sense of how I might describe the experience of other men, or the public world which they and I inhabit. To find the 'essence' of our mental states we must look not inwards but outwards, to their expression in activity and in language, to the publicly recognizable practices in which they have their life. It is only what is publicly accessible that can be publicly described, and it is only what is publicly accessible that is important: nothing else, I should like to argue, can make any difference to our lives.[15]

But there is something that remains to the 'method' of phenomenology and which is of considerable importance in our present study. This thing will become clear in the light of what I think is a conclusive objection to any theory which claims to derive the essence of experience from a study of the first-person case. Such a study cannot present us with the essence of experience but only with the peculiarities of *self-conscious* experience. In phenomenological analysis, the 'I' is already posited. But if that is so, how can we be sure that phenomenology actually provides us with a description of processes which might exist in the absence of a self, processes for which there is no 'I', and no reflection? Now perception does not require a 'self', in the sense implied in the usage of 'I'. For there is perception that is not self-conscious. The self is an elaborate social construct, and my knowledge of myself as 'I' is a corollary of my intercourse with others.[16] My dog, not being in that sense a *zōon politikon*, must lack both the knowledge and the concept of self: in the normal sense, he *has* no self. Therefore there can be no phenomenology of his experience. Yet he sees me in the garden, hears me calling to him, smells me as he approaches. In other words, he has perceptual experience, just as I have. Yet while most animals perceive, only some animals imagine. Imagination is in fact peculiar to self-conscious beings, beings whose intellectual capacities transcend the fixation with the immediate that is characteristic of merely animal existence.

To establish the last point would be to demolish the general theory of imagination. For if one continues to insist that there is some common process involved in all perception and experience, then one must go on to say, either that such a process is not after all identical with imagination, or that it is, and that my dog, who lacks imagination, cannot see. And it is clear which alternative we should choose. But should we accept that last point? It seems to me that we must. For if we admit the existence of mental states which are not inherently self-conscious, mental states, like those of my dog, which have no phenomenological reality, then we must concede that imagination is not one of the capacities that an unselfconscious being could have. To show this is to show what is valid as well as what is invalid in the method of phenomenology.

It is wrong to say that animals have imaginative experience because we could never have grounds for attributing imagination to a creature who lacks the ability to reflect on its own experience. To apply the concept of imagination to animal experience is to use the concept in the absence of any behaviour which it could describe: it is to speak redundantly, using a complex concept where a simpler one would do. The simple concept is that of 'literal' perception, perception which is subordinate to belief. For consider how it is that we come to attribute perception to animals. The principal reason for doing so is that we recognize causal connections between things in the world and an animal's beliefs. A mouse hides behind a stone, and this causes the cat, who is watching, to believe that a mouse is hiding behind the stone. A pattern is established, of causal relation between environment and information; it is this pattern that we have in mind when we speak of animals perceiving things, and it is for this reason that we can use the concept of perception to explain an animal's behaviour.[17]

Now consider the case of a self-conscious being. Here there is an additional capacity to reflect on experience, to interpose between experience and belief thoughts that are determined by neither. I shall explain what I mean through the example of music, which will bring us back to the experience of architecture, and so serve to show that the experience of architecture belongs not to literal but to imaginative perception. I shall argue that animals are not capable of hearing music, since to hear music is to exercise a kind of imaginative understanding of which animals are incapable. It may seem absurd to say this, since it has the corollary that birds do not sing. Nevertheless I think that it is true.

Let us grant (what seems incontrovertible) that birds, like cats and dogs, can see and hear. How are we to describe *what* they hear? This seems a simple question, until we realize that the phrase 'what is heard' is systematically ambiguous. It may refer to the sound that is heard, or to the way of hearing it (the appearance). And since birds, like men, may occasionally suffer from hallucinations and misperceptions, their way of hearing may not correspond to the way things are.[18] How, then, would we describe the way things sound to a bird? If we can answer that question then we will know that phenomenological analysis (construed as akin to introspection) is wholly unnecessary in order to describe appearances, since there can be no phenomenology of a bird's experience.[19]

In fact we *can* answer the question, because we can recognize, from a bird's behaviour, its capacities to discriminate between different sounds. On that basis, we can ascribe certain classifications, or 'concepts'.[20] For example, a bird may discriminate between middle C and the C sharp above (and we might discover this at once if it takes the first as a warning, the second as a territorial display). For such a bird we could say that, on some given occasion, it misheard C sharp as C: in other words, we can describe *how* it hears a certain sound, without implying that the actual sound corresponds to its experience. Nevertheless, we are limited in our description of how things appear to a bird by a very narrow account of how things are. In the animal world, the possibilities of appearance are governed by the possibilities of belief, and our attributions of beliefs to animals depend upon our classifications of the objects of belief, these classifications being, in turn, subordinate to the enterprise of explaining animal behaviour. For a human being, however, the world of appearance responds also to self-conscious reflection. The way things appear to us may not be accurately captured by a belief about how they are, and certainly not by any scientifically acceptable description designed purely to explain our behaviour.

This becomes clear when we consider the distinction – apparent to a man, but not to a bird – between a sound and a note. Hearing a note is like hearing a word in language – it is hearing a sound imbued with implications. (My dog hears the sound 'walk' and is triggered into Pavlovian excitement; but the sound is not for him what it is for me, the point of intersection of indefinitely many meanings.) When I hear a note I hear a sound that is pregnant with musical meaning: it suggests harmony, melody, movement. Consider the most basic of these, the phenomenon of musical movement. If I hear two notes, say middle C followed by the A above, then what I hear, speaking literally, is two pitched sounds, separated by the interval of a major sixth. That literal description may equally characterize the experience of a bird. Unlike the bird, however, I may also hear a movement from C to A. Something begins at the first note and rises upward to the second. If I could not hear such movement, then I could not hear melody or sequence: I would be deaf to music. But *what* moves? We may find ourselves at a loss for an answer to that question; for, literally speaking, nothing *does* move. There is one note, and then another; movement, however, demands *one* thing, which passes from place to place.[21]

A certain scepticism might arise here, in response to the thought that music is constituted in some sense as a spatial dimension. And if music is a form of space, there ought to be movement in musical space. There are measurable distances in music, and in this respect, the musical spectrum constitutes a genuine dimension and not a mere gradation. It is for this reason that there can be a 'mirror' in auditory space. The following two chords exactly mirror each other:

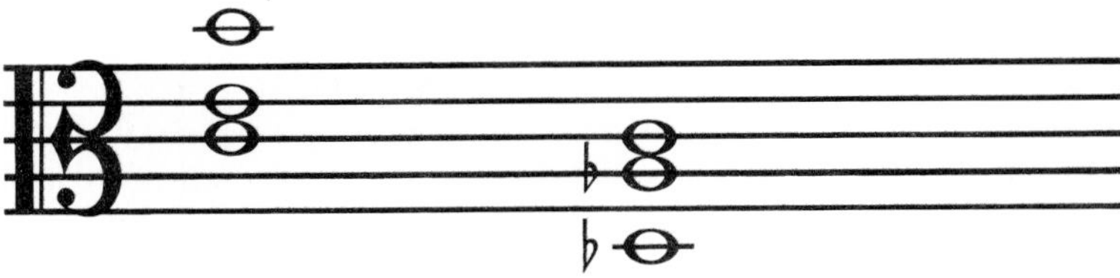

and like all mirror images they form 'incompatible counterparts'. They cannot be shifted in space in such a way as to exactly coincide, even though the spatial relations among their parts are precisely the same. (It was Kant who first pointed to this remarkable feature of 'dimension', a feature which distinguishes it from the mere gradation of properties, and constitutes part of what we mean when we say that space is something *in* which things occur, rather than a property which things possess.[22])

But despite this analogy with space, we have to recognize that musical space is unlike ordinary space in a way that forbids any literal interpretation of the concept of musical movement. For there are two essential properties of physical space, at least one of which must be absent from musical space. This fact will be seen to present an important difficulty for any theory of musical movement. The first property is that no two particulars can be in the same place at the same time (an axiom of great philosophical significance, although one that allows certain rather peculiar counter-examples).[23] Is this true of musical space? The question is difficult to answer, and the difficulty is of a piece with the difficulty of deciding what are the individual entities which *occupy* musical space. Suppose that a violin and a flute play in unison. Is the result one note or two? If the latter, then of course our axiom of spatiality is contravened. So perhaps we should say the former, that there is only one note, whose colour or timbre depends upon its mode of production, but whose identity depends only on its pitch. I suspect that many difficulties will arise if we attempt to individuate notes by their pitch, without reference to their mode of production; for one thing, this contravenes an accepted way of counting the notes in music. But, even if we can accept the suggestion, it only serves to exacerbate the second asymmetry with physical space, which is that no individual in auditory space can be at two different places at different times. For the individuating feature of a note – its pitch – is precisely the feature which determines its 'spatial' location. There is no way of separating the note from the place that it occupies. It becomes senseless to say that the same note could occur at another pitch; hence if notes are the fundamental individuals in musical space, nothing in musical space can actually *move*. But this contradicts our sense that music is a form of movement.

How do we resolve that contradiction? One suggestion would be this – that we should ignore the claims of music to any kind of spatial organization and simply accept that nothing in music really moves. What we hear in music is not movement, since there is no space and no objects that move in it; we hear only processes, events which take time, but do not change place. But to take such a line would be to misdescribe musical experience. For sounds, too, belong to processes – indeed, they *are* processes. Sounds can be combined sequentially and heard in sequence, even when they are not heard as music. When we hear music we hear something more than sequence; we hear movement, movement not in space but only in time (cf. T. S. Eliot's *Four Quartets*, I, V). And because we hear this movement we are disposed to describe *places* in the musical space; we speak of a melody moving towards or away from those places. These spatial metaphors are far from accidental; they are essential to the phenomenology of what we hear. It is a phenomenological truth that music moves, but it is a truth that corresponds to no physical reality. It is difficult to see, therefore, that we could ever have a use for this concept of musical movement in describing the experience of a bird. The 'movement' which is of the essence of music is not a proper object of literal perception. To say that musical movement is a phenomenological fact is to say that it is a fact about the experience of a being that can reflect on its own experience. If there is a valid study of phenomenology it is in the description of what is peculiar to self-consciousness, in the description of that 'phenomenal' residue which survives when all literal belief and experience has been subtracted. The appearances which constitute literal perception will be characterized only in terms of the beliefs expressed in it, and we can have no grounds to attribute to a creature any more complex belief than is strictly necessary in order to explain its behaviour. In explaining the behaviour of birds it is impossible to invoke the concept of musical movement, since this movement is not a constituent part of the reality in terms of which the bird's behaviour and beliefs are to be explained. Musical movement is not part of the material world and therefore not something of which a bird could take cognizance. No scientific description of the world of sound need mention – as an independent fact of the matter – the phenomenon of musical movement. There is no explanatory function to be fulfilled by the concept of musical movement that will not be fulfilled by the concept of auditory sequence. No scientific method (no method for discovering causal relations) could possibly discriminate between the two. From the scientific point of view the only *fact* of the matter here is the fact that beings of a certain sort *hear* movement in music.

I have tried to suggest that this certain sort of being is to be described in terms of self-consciousness, in terms of the ability to transcend the immediate, in terms of those capacities which we might wish to say were seen at their most explicit in imaginative perception. We can now see why that is so. The purely 'phenomenological' residue of musical experience exhibits the obvious marks of imaginative understanding. For one thing it involves an imaginative leap comparable to that involved in seeing the face in a picture. The concept of movement is a concept that is transferred to music from the realm of literal understanding and applied independently of any belief that something moves. It is not that we hear the same thing at two different places and so derive our concept of musical movement from *that*: the concept of musical movement is something like an entrenched metaphor. Similarly the experience of music exhibits the kind of freedom that is characteristic of imagination. I can choose how to hear the musical movement: as beginning here, or here.[24] But perhaps this point will be clearer when we return to the description of architecture. For in architecture too, experience manifests an imaginative structure. In the course of describing that structure we will not only justify the age-old analogy between architecture and music (the analogy which led Schelling to describe architecture as 'frozen music'), we will also be able to show more clearly that what matters in imaginative experience is not so much the 'knowing misapplication of a concept', but rather the structure of attention which makes this misapplication possible.

A final word about method will be in place before we leave this digression into the philosophy of perception. It is important to recognize that our results do not depend upon any process of close attention, introspection or self-analysis. The kind of 'analysis' of perceptual experience that I am proposing is to be distinguished from introspective psychology as from every other kind of empirical investigation. Its aim is the understanding of a concept, and, since that concept belongs to a public language, the proper method of analysis is a public one, a method which depends not on introspection, but on the publicly accepted and publicly recognizable distinctions which speakers of the language observe, not just in describing their *own* experience, but in describing the experience of others and of animals. The criterion of success is not truth to the facts, but the provision of a useful concept, a concept which enables us to distinguish things that are observably distinct, and to formulate the facts which make them so. Our results are based not on the private study of personal experience but on the observation of public practice – the practice of attention, command, study and reasoning which distinguishes the realm of imagination and which can be observed as well in the behaviour of another as introspectively in ourselves. In returning now to the experience of architecture, we shall be able to see in more detail just what these publicly recognizable features of imaginative experience are, and just what kind of importance attaches to them.

Now imaginative experience, as I have so far described it, can certainly have architecture as one of its objects. If we return to the theory of the Gothic aedicule, we can see, in the experience to which Summerson refers, a prime example of imagination – of seeing a building in terms of a concept that one knows not to apply to it. Consider, for example, the West Front of Amiens Cathedral (Plate 24). It is possible to see the three porches here as three continuous edifices, the pinnacles between them as separate edifices, the arcade above as a sequence of little shelters joined together, and so on. Seeing the cathedral in that way will not be a matter of believing; we see it as we know it not to be. Our perception is imbued with the thought of something absent, just like the perception of a painting or a sculpture. And, being imaginative, our perception is also free: for it is subordinate to patterns of thought and attention that we are in no way compelled by what we see to engage in.

We are compelled to believe that what we see is a mass of masonry, and therefore to see that it is so. But we are not compelled to attend to the building in such a way that the thought of the celestial city seems an apt or appropriate expression of our experience. It is an activity of ours to attend to the cathedral in that way, and it is an activity that we might choose not to engage in.

PLATE 24 Cathedral, Amiens, West Front

This point is brought home by seeing that imaginative experiences of this kind – unlike ordinary perceptions – may be inherently ambiguous. Consider the tracery from the central loggia on the upper floor of the Palazzo Pisani-Moretta in Venice, illustrated in Plate 25. This arrangement may be seen in at least two ways, depending upon how the observer directs his attention. He may form aedicules from neighbouring columns, or from columns joined by the semi-circle of tracery

PLATE 25 Palazzo Pisani-Moretta, Venice

in the upper parts. Once aware of the ambiguity he can readily alternate the two interpretations (just as with the famous ambiguous figures investigated by Gestalt psychologists,[25] or with the ambiguous melodies, such as those that delighted Beethoven, which can be heard to begin either on an upbeat or on a downbeat). In fact it is misleading to talk of a choice of 'interpretations'; for what one is choosing here is not the interpretation alone, but also the experience which embodies it. And it is the most remarkable feature of imagination that imaginative experience may be *chosen* in this way.

In the case of literal perception, where normally seeing is believing, and where knowledge is the fundamental aim, we do not notice this 'choice'. I cannot choose to see what I know to be a tree in some other way; I cannot will myself to see it to be a man, a face or an animal. What I see is inextricably entwined with what I believe, and over my beliefs I have no control. If I can see the tree 'as' a face, say, while still believing it to be a tree, I have once again stepped outside the realm of literal perception into that of the imagination. I am seeing imaginatively, for my experience now depends upon a particular act of imaginative attention, and, in virtue of that, must be described in terms of a concept that in no way corresponds to my belief. It is not merely that in imaginative experience concepts are being deliberately misapplied: it is rather that such experience reflects a special mode of attention and a special intellectual aim. Literal perception *aims* at belief, and the act of attention here is also a desire to 'find out'. Imaginative experience aims not at belief but at a different kind of understanding; it is one of my purposes in this book to say what that understanding is, and why it is important. The act of imaginative attention is therefore characterized by no specific desire to 'find out', no special preoccupation with facts, since while these may be a necessary pre-condition for its exercise, their knowledge is no part of its aim.

We have already seen, from the example of musical understanding, that there may be objects which can only be perceived imaginatively, since the most basic experiences involved in their perception may depend upon acts of attention that transcend the aims of literal understanding. The same, I think, is true of architecture. It is not merely that architecture is the occasional object of imaginative experience (for what is not?), but rather that it is a proper object of that experience, and that it cannot be understood except in imaginative terms. This is shown by abstracting from all 'interpretation', from all 'seeing as' of the kind exemplified in our Gothic example, and turning to the basic forms of architectural experience, just as we explored the basic forms of the musical 'space'. We find that, however much we divest our experience of interpretation, it retains the character of freedom which is one of the distinguishing marks of an imaginative act. Consider the ambiguous arrangement of columns employed by Peruzzi in the entrance loggia to the Palazzo Massimi (Plate 26). This ambiguity – caused by the classically accepted[26] widening of the intercolumniation to mark the door – is made specially apparent by the bold curve of Peruzzi's façade. We find that there are two ways of seeing the six columns, both equally stable. We may see them as four pairs, taken together with the two pilasters contiguous to them, or as three pairs, one framing the door and the others supporting (by unseen connecting lines) the outer frames of the windows on the floor above. The ambiguity might be immediately removed in another context, say by placing pilasters in the upper wall, so that the columns follow their rhythm, or by approaching the loggia from the side. More subtle rhythms are achieved by lessening the disparity between central and peripheral

PLATE 26 Baldassare Peruzzi: Palazzo Massimi alle Colonne, Rome

spaces, and by counterpointing the emphasis with a cornice, the modillions of which fail to correspond to the centres of the columns, as in Palladio's hexastyle pronaos to the Villa Cornaro (Plate 27).

I add the example from Palladio partly in order to show that this ambiguity is not a rare phenomenon; in fact it is of the essence of Mannerist architecture and indispensible to some of the finest effects of the baroque. Moreover, it is through understanding this kind of example that we are able to form a proper conception of the normal case. The 'ambiguity' of Peruzzi's arrangement comes about partly through the absence of 'interpretation'. It therefore indicates a basic truth about architectural experience, about how we are constrained to see the buildings at which we look when we study them as architecture. It is this way of seeing buildings that reflects the act of attention of which they are the proper object. We have then, in this example, a

PLATE 27 Andrea Palladio: Villa Cornaro, Piombino Dese

paradigm of architectural experience: the experience can never be 'purer', less interpreted, than this.

Let us then use the example to extract some of those essential features of imaginative perception at which, in discussing the musical example, we only hinted. I shall mention what I take to be the most important.[27] First, our experience of form has a precise duration. The columns seem to be grouped in one way for a certain length of time, and then the 'aspect' changes, and they look different for a further length of time. My seeing them in either way is a phenomenon that can be precisely dated, and in this respect it shares one of the general characteristics of experience – one of the characteristics whereby we distinguish experiences from other states of mind, such as thoughts, emotions and desires.

A further feature shows clearly that our grasp of architectural form is a type of 'seeing': this is, trivially enough, its strict dependence on what is seen. Without eyes the effect to which I refer could not be apprehended. It is not a mere 'thought' or 'concept', available to anyone who can think in terms of order and relation. It is something *seen*; it does not survive the perception of the columns, and disappears as soon as the columns are seen in another incompatible way. Thus while one may *think* of the columns under both 'groupings' at once, one can see the groupings only one at a time. Furthermore, the effect has the feature of 'intensity' that is characteristic of experience; one aspect may stand out as more intense or striking than the other.

On the other hand, the experience is of a peculiar kind in that it can be, and in this case actually is, directly subject to the will. It makes sense to ask someone to see the columns now one way, now another, and this request can be obeyed directly: there is nothing else that has to be done first in order to comply with it. In this respect the experience shares one of the fundamental properties of imaginative thought (as when I ask someone to 'think of it in this way . . .'): the property of voluntariness. And it possesses this property despite the fact that there is no easily identifiable concept (such as the concept of an aedicule, or the concept of movement) which is here being consciously misapplied. The experience is voluntary purely because a particular act of attention is involved in its existence. It is, therefore, not an accident that the experience of the columns should be affected by the way we think of them. It will change, for example, under the influence of comparisons we might make with other structures, say with the Palladio example in Plate 27. It follows – as I shall show in more detail in the next chapter – that the experience of 'seeing' will here acquire a certain 'rational' character. By this I mean that one will be able to give reasons for and against a certain way of seeing (reasons which might connect with how the building should be understood). So there is such a thing as accepting a reason through an experience; and the importance of this point must not be underestimated.

It is true that one does not normally have the kind of complete control over experience that is exemplified by these ambiguous patterns. Nevertheless, the imaginative character of the experience is present even when the control is not. When I see the equal rhythm of the columns in S. Spirito I am engaged in an imaginative act, just as I am when I 'group' the columns of the loggia of the Palazzo Massimi (see Plate 11, p. 47). It is of course difficult to see Brunelleschi's columns except as evenly rhythmical: they demand an equal value. But that in itself proves nothing, and certainly does not warrant the strange assertion of some architectural historians that visual ambiguity was an invention of the Mannerists, unknown in European architecture before

PLATE 28 S. Spirito, colonnade: a way of seeing

Giulio Romano and Peruzzi.[28] For one thing, it is worth noting that we speak of the colonnade of S. Spirito as *demanding* this equal emphasis, as though what it compels is also something that we *give*. More importantly, there is as much in the experience of Brunelleschi's columns that lies in our power to change as there is in any of the mannerist examples. And this is not simply a fact about Brunelleschi's style: it is an inevitable consequence of the way in which we experience architecture. Consider, for example, the various ways in which one might see the point of rest in this composition, the point where arch and column come together. One might see the arches as springing from the top of the Corinthian capitals, and as resting their weight there, so that the dosserets are pierced by the movement of the arch. Alternatively, one might imaginatively 'fill in' the gap between the dosserets, and come to see them as a broken entablature (Plate 28). In such a case the arches will seem to spring from above the mouldings, as they seem to spring from above the impost blocks of the columns at S. Apollinare Nuovo (Plate 29). (An addict of ambiguity might wish to make further comparisons: say with the early Christian churches of S. Sabina (Plate 30) and S. Giorgio in Velabro in Rome, where masonry is placed directly onto the tops of borrowed columns; all such comparisons may enrich and modify the experience, though of course to make them is the critic's and not the philosopher's concern.) Here, not only is it possible to choose one's interpretation, in the sense of choosing the experience

PLATE 29 S. Apollinare Nuovo, Ravenna, view of nave

that is most satisfying; one can also begin to see how the notion of a *correct* experience might arise, the notion of an experience that leads to an understanding and appreciation of the building. For it is surely the presence of this unseen entablature that leads to the serene horizontal movement of S. Spirito, and which accounts for its superiority over the same master's interior at S. Lorenzo, where the swelled and embellished friezes of the dosserets make the perception of their unseen juncture impossible. (Although there is classical authority for the swelling of the dosserets: e.g. the Roman church of S. Costanza.)

In the next chapter I shall consider this notion of a 'correct' experience in detail. But it is worth providing one or two more illustrations at this juncture, in order to convince the reader that there is no aspect of architectural experience that does not exemplify the imaginative structure which the idea of 'correctness' implies. Consider then the relation between column and wall. The early Renaissance theorists took their understanding of the Orders from an inspection of the Roman remains, and from a reading of the obscure Vitruvius. Now clearly it is possible to see the half-columns and pilasters of a building like the theatre of Marcellus (Plate 31) as vertical decorations to the wall, just as it is possible to see the wall as a filling-in between columnar supports. The latter, as we know, is the experience intended: Alberti, however, saw this building in the first way, as is evidenced both by his treatise[29] and by his own use of the Orders at the Palazzo Rucellai. One might

PLATE 30 S. Sabina, Rome, capitals of nave

say that, as the true origin of the column became more firmly appreciated, Renaissance builders learned to see the column as a supporting member rather than as an ornament. Later Renaissance buildings leave no doubt about the matter, as can be seen, for example, from the upper wall of the Palazzo Chiericati by Palladio (Plate 32), a composition which forbids this particular ambiguity. There is no doubt about the correctness of Palladio's interpretation: not because it accurately represents the history of the column and its derivation from the peristyle temple, but because to see the column in this way is to open the possibility of a richness of meaning that would otherwise be missed. The dialogue between wall and column enables the aesthetic properties of the column – which it derives precisely because we see it as standing free, holding itself and its entablature unaidedly upright – to be spread across the wall. The wall therefore partakes of the implications of the columnar Order, and the subtleties of suggestion which the divisions of the Order imply. It is even possible to refine the column out of

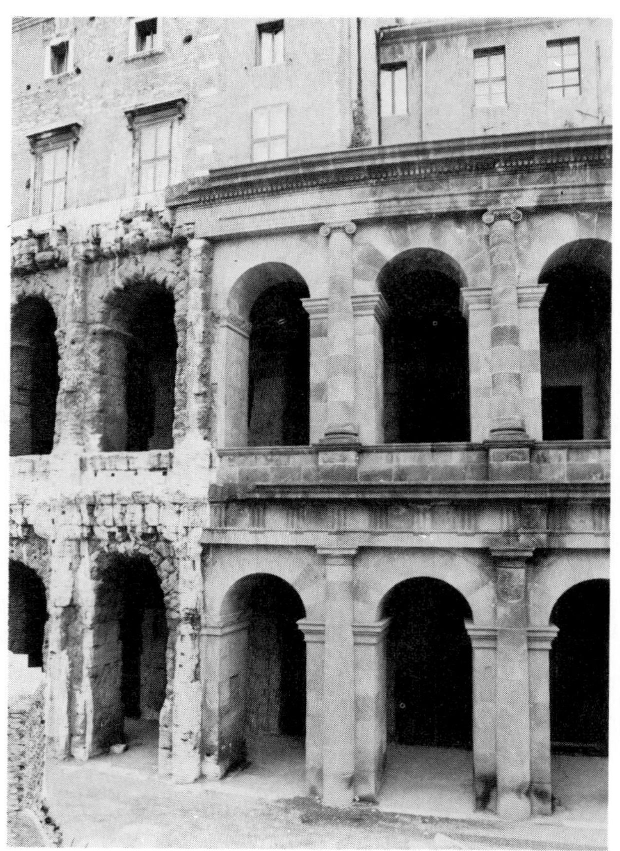

PLATE 31 Theatre of Marcellus, Rome (partly restored)

existence – to remove every direct representation of it – and still be left with a wall imbued with the implications of the Order, as in the wall of a Georgian house, the organization of which becomes vivid when we see in it a reflection of the column from which it is derived.[30] (Thus one may see Gower Street, for example, as a kind of unspoken colonnade.) It is not that Alberti made a *mistake* at the Palazzo Rucellai: but there are persuasive arguments against his way of seeing the Roman prototypes, arguments which derive from the relative value of competing experiences.

In all architectural experience the active participation of the observer is required for its completion. Each determinacy that is offered provides the basis for a further choice, and the idea of a building that can be experienced in its entirety in only one way is an absurdity. It is impossible to banish the imaginative ordering of experience that I have described: the experience is active even when it is compelled. For although I am compelled, when I attend to the colonnade of S. Spirito, to perceive a regular rhythm established and passed on from part to part, it is no part of seeing the material object before me – the disposition of masonry – that I should see this rhythm. It is my own imaginative attention that enables me to see it, and a creature incapable of that

PLATE 32 Andrea Palladio: Palazzo Chiericati, Vicenza

attention would no more see the rhythm than a bird hears music. This explains the active nature of architectural experience, even at its most involuntary. Ordinary perceptual experience – the experience of animals, and our own experience of the day-to-day (when it is not subjected to self-reflection) – is compelled by its object. We are passive in respect of such experience as we are passive in respect of our beliefs. But we are not passive in respect of the experience of architecture, which arises only as the result of a certain species of attention. Our beliefs are not changed when we change the 'grouping' of a sequence of columns, nor need they be changed by any of the acts of attention which we direct at architecture. Our aim is not knowledge, but the enjoyment of the appearance of a thing already known.

We have arrived at an important conclusion. We have discovered that a vital part of our experience of architecture is imaginative; as such it admits of argument and proof, can be described as right, wrong, appropriate and misleading, can reflect a conception of its object that is in no way tied down to the literal significances explored in common perception. As I shall argue, if the experience of architecture has this imaginative structure, then it is also primarily aesthetic, and involves an inevitable exercise of taste. Taste and aesthetic discrimination become the dominant ideas in our theory of architecture. But before we move on to consider those ideas, we must pause to take stock of certain difficulties which arise from the fact that we have given too narrow a description of the experience of architecture. In fact we have considered only the visual aspect of architecture, and confined our discussion, even of that aspect, to one particular part, the experience of form. But there is more to architecture than visual pattern and visual form. We do not treat buildings simply as static façades; the sequence of experiences consequent on movement through a building may be essential to its effect, and may be the object of profound architectural study, a point made evident by Palladio's church of the Redentore in Venice.[31] We also listen to buildings, hearing echoes, murmurs, silences, all of which may contribute to our impression of the whole. It is doubtful that a purely visual experience could reveal to us the full power of St Peter's in Rome or, for example, the intimacy of Bramante's cloister at S. Maria della Pace, with its particular deadened echo that leads one to perambulate quietly around. And again, even our visual experience is qualified by reference to the other senses. As many critics have pointed out,[32] materials and forms are often endowed with a visual appearance that 'translates', as it were, their functional and tactile qualities. Rough-cast concrete has an unfriendly look, because we anticipate the scouring and bruising which result from touching it, while the wood and paper of a Japanese house are 'friendly' materials, from which we anticipate no harm.

These 'anticipatory' appearances are of fundamental importance, and we shall have cause to return to them. They arise because we can see objects in terms of concepts that denote no strictly visual property: a fact that few philosophers have been able to account for. I may see a shape as 'hard' or 'soft', as 'welcoming' or 'hostile'. This general ability to see things under non-visual concepts is not peculiar to architecture. Of course, it is no easy matter to determine what is to count as a visual, and what as a non-visual property.[33] But on any view it must be possible to see not only colours and shapes, but also such properties as warmth, mass, solidity and distance. How much more, then, can be seen when one's aim is not confined to any literal understanding, but ranges freely over every imaginative conception? For certainly we should not think of all these experiences of anticipation in terms of changed belief. That would be to ignore the difference between literal and imaginative perception. When I see a material as warm, soft or hostile this may not be a matter of believing it to be warm, soft or hostile. I do not anticipate that it would be more painful to strike my head against the wall of the Pitti Palace than against the wall of the Florentine Baptistery; but the first of these has a 'painful' look which the second does not. Anticipation here is a property of the experience and not of any judgement to which it gives rise. And it is worth pointing out that the same might be true of an experience of 'function'. If the functionalist means to say that a building should express a function, meaning that we should be able to *see* the function in the building's form, then it follows that a building might express a function that it does not possess and which the observer knows it not to possess. An example of this is the colonnade in the undercroft of Wren's library at Trinity College, Cambridge, added in answer to donnish unease, and designed to express a fictitious function so as to satisfy purely visual qualms.

Clearly our theory of imaginative perception can enable us to incorporate, in some such way, most anticipatory experiences into the single visual experience which it is best designed to analyse. But why should we attach that experience specifically to architecture? If we cannot answer that question, we shall not know how these other features of architectural experience – the features of movement, sound, change and touch – form part of a unified totality. And if we cannot show that, then we shall have failed to provide a satisfactory account of the experience of architecture, an account which embraces the full reality of its object. Clearly, my remarks could apply to any of the decorative arts in which an experience of 'pattern' plays a dominant role – to embroidery and clothing, as well as to colonnades. As is shown by the encrusted façades of the Florentine churches, and of the Arab mosques, and by our own Suffolk flushwork, architecture need not be far removed from the other arts of decoration. But it is always something more than decoration.

Here again functionalist doctrines may seem to provide a useful recourse, in describing what makes a pattern into architecture, rather than ornament. The functionalist might attempt to redescribe our pleasure in pattern as a kind of pleasure in the structure which it articulates. But again that will not do. (For example, the piazza of the Campidoglio in Rome relies for its harmony on an inlaid pavement, the pattern of which strikes up a vivid counterpoint between the buildings, while wholly lacking in structural significance: Plate 33.) Nor will the functionalist doctrine help us to extend our account to embrace those visual aspects of architecture which are not aspects of 'pattern' or 'form'. Consider the feature of colour: this is not simply a means of clarifying structure, as the Arab mosque clearly demonstrates. Even the Greeks, admired above all for the harmonious composition of their temples, are known to have painted them in bright, garish colours that

PLATE 33 Michelangelo: Piazza del Campidoglio, Rome

could hardly have served the function of 'clarifying' a form that is already clearer and more impressive than all the forms which later architects devised.

Now the last example has sometimes seemed rather strange to modern critics.[34] We have an expectation that colour and material should be in some way conjoined, like the colour of brick, of variegated limestone, of serpentine. A merely painted surface seems to contain something in excess of architecture: it is architecture 'decked out', as it were – the habit of painting temples was perhaps not so very different from the habit of hanging them with garlands. A more subtle example of the distinction between 'pure' and 'ornamented' architecture might be seen in the example of statuary. Here, too, we often feel inclined to distinguish the use of statuary to 'deck out' an architectural form, and its use as a proper and inseparable part of architectural meaning. It is important to understand that distinction.

Consider again the view which sees the fundamental experience of architecture as lying in structural pattern. Statuary, like any other detail, would now be regarded, either as a mere embellishment, or else as a means for emphasizing pattern. Every interesting pattern requires obstruction to visual grasp. It requires points of complexity where the eye can pause, where lines and figures entangle and separate, like the crossed mouldings of Gothic tracery. Without such necessary ornaments, the experience of pattern is simplified to the point of vacuity, as in the monotonous slabs of a concrete bunker. On such a view, statuary, considered as a significant part of architecture, is no more than structural pattern become representational, and its representational meaning will presumably be secondary, like the representational meaning of the formalized animals in Caucasian carpets. Such a view enables us to distinguish architectural statuary (as in the North Porch of Chartres) from autonomous sculpture (such as Epstein's St Michael which hangs, seemingly without support, on the bare wall of Coventry Cathedral). In the one case sculpture obeys the imperatives of its architectural frame, and emphasizes a pre-existing pattern; in the other case it remains detached, and both building and scrulpture are comprehensible separately. The two rival modes of understanding are well illustrated in Verrochio's group of Doubting Thomas, on the façade of Or San Michele (Plate 34), where the saint's foot emerging from the frame gives to the figure a unique sense of startled understanding, precisely because of its refusal to be fixed in the architectural surround. (It should be pointed out that this effect, although often admired, was probably not intentional, the Verrochio having been placed in the niche after a smaller statue had been removed from it.) Without the contrast between architectural and sculptural ways of seeing, this effect would be invisible.

As the example demonstrates, there is a distinction between the architectural and the sculptural approach to statuary. And again functionalism clearly illustrates, although it does not solve, the important theoretical problem which that distinction presents: the problem of locating what is central in the experience of architecture, and of explaining the unity which we acknowledge in its object. It is possible for a building to owe part of its architectural effect to the quality of its sculpture: the value of Chartres as architecture would not be unchanged had the statuary been remade by an apprentice of Gilbert Scott. Similarly, it is possible for sculpture to derive part of its quality, and even its representational significance, from an architectural frame, as the Verrochio and again Chartres illustrate. How, then, do we

PLATE 34 Verrochio: Doubting Thomas, Or San Michele, Florence

distinguish the essential from the inessential in architecture? Alberti, aware of this problem, made a distinction between beauty and ornament.[35] Beauty exists only when no part is detachable, when no alteration can be effected in one part without detriment to the whole. Ornament, by contrast, is aesthetically detachable, and may be added to a building, but does not become, aesthetically speaking, a proper part of it. (Consider the jewels around the neck of a pretty girl, which neither add to her charm nor lose the charm of their own when strung about the neck of a withered crone.)

Alberti's distinction occurs in the course of an attempt to *define* 'beauty', and as such I shall return to it in chapter 9, when the problem of the meaning of such aesthetic terms will be one of my principal preoccupations. But the distinction to which he refers is already of the first importance, and illustrates the recurrent search for what is central in the experience of architecture. As I have expressed it, the distinction is not so much between Beauty and Ornament, as between the essential and the accidental in architecture. If we can make such a distinction it is because there are two ways of understanding what we see. Sculpture may enter into our understanding of architecture, to the extent that our experience of a building as a whole may depend upon an experience of the sculptural significance of its parts. Fine Gothic statuary, adapted to its niche, in an extended and ceremonial arrangement dispersed over a dignified façade – such sculpture as we find in Nôtre Dame de Paris – is essentially architectural and to be understood accordingly. There are also sculptures which add nothing to their architectural context and gain nothing from their architectural frame. It is not, as my imaginary functionalist supposes, that statuary becomes architectural when it contributed to structural clarity – such a theory would provide no account of the eminently architectural statuary that surmounts Bernini's colonnade. The question is rather one of the autonomy of understanding.

But now, it will be asked, what is meant by 'understanding'? So far I have spoken primarily of an *experience* of architecture, and have presented the problem of the unity of architectural effects as though it were a problem about the internal structure of experience. So why speak of 'understanding' as the source of unity? In fact the question answers itself. It is one of the most striking features of imaginative attention as I have described it, that experience and understanding follow each other. An intellectual grasp which leads to no experience of unity is not yet an act of understanding. It will never suffice to be told of some abstract significance in the sculpture attached to a building which makes it appropriate to the use. Only if that significance affects the act of imaginative attention, and so changes the experience, will it enter into understanding. For examples of this interpenetration of significance and experience, embracing both sculpture and architecture (the kind of interpenetration that Bernini had in mind in referring to the architectural *concetto*[36]) the reader is referred to chapter 8. All that is necessary for the moment is to realize that we must allow precedence to the visual aspect in architecture: it is this which forms the basis and the necessary precondition to all the other parts. And if we allow that, then there will be no problem in giving a comprehensive account of architectural understanding or in separating architectural understanding from rival kinds. We shall be able to do this as Alberti did, by pointing to the act of imaginative attention which is the most complete and satisfying, the act from which the least can be subtracted without destroying the whole. And then we should not be surprised to find that not only pattern, but also colour, light, statuary and material, can enter into and determine the true experience of buildings.

There ought to be no real problem, therefore, as to how the experience of architecture may form a unity, despite its covering so many separate things. Once we abstract from day-to-day perception and enter the world of imagination, our experience ceases to obey normal theoretical and practical strictures. It is neither an instrument of knowledge nor a premise to action. Whatever unity the experience achieves will depend upon a corresponding unity imposed upon its object. It is the desire for unity, and a puzzlement as to how to achieve it, which led to the theories discussed in the last chapter, and we must beware of following them in reducing all the aims of architecture to a single 'essence'. Imaginative experience borrows its unity from the unity attributed to its object. So long as it is possible to attend to the object under a unified conception, so will the experience which expresses that conception retain its integrity. There will be no more difficulty in postulating a unity between the experience of a façade and the experience of the interior than between the experience of the first act of a play and the experience of its sequel. The unity depends upon bringing both experiences under a single conception, and upon accommodating experience to conception, as one accommodates experience to conception in seeing a group of lines as a pattern or a face. As I walk down the aisle of S. Spirito my experience constantly changes; but because I can see each round arch as continuing or varying a rhythm established by its predecessor, my experience 'hangs together', just as when I hear a melody in music. And so too does my experience of statuary on the North Porch of Chartres hang together with my experience of architectural forms, since how I see the statues, and how I see the forms, are determined by the same set of religious thoughts. Because my experience is not constrained by the needs of literal perception, it ranges freely over its object, and imposes on the object whatever unity it will bear.

We have established two important points. First, that there is a radical distinction between imaginative and 'literal' experience and that the experience of architecture firmly exemplifies the first of these. Second, that the experience of architecture – because it reflects an underlying act of imaginative attention – belongs to the active and not the passive part of mind. It is, in a certain sense, free; it can therefore express the full burden of our intellectual conceptions, can be altered and amended through argument, can impose unity and order on its object when the literal mind would see nothing but disjointedness or chaos. It seems to follow, therefore, that there can be no experience of architecture that is not also an exercise of taste. For if the experience can be spoken of as 'right' or 'wrong', does it not already presuppose a certain choice? And does it not lead us naturally towards the attempt to find its best or appropriate object? It seems then that we can only expect to understand architecture if we first investigate the workings of taste. Perhaps there are established principles of taste; if that is so, then we shall also know how to build.

5

JUDGING ARCHITECTURE

It is important, first, to dismiss a certain popular idea of aesthetic taste, the idea enshrined in the familiar maxim that *de gustibus non est disputandum.* 'It's all a matter of taste', men say, thinking in this way to bring argument to an end and at the same time to secure whatever validity they can for their own idiosyncracies. Clearly no one really believes in the Latin maxim: it is precisely over matters of taste that men are most prone to argue. Reasons are given, relations established; the ideas of right and wrong, correct and incorrect, are bandied about with no suspicion that here they might be inappropriate. Societies are formed for the preservation of buildings to which the majority of people are thought to be indifferent. Anger is expressed at the erection of a skyscraper in Paris, or a shopping precinct in some quiet cathedral town. This anger has many causes, not all of them specifically 'aesthetic'; but, on the face of it, it is quite incompatible with the assumption that in matters of taste dispute is pointless, that each man has the right to his own opinion, that nothing is objective, nothing right or wrong. In science, too, we find differences of opinion. Perhaps some people believe that the earth is flat, and form societies to protect themselves from the abundant evidence to the contrary. But at least we know that such a belief is the sign of a diminished understanding. Why should we not say, then, that a preference for the Einstein Tower over Giotto's campanile is simply incompatible with a full understanding of architecture? It could be said that there is more to be seen in the Giotto, that it possesses a visual and intellectual richness, a delicate proportionality, an intricacy of detail, that it is beautiful not only as form but in all its parts and matter, that every meaning which attaches to it upholds and embellishes its aesthetic power. A man who notices and takes delight in those things is unlikely to believe that the Mendelsohn bears comparison, even if he should admire its smooth contour and thorough conception. When we study these buildings our attitude is not simply one of curiosity, accompanied by some indefinable pleasure or dissatisfaction. Inwardly, we affirm our preference as valid, and if we did not do so, it is hard to see how we might be seriously guided by it, how we might rely on it to fill in the gaps left by functional reflections in the operation of practical knowledge. Our preference means something more to us than mere pleasure or satisfaction. It is the outcome of thought and education; it is expressive of moral, religious and political feelings, of an entire *Weltanschauung*, with which our identity is mingled. Our deepest convictions seek confirmation in the experience of architecture, and it is simply not open to us to dismiss these convictions as matters of arbitrary preference about which others are free to make up their minds, any more than it is open to us to think the same of our feelings about murder, rape or genocide. Just as in matters of morality, and matters of science, we cannot engage in aesthetic argument without feeling that our opponent is wrong. 'I had always', wrote Ruskin, a clear conviction that there *was* a law in this matter: that good architecture might be indisputedly discerned and divided from the bad; and that we were all of us just as unwise in disputing about the matter without reference to principle, as we should be for debating about the genuineness of a coin without ringing it.'[1] I should like to agree with Ruskin, if only because I am convinced that, in so many matters of architectural taste, his own opinions were fundamentally wrong.

Two features of taste deserve mention at the outset: first, that only a rational being may have taste; second, that taste is changed not through training but rather through education. The two features belong, not surprisingly, together. Taste is something that is both exercised in thought and changed through thought. The dog who prefers 'Doggo' to 'Chump' is making no conscious comparison between them, and has no reason for his preference. His preference is a brute fact: it arises from no reflection upon the nature of 'Chump' or upon the nature of 'Doggo'. In rational beings, however, we may discover preferences that are not only influenced by reflection and comparison, but in many cases arise from that reflection much as do the conclusions of a reasoned argument. Such preferences may be educated; they are not as a rule the outcome of a process of training such as would be administered to a horse or a dog. On the contrary, tastes are acquired through instruction, through the acquisition of knowledge and the development of values. If taste were so simple a matter as the Latin adage implies, would it not be surprising that a man can be brought to a love of the modern style through understanding the ideas behind it, or that he could come to hate neo-classicism, as Ruskin and Pugin hated it, in the interests of moral and religious convictions? Indeed, I shall argue that changes in taste are continuous with, and indeed inseparable from, changes in one's whole outlook on the world, and that taste is as much a part of one's rational nature as are scientific judgements, social conventions and moral ideals.

It is part of the philosophy of mind – as this was adumbrated in chapter 1 – to impose on the human mind a fundamental division into categories: for example, into the categories of thought, feeling and will, or into the categories of experience, judgement and desire. The point of such divisions is not to arrive at a scientific theory of the mind, nor to divide mental processes into neatly separable compartments, associated one with another only contingently, and capable of autonomous existence. It is, rather, to understand the fundamental *powers* of the mind: not what the mind is, but what it can do. And it is no part of this aim that the powers should be truly separable – that they should be either understood or exercised in isolation. The description of mental powers is therefore a conceptual enterprise, in the way that all philosophy is conceptual: it involves exploring how we might identify and describe the phenomena that surround us, before we have even begun the task of explaining them. Now suppose we ask the question – to which category should the phenomenon of taste be assigned? We find that our intuitions present no simple answer: there is no accepted category to which taste belongs. Indeed, we find that taste is the least 'extricable' of all mental phenomena, the most spread out over our several mental capacities. As we reflect on this, we shall begin to understand the value of taste, its value as bringing together and harmonizing the separate functions exercised in practical understanding. I shall consider in turn the relation of taste to the three principal categories of experience, preference and thought.

First, then, the relation of taste to experience. This would be undeserving of discussion were it not for the fact, already remarked on, that the experience of architecture has so often been misdescribed, or even ignored altogether, in the various attempts to establish comprehensive canons of architectural judgement. Thus the cruder forms of functionalism would seem to ignore the appeal to how a building is seen, finding the only true canon of taste in the *intellectual* relation of means to end. Recognizing, however, that it is really most strange to rule *a priori* against virtually every building that has ever been admired, a more subtle form of functionalism evolved, according to which the experience *is* the most important thing, but that the experience of architecture – or at least the *true* experience of architecture – simply *is* an experience of function. But even that view, as we shall see, is wrong.

The argument of the last chapter showed the element of experience to be a vital constituent in the exercise of taste. We cannot be affected in our judgement of a building by its abstract significance unless that significance first affects our experience of the building. If I support my favourable judgement of a building by reference to its meaning, then this reason can only justify my preference, and indeed can only be part of what leads me to that preference (a part of *my* reason for the preference) if the meaning is revealed in an experience. To refer to history, anecdote, association, function and so on – all this must be irrelevant in the justification of one architectural preference against another until it is shown how the interpretation modifies the experience of a building. For until that is shown we have not given a reason for looking at one building in preference to the other, rather than a reason for thinking of one and not the other, writing a book about the one but not about the other, and so on. Hence we have given no support to the aesthetic judgement, the judgement which favours the building as an object of experience.

As I tried to show, our experience of architecture, being based on an act of imaginative attention to its object, is essentially open to emendation in the light of reasoned reflection. Consider, for example, Geoffrey Scott's description of the church of S. Maria della Salute in Venice (Plate 35):

> [The] ingenious paring [of the volutes] makes a perfect transition from the circular plan to the octagonal. Their heaped and rolling form is like that of a heavy substance that has slidden to its final and true adjustment. The great statues and pedestals which they support appear to arrest the outward movement of the volutes and to pin them down upon the church. In silhouette, the statues serve (like the obelisks of the lantern) to give a pyramidal contour to the composition, a line which more than any other gives mass its unity and strength . . . there is hardly an element in the church which does not proclaim the beauty of mass and the power of mass to give essential simplicity and dignity even to the richest and most fantastic dreams of the baroque.[2]

At every point in this description Scott refers to some visual aspect of

PLATE 35 B. Longhena: S. Maria della Salute, Venice

the building, and he allows himself the benefit of no abstract idea that does not find its immediate correlate in experience. Suppose, then, that someone, having read Scott's description, remarks, on returning to the church, that it looks just the same to him – its aspect simply has not changed, and however hard he tries he cannot see it as Scott requires him to. Like Ruskin, he sees it as an incongruous jumble of unmeaning parts,[3] nothing more than an unstable juxtaposition of octagon and circle, with sixteen lumps of stone balanced at the corners. To such a man Scott's criticism has made no difference: it is not that he has been persuaded by it, but remained unable to adjust his experience. It is rather that he *has not been persuaded*. The mark of persuasion *is* the changed experience. For a man really to accept what Scott says, having previously been of another mind, his experience must change. To accept the criticism is to come to see the church in a certain way, in such a way, namely, that the description seems immediately apt, having become, for the subject, his preferred way of describing what he sees, of describing, as a philosopher might put it, the intentional object of perception.[4] Unless Scott's description has this relation to experience, it cannot serve as a reason for the judgement of taste. It would be at best an explanation, with no justifying force.

Scott's criticism is relatively concrete. But the same principle applies even in the most abstract of architectural judgements, and, properly understood, can be used to redeem from the obscurity which surrounds them, the doctrines of space, function and *Kunstgeschichte* which I criticized in chapter 3. It is impossible to avoid the sense that an idea, while in itself wholly abstract, may nonetheless find something akin to an architectural *expression*, and gain validity as a result. For example, one might think of a Romanesque cloister in terms of the industrious piety of its former inhabitants: in terms of an historical identity, a way of life, with which this habit of building was associated. But were a man to present this as his reason for looking favourably on some particular cloister, say that of S. Paolo Fuori le Mura in Rome (Plate 36), then the onus lies on him to show exactly how such an idea finds confirmation in an experience of the building. Perhaps he could go on to refer to the variety of forms employed in the columns, to their fine industrious detailing, and to the way in which none of this abundance of observation disturbs the restful harmony of the design. He might trace the rhythm of the arcade, and describe the Cosmatesque mosaic, with its bright and childlike inventiveness that never transgresses the bounds of sensible ornamentation. In all this, he might say, we see how energetic observation and monastic piety may be successfully combined. A certain idea of monasticism becomes a visible reality: the idea is not merely a personal association occasioned by some anecdotal or historical reminiscence: we *see* it in the details of the building.

I have said that taste may involve the adducing of reasons. We may note, therefore, that whatever reasons are brought forward in support of the judgement of taste – however we may wish to defend our preferences – these reasons can be valid reasons only in so far as they enter into and affect our experience of a building. It is pointless to argue with someone about the structural honesty, social function, or spiritual meaning of a building when, even if he agrees with what one

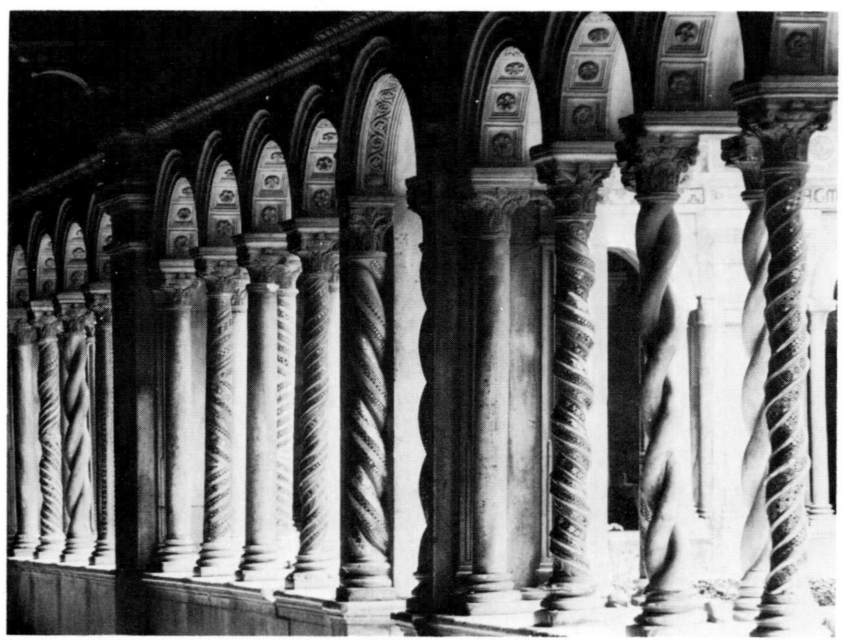

PLATE 36 S. Paolo Fouri le Mura, Rome, cloister

says, he is unable to experience the building differently. For until he experiences it differently one's reasons will have failed to change his aesthetic point of view: here the point of view *is* the experience. Some philosophers have been so puzzled by the idea that a process of reasoning might have as its end-point not a judgement but an experience that they have wished to deny that what we call reasoning in criticism really deserves the name.[5] But the argument of the last chapter should enable us to see that the suggestion is far from paradoxical; for our experiences may be subject to the will, and the product of specific forms of attention. They can constitute part of the *activity* of mind. It follows that an experience, like an action, may be the conclusion of an argument.[6] If criticism is not reasoning, then, what is it? Certainly critical comments may be proper answers to the question 'why?' Moreover, they are not intended as *explanations*: they give reasons, not causes, as I shall later show. It is possible that they cannot be elevated to the status of universal criteria; and it is possible that they do not have 'objective validity': at any rate, these are matters which we have yet to consider. But neither of those possibilities should lead us to deny that the observations of a critic can be adduced as reasons for the response or experience which he recommends.

I turn now to the connection between taste and preference. With what kind of preference are we dealing here? A simple answer would be this: the experience of one building is preferred to that of another because it is more pleasant. But what do we mean by pleasure? Those philosophers who emphasize the place of pleasure in ethics and in art (empiricists, utilitarians, and their progeny), usually end, either by making the notion of pleasure primitive and inexplicable, or else by identifying pleasure in terms of preference. In other words, they propose as the criterion for a man's taking pleasure in something that he should prefer it to alternatives. As an explanation of preference, and if not further analysed, the mention of pleasure then becomes entirely empty. I think we should hesitate to lay the burden of our aesthetics, as so many empiricists have done, on a concept that is taken to be self-explanatory, but which is in fact entirely vacuous.

There are various ways in which an experience might be related to pleasure. We can imagine a purely causal relation: a certain experience causes pleasure, brings pleasure in its train, or is part of a process in which pleasure is included. When a rich man surveys his palace, it may cause him to reflect with pride on his own magnificence; and in this thought is pleasure. Here the pleasure is aroused by the experience of the building, but does not lie in that experience. It seems that, in contrast to this case, aesthetic pleasure must be internally linked to aesthetic experience. If it were not so linked, then we should be in danger of offending against the autonomy of aesthetic interest; in danger of saying that we seek aesthetic experience, and so are interested in its object only as a means to some separate effect.[7] If that were so, then the work of art becomes redundant: it would be a mere accident if the pleasure we obtain from reading *Paradise Lost* is obtained in that way, rather than from an injection or a tablet. It is true that certain people have compared the experience of art and the experience of drugs: but if their arguments have contained any sense, it is because they have been speaking, not of the pleasure of drug-taking, but of the pleasure in other things which, for some reason, the drug makes available. (As when, after a glass of wine, a man may look with more pleasure on a flower: here what he takes pleasure in is not the wine but the flower. The wine, as mere cause of his pleasure, has ceased to be its object.)

An experience may be internally related to pleasure by being itself essentially pleasurable (or essentially painful). Certain experiences, in other words, are simply *species* of pleasure: sexual experiences present perhaps the most obvious example. Other experiences, while not essentially pleasurable, are, when pleasurable, pleasurable in themselves rather than in their effects: for example, the experience of warmth. Aesthetic experiences are of such a kind: they may be neither pleasant nor unpleasant. Nevertheless, unlike the experience of warmth, their relation to pleasure is not merely a contingent one. Unless a man sometimes enjoys aesthetic experience he cannot, I think, ever be said to have it. Aesthetic experience is not *just* a form of pleasure, but nor is its connection with pleasure a mere matter of fact.[8]

A distinction should here be observed. To say that an aesthetic experience is pleasant might seem to imply that a man takes pleasure *in* the experience, as though it were the experience, rather than its object, that constituted the prime focus of his attention. But lovers of architecture take pleasure in buildings, not in the experiences that are obtained from buildings. Their pleasure is of the kind roughly described at the beginning of the last chapter; it is a pleasure founded on understanding, pleasure which has an object, and not just a cause. And here pleasure is directed outwards to the world, not inwards to one's own state of mind. The pleasure of aesthetic experience is inseparable from the act of attention to its object; it is not the kind of pleasure characteristic of mere sensation, such as the pleasure of a hot bath or a good cigar. In other words, aesthetic pleasures are not merely *accompanied* by attention to an object. They are essentially connected with that attention, and when attention ceases, whatever pleasure continues can no longer be an exercise of taste. This is part of what might lead one to say that, here, pleasure is not so much an effect of its object, as a *mode of understanding it.*[9]

Now, someone might argue that people absorb from the organic contours of our ancient towns, with their human details, their softened lines and their 'worked' appearance, a kind of pleasure that sustains them in their daily lives; while in the bleak environment of the modern city a dissatisfaction is felt that disturbs people without their knowing why. Even if this were true, it is not necessarily relevant to aesthetic judgement. Such inarticulate pleasures and displeasures have little in common with architectural taste and give us no guidance in the practice of criticism. They can be accommodated, I suspect, only on the level of human 'need', and as we have seen, that is not the level where aesthetic values occur. Of course, were we to take a wider conception of human 'need', a conception that transcends the boundaries of popular biology, then we might certainly find that there is a real issue here. And if we allow human values into the realm of human 'needs' then it becomes impossible to speak of a need for light, air and sanitation, and at the same time to ignore the deeper need to see in one's surroundings the real imprint of human labour and the workings of human history. But until we can connect these things with the values implicit in aesthetic attention, we have advanced no further with the practice of criticism. In chapter 10 I shall make that connection; but it will be made in a way that removes all force from these merely sociological observations.

This last feature – the connection between aesthetic pleasure and attention – is one of the many reasons for distinguishing taste in the aesthetic sense from another phenomenon that often goes by the same name, the discriminating palate in food and wine. For although the connoisseur of wine may 'attend to' the qualities of what he drinks, his pleasure, when he does so, is not of a different kind from that of his ignorant companion, who takes no interest in the wine beyond enjoying its taste. The connection between pleasure and attention is here only external: gustatory pleasure does not *demand* an intellectual act.

However, it is no accident that we use the word 'taste', to refer to both sensuous and aesthetic pleasures. Reflection on this fact leads us to qualify the distinction made at the outset of the last chapter between sensuous and intellectual pleasure. I distinguished pleasure which is internally related to thought from pleasure which depends on thought only accidentally. And it seemed that the pleasures of architecture could not belong to the second kind, since they cannot exist in the absence of attention. However, even if we accept this distinction, we cannot say that all intellectual pleasures are 'aesthetic'. Plato considered aesthetic pleasure to be a kind of intermediary between the sensuous and the intellectual, and the pursuit of beauty to be one mode of ascent from the lower to the higher realms of mind.[10] In this theory he recognized that there are pleasures which are internally related both to thought and to sensation. A clear example is that of the 'aesthetic' interest in a painting, where intellectual apprehension is fundamental to pleasure, but no more fundamental than the sensory experience with which it is combined. The case might be contrasted with one of Plato's favourite examples, the purely intellectual pleasure of mathematics, the enjoyment of which may be obtained through reading, listening, or fingering Braille; even through pure thought alone.

But not every 'sense' lends itself to aesthetic pleasure. The experience must be such that, in attending to it, one attends also to its object. In particular, we should note how different in this respect are the eye and the ear from the other senses. It seems to me that there is probably no such thing as savouring a visual impression while remaining incurious about its object – as though one could savour the sensation of red, while remaining uninterested in the red thing that one sees. Visual experience is so essentially cognitive, so 'opened out', as it were, on to the objective world, that our attention passes through and seizes on its object to the exclusion of all impressions of sense. Now it is difficult to describe the difference here, between vision and hearing on the one hand, and taste, smell, perhaps even touch, on the other. But the fact in question is clear enough, and has been noticed by philosophers from Aquinas to the present day.[11] Vision and hearing, unlike taste and smell, may sometimes be forms of objective contemplation. In tasting and smelling I contemplate not the object but the experience derived from it. A further distinguishing feature might also be mentioned, which is that in tasting, both the object and the desire for it are steadily consumed. No such thing is true of aesthetic attention. I do not propose to study these features; were one to do so, however, the full complexity of the distinction between sensuous and aesthetic pleasure would become apparent. And it would also become apparent that aesthetic experience (as has often been noticed) is the prerogative of the eye and the ear.

The contrast between aesthetic and sensuous pleasure can be made, however, without going into those complexities. It suffices to study the notion of value. As I suggested earlier, values are more significant than preferences. Values play a part, not only in the processes of practical reasoning that issue in action (which might be concerned purely with the agent's own individual interest, without reference to the interests of any other man); they also enter into the process of reasoning whereby we justify action, not just to ourselves, but to others who observe and are affected by it. And until we have this habit of justifying action, we shall never acquire a conception of its end. We must see the end as desirable, and not just as desired; otherwise we are only half engaged in the pursuit of it. Without values, it is hard to imagine that there could be rational behaviour, behaviour which is motivated by an understanding not of the means only but also of the end. Not only do we try to support our values with reasons when called upon to do so, we also learn to see and understand the world in terms of them. Now, I have not said enough about the distinction between value and mere desire, for the distinction is difficult to capture in a simple formula and will become clear only gradually as we proceed. But it cannot be doubted that there *are* desires which we are prone to justify and recommend to others, as well as desires which we regard as personal idiosyncracies. The former have a more intimate connection with our self-identity, and involve a deeper sense of ourselves as creatures responsible for our past and future; later I shall show why that is so.

The best way to begin the study of value is through examples. In culinary matters we are not dealing with values. You happen to like oysters, I happen to dislike them. You happen to like white wine, I prefer red; and so on. If is felt that these are ultimate facts, beyond which one cannot go. And it is further held, on account of this, that here there can be little point in employing ideas of 'right' and 'wrong', of 'good' taste and 'bad'.[12]

Such a claim is of course exaggerated. We do talk of good and bad taste in food and wine. Nevertheless, we do not normally believe that we make reference in doing so to anything like a standard of taste, which it is incumbent upon others to accept. Certainly we discuss matters of culinary taste, and we regard such tastes as in some sense capable of education. But we do not think that there are reasons which will support one culinary preference against another. For if we look at the matter closely, we find that the notion that a reason might actually give *support* to a preference of this kind is a contentious one. If one man prefers claret to burgundy (or, to be more specific, Mouton to Latour), there is no sense in which this disagreement can be resolved into some other, more basic one, without ceasing to be a disagreement about the gustatory qualities of the wines and becoming instead a disagreement about something else, for example, about their medicinal properties or social standing. Of course, there is discussion of wine. The enjoyment of wine may even aspire to those levels of self-conscious sophistication pursued by Huysman's Des Esseintes, in his (I think logically impossible) 'symphony' of perfumes. But even if one were to take the chatter of wine snobbery with all the seriousness that such an example (or the more English example provided by George Meredith in *The Egoist*) might suggest, this would still not suffice to turn *discussion* into *reasoning*. For here no disagreement can be resolved simply by coming to an agreement over some *other* matter of œnological preference. Such preferences are essentially particular, and logically wholly independent of one another: there is no logical order, as one might say, among preferences of this kind. It is never possibly to say: 'But you agree with me in preferring Moselle to Hock and therefore, because of the proved similarity of the choice, you simply *must* agree in preferring claret to burgundy.' Such a remark is close to nonsense. Moreover, there is no sense in which a change of experience can here be the true *conclusion* of a process of reasoning. It is, logically speaking, a mere accident if the discussion of a wine changes its taste: the changed taste might have been caused by the reasoning which preceded it, but it bears no intellectual relation to that reasoning, and cannot in any sense be considered as its logical outcome or expression.

Compare the case of moral sentiments – the prime example of

values. There would be something most odd in a moral argument which concluded with the words: 'I grant all that you have said about murder, but it still appeals to me; and therefore I cannot help but approve of it.' That is not the sincere expression of a moral point of view. We do not, and cannot, treat moral opinions as though they were isolated and idiosyncratic preferences that bear no necessary relation to one another. Thus moral sentiments, unlike preferences in food and wine, may be inconsistent with each other, they may be supported by reasons which seem conclusive, or refuted and abandoned purely on the basis of thought.

Aesthetic tastes are like tastes in food and wine, in that they are never actually logically inconsistent. I may like St Paul's today but not tomorrow. I may very much like St Bride's and very much dislike St Mary le Bow. However, the matter does not, and cannot end there. Mere caprice cannot take the place of aesthetic judgement; a preference that is merely capricious cannot be described as an exercise of aesthetic taste, for it lacks the origin, the aim and the reward of taste. A man exercises taste when he regards his enjoyment of one building as part of an aesthetic outlook, and hence as in principle justifiable by reasons that might also apply to another building.[13] It would be most odd if a man thought that there was nothing in the basis for his dislike of St Mary le Bow that would not equally provide him with a reason for disliking St Bride's (Plates 37 and 38). Does he regard the baroque steeple as an unhappy stylistic compromise? In that case he must dislike both the churches. Moreover, if he has that dislike, it is perhaps because he has not understood the need for a variegated sky-line, has not understood how much the baroque forms depend for their true exuberance on an excess of light, an excess that in England is obtained only far above the level of the street. In coming to understand that, he may understand too the correctness of inspiration in the Gothic revival – correctness, that is, as an answer to the stylistic problem posed by large buildings and endless cities, crowded beneath fogs and rains and gloomy Northern skies. Again, our dissenter might consider that Wren's inventiveness is a cold and contrived phenomenon, in comparison, say, with the inventiveness of Hawksmoor, which involves the less obvious but more subtle disposition of mass, and a finish which is consequently firmer and crisper (Plate 39). But again he ought to dislike *both* the Wren churches, and again he could be reasoned with. For has he really noticed the effectiveness of the play of light devised by Wren, and the springing upward movement of the boundaries? All this suggests that, while he may indeed *prefer* one of Wren's churches

PLATE 37 (*left*) Sir Christopher Wren: St Mary le Bow, London, steeple
PLATE 38 (*right*) Sir Christopher Wren: St Bride's, London, steeple

to the other, he cannot strongly dislike the one and think that this gives him *no* reason not to strongly admire the other, unless he can make some adequate distinction between the two. While there is no true inconsistency between architectural tastes, it is always possible to construct these 'bridges' of reasoning from one taste to another; and therefore there may always be a pressure of reason to bring one's judgements into line.

I envisage an important objection here, which is that I have not yet sufficiently distinguished the discussion of architecture from the discussion of wine. The examples given, it might be said, are not really examples of reasoning, but rather of *ex post facto* explanation of an immediate, and in itself inarticulate, response. We admit such wealth of detailed discussion in the present case only because the matter is important to us, not because there is any real possibility of rational debate.

PLATE 39 Nicholas Hawksmoor: St Anne, Limehouse, London, steeple

It is true that aesthetic interest may often be as the objection implies; what it contains by way of discussion may be not reasoned justification but an attempt to explain or make articulate an unreflecting impression. However, aesthetic interest need not be like that, and indeed has an intrinsic tendency to be something else, something that exhibits genuine reasoning. It is reasoning because its aim is justification, not explanation. Justification is possible here because of the active nature of the experience, which is both partly voluntary, and in any event dependent upon an activity of imaginative attention. I can reason in favour of such experience, just as I reason in favour of actions, emotions, attitudes and beliefs. Architectural tastes need not, therefore, be spontaneous. Indeed, in so far as they are *tastes* in the aesthetic sense, they inevitably make way for deliberation and comparison. And here deliberation does not mean the cultivation of a vast and varied experience, like that of the over-travelled connoisseur. It denotes not the fevered acquisition of experience, but rather the reflective attention to what one has.[14] A man might know only a few significant buildings – as did the builders of many of our great cathedrals – and yet be possessed of everything necessary to the development of taste. It suffices only that he should reflect on the nature of those choices that are available to him and on the experiences that he might obtain. Consider, for example, the development of Lincoln cathedral from nave to transept and transept to choir, where we may observe a basic architectural vocabulary being used with greater and greater refinement, with more and more subtle detailing and more and more harmony of effect. Once the Lincoln style had been established, later architects had all that they needed in order to distinguish the successful from the unsuccessful extrapolations of it. The same is even true of the bare style established by Gropius and his followers at the Bauhaus, a style which has been the stock in trade of many architects since the war, and which still can acquire its tasteful and appropriate continuations, as can be seen from comparing the factories which spread from London along the Western Road. Moreover architectural taste, like moral opinion, will be based on other attitudes and judgements. To return to a previous example: it may be that a certain monastic idea becomes appealing because it is expressed by the cloister of S. Paolo; it may also be that a man's previous allegiance to the monastic idea serves as reason for his admiration of the cloister.

But it is here that the notion of taste becomes puzzling. Certainly the clarity that attaches – or seems to attach – to much moral argument, the sense of clear premises and inexorable conclusions, does not here prevail. For example, it does not follow by logic that if I understand the baroque idiom and know how much it harmonizes with my other predilections, then I simply *must* come to like it. I may not like it all the same. But the peculiarity of architectural (as of all truly aesthetic) preference is that I *will* come to like it; or rather, I shall feel a weight of reason in its favour. And this is not in fact so surprising. For my experience of a building, or of an architectural idiom, may change as my conception of it changes. And as my experience changes, so must my taste. We have seen that such a change of experience is precisely the aim of architectural criticism. But exactly what kind of reasoning supports it? The examples in the last chapter seemed to suggest that criticism involves a search for the 'correct' or 'balanced' perception, the perception in which ambiguities are resolved and harmonies established, allowing the kind of pervasive visual satisfaction which I hinted at. But that cannot be all. The conceptions which influence our experience of architecture are as far-reaching as the conceptions which govern our lives. How else is it possible for an architect like Pugin to think that it was incumbent upon him as a Christian to explore the intricacies of finials, pinnacles and tracery?

Suppose that a man claims not to like Borromini's Oratory in Rome. A natural response might be to say that if he does not like it, then he does not understand it. This notion of 'understanding' is an important one, and I shall shortly return to it: but notice how strange it would be to regard a man who honestly preferred beer to Château Lafite as deficient in understanding: that would be to ascribe to such a taste precisely the intellectual dimension which it lacks. The question then arises how one might bring such a man to a sufficient understanding of Borromini's building. And here it is significant that his misunderstanding might, after all, have a basis which is quite remote from any incompetence in his experience of architectural composition. An historical understanding – and a corresponding lack of sympathy – might very well be at the root of his aesthetic error. (Here one begins to see the legitimate sphere of art-historical criticism.) The Oratory was designed to house one of the most vital institutions of the late Counter-Reformation, and to give expression to its remarkable combination of civilized self-confidence and spiritual humility.[15] It is true that, in this building, modesty was often imposed by an official parsimony against which (as was his manner) Borromini constantly grumbled, but one can hardly doubt that a certain modesty is there, too, in his fundamental artistic conception. The bold rhythmical façade sweeps its arms outward to the street, but its clear-cut forms are of modest brick, finely laid (see Plate 40). Its angles and corners are banded with the meeting of innumerable mouldings, combined with consummate elegance; and yet their forms are retiring and softened, seeming to accommodate themselves to the movements of passers-by (Plate 41). It is important to see in these forms the balance of competing claims, of worldly competence and spiritual grace. Now the language of Borromini, while it speaks to us outwardly in definite and self-confident accents, embraces, too, a powerful subjectivity of outlook. It is not absurd to see in this a correlate of the earlier Counter-Reformation attempts to reconcile the outward show of the church with the rise of an inner conscience, and certainly not absurd to see that spirit in a building dedicated to the order of St Philip Neri. When we understand the nature of this wrestling and reconciling between outer and inner we see just how significant is the visual achievement of the Oratory. Here we find a perfect marriage between the inventive and flexible exterior, in which elegant variety is presented as at the same time a species of unassuming simplicity, and a quiet ponderous quality

PLATE 40 Francesco Borromini: Oratorio di San Filippo Neri

within, in those parts designed for the contemplative life of the Filippini. Compare, for example, the powerful movement of the cloister (not finished, unfortunately, as Borromini had designed it) with its overmastering colossal Order whose rhythm is taken subtly and effectively round the corners by curved pilasters finely worked in *mattone* – with the interior, where the very same modest vitality is represented as an inner state. Consider, for example, the restful corridor, into which an indented window suddenly penetrates, without disturbing the studied and reflective detailing of the frame; or the recreation room, with its fine chimney piece and subtle mouldings, which create an illuminated space and a strangely mobile whiteness of wall, that seem the perfect symbol of inwardness (Plates 42–4). There is no doubt that when Borromini wrote of the stylistic need to *fantasticare*[16] he meant to refer, not to some arbitrary over-spilling of exuberant forms, but rather to the constant need to alter and amend, to make bold gestures and steady variations, and so to transform decorative invention into expressive art.

PLATE 41 Francesco Borromini: Oratorio di San Filippo Neri

To speak in such a way of Borromini's Oratory is to risk offending the architectural purist. It has been said that to interpret a building in terms of some underlying 'idea' is either to indulge in an irrelevant rhapsody that bears no relation to the visual qualities of the building, or else merely to make a fanciful and unverifiable speculation about the psychology of the architect.[17] But surely, Borromini had no intention that we should see his work in the way that I have suggested, and even if he had that intention, this would be purely incidental to the aesthetic quality of his building?[18] Familiar as we are with the simplistic interpretations of the Gothic that have swept in such rapid succession over the field of architectural history, we are perhaps somewhat reluctant now to concede the relevance to architectural criticism of the 'history of ideas'. However, in our zeal to discredit the enthusiastic bigotries of our ancestors, we should not take refuge in pure hedonism, excluding altogether from the discussion of architecture the ideas that so often lead us to an interest in it. We should realize that, in relating our visual experience in this way to an abstract idea, we are not necessarily describing the architect's intentions, nor are we proposing a definitive interpretation, valid irrebuttably for all succeeding times. Rather, we are attempting to show that the spectator's knowledge of, and sympathy with, a particular state of

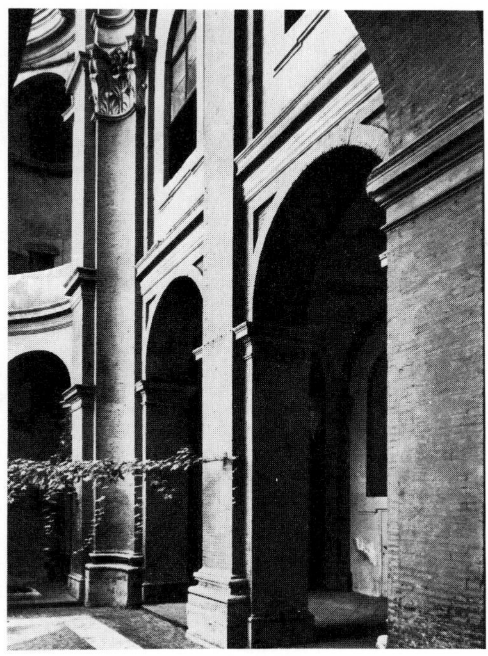

PLATE 42 Francesco Borromini: Oratorio di San Filippo Neri

mind, may modify and enrich his perception of a building. The validity of such an attempt must rest not in the architect's intention but in the transformation of the spectator's experience. For an idea to be a successful instrument of criticism it must find a detailed, and not merely a schematic, correspondence in our perceptions.

These thoughts are vague as yet, and I shall go on to clarify them. But already we may see in them both the strengths and the weaknesses of the art-historical criticism that was discussed in chapter 3. On the one hand it is clearly true that an historical understanding can transform our experience of architecture; on the other hand, it cannot be assumed, in advance of a critical description of the individual case, that this transformation will be either possible or reasonable. We cannot arrive mechanically at historical significance, simply by throwing every object back into the nest of ideas and feelings which surrounded its birth. The relation of a building to an historical, spiritual or moral interpretation is a critical achievement; it is *created* by the critic, in drawing comparisons, and in deriving significances, that penetrate down into the smallest detail of architectural understanding. (Such criticism is rare in the discussion of architecture, for reasons which were mentioned in chapter 1. Among the few examples one might mention again Panofsky's study of the Gothic style, and Ruskin's description of the Doge's Palace.) And it is clear that it is only for certain buildings, and largely for those of a public or symbolic character, that this critical transformation can be effected. Criticism of the

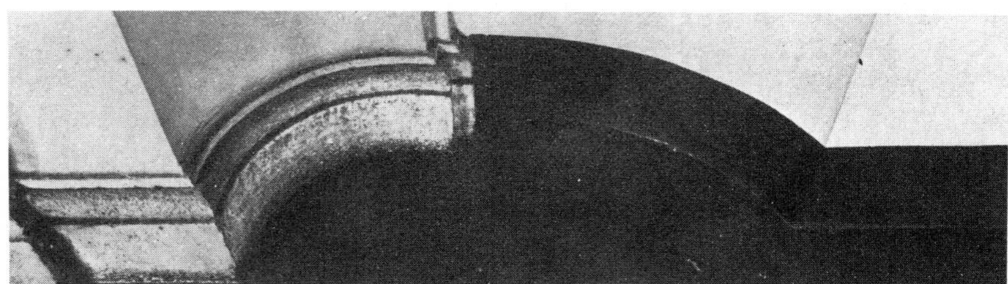

PLATE 43 Francesco Borromini: Oratorio di San Filippo Neri

commonplace or vernacular style must make use of other concepts than the elevated abstractions of art-history. One of the major questions which I shall consider in the second part of this book, is the question of what is common to critical procedures. What kind of 'significance' does the critic discover? And why should it be an important part of architectural experience?

A significant point has been revealed in this discussion, which is that the connection, in aesthetic taste, between experience, preference and thought, is in some way inextricable. At no point can any one of these be truly separated from the others, or the meaning and value of the one be fully characterized without reference to the meaning and value of the others. It will help the reader to appreciate the point if we return briefly to a consideration of the functionalist doctrines, and ask ourselves how they might be redeemed from the sterile *a priorism* of their advocates and given serious critical grounding.

PLATE 44 Francesco Borromini: Oratorio di San Filippo Neri

Now the single most powerful impetus behind the functionalist movement was the revolt against superfluous or 'useless' ornament. We have already seen that Alberti saw fit – and for very good reasons – to distinguish beauty and ornament, to distinguish that which is proper to architectural understanding from that which is not. And, as we also saw, the functionalist proposes an account of what architectural understanding consists in, an account which can be applied step by step in the criticism of individual buildings. It was the Gothic revivalists (paradoxically enough) who first gave vigorous expression to the doctrine, and first directed it against the useless accretion of ornament at the expense of structure and form. To Pugin and his followers[19] it was intolerable that people should think of architectural detail as *purely* ornamental, an idle surface, stuck over a functional frame but detachable from the true structure of the building. It seemed intolerable, for example, that one could have two buildings of identical structure, one in the Gothic 'style', the other purely 'classical', as though 'style' were a matter merely of sculptural veneer rather than architectural achievement. (Compare again Schinkel's two designs for the Werdersche Kirche, Plates 7 and 8, p. 42.) In opposition to such suggestions Pugin – and Ruskin in *The Stones of Venice* – attempted to demonstrate how the ornamental and stylistic details of the Gothic were by no means idle superfluities but on the contrary natural, and even inevitable, developments from the structural and social requirements that the Gothic builders had to meet. Ruskin went further,[20] attempting to show that the love of stone which is the single origin of all serious ornament, and the respect for sound construction, are of identical origin; that the process of building and the process of ornamentation are contiguous parts of a single enterprise, not to be understood independently. There is no such thing as an appreciation of ornament that is not at the same time an appreciation of function.

To understand the critical force of this account we must make a distinction between actual structure and actual function, on the one hand, and what we might call – borrowing a term from Suzanne Langer[21] – virtual structure and virtual function, on the other. That is, we make a distinction – obvious in the light of the discussion in chapter 3 – between how a building is in fact constructed and how that construction is experienced. Our discussion of taste has shown that actual structure is irrelevant to aesthetic judgement except and in so far as it is revealed in virtual structure. But how can structure or function form part of an appearance? And how can they affect the exercise of taste? Perhaps an example will make this clear. Consider, then, the stern of a seventeenth-century ship embellished with all the magnificent trappings of the contemporary baroque (see Plate 45 – loosely adapted from

PLATE 45 'Le Roi Soleil', stern

Le Roi Soleil). Such a composition, jutting from the façade of a house, is unlikely to strike us as tasteful or harmonious. And one might plausibly say that part of the explanation would lie in the consequent abuse of virtual structure. However well supported this pile might be on land, its *apparent* structure is one that makes proper sense only when resting upon an ubiquitous cushion of sea. We must see the boat as supported in this way from below, floating freely, so that the pilasters and structural lines appear to bind the horizontal stages together. They do not then seem directly to 'support' the horizontals, as they would if it were rigidly fixed to land. The example shows, I think, how readily our conception of structure translates itself into experience, and how our awareness of structural vectors may be inextricably connected to our sense of what is aesthetically correct. As part of a house the given structure would be bulbous and disjointed. As a boat floating free in the ocean it is the very perfection of harmony: all the details then make perfect sense.

The question which the functionalist critic now has to answer is how far his critical *aperçu* may be extended. Naturally, there is no end to the possibility of its applications. Virtual structure is in the centre of our experience whenever we accept or reject a new advance in architecture. It is this – far more than any Corbusian desire for endless football grounds – which gave rise to the taste for glass towers raised on pilotis. If you must have high towers, then at least build them in such a way that they do not seem to bear down on the observer with a crushing weight. The accepted composition, in its most successful examples (those, for example, of Mies Van Der Rohe), compels one to see the building as a light screen or curtain strung upon thin bands of unbroken upward force. At all periods of history it has been through the problem of virtual structure that each new canon of visual taste has been forced to evolve and compromise. Compare the helpless corners of Michelozzo's cortile at the Palazzo Medici – an attempt to translate Brunelleschi's quiet rhythms at the Innocenti from straight into quadrangular form, leading to a strange amalgamation of the archivolts, and a sense of trembling weakness at the corners – with the equivalent detail from the Palazzo Venezia, built some 20 years later in Rome (Plates 46 and 47).[22] Here the aesthetic problem – the problem of building an inner courtyard conforming to the classical style – is at the same time a problem of virtual structure, and the 'right' appearance differed from its predecessors precisely in its apparent strength. In such cases, thoughts about function, experience of form, and resulting preference, all arise from the same considerations, and co-exist in unity. That is the outstanding characteristic of all aesthetic judgement, and shows the true critical application of the functionalist doctrine.

But we must again remind ourselves of our strictures against impetuous generality. The theory of virtual structure could never provide an *analysis* of the concept of aesthetic taste, nor could it provide a complete and general principle of construction, despite at least one honourable philosophical attempt to defend it as the sole truth about architecture (that of Schopenhauer[23]). Such theories can never be extended to give universal principles of validity that do not seem arbitrary or partisan. For example, it would be natural to explain the significance of mouldings in a cornice, architrave or string course in terms of the gathering together and arresting of virtual forces and the carefully modulated emphasis on horizontal lines which that requires. Thus an entablature surmounted by an upper story should be both horizontal and properly moulded – it might be said – because if it is so,

PLATE 46 Michelozzo Michelozzi: Medici Palace, Florence, courtyard

the structural vectors of the upper wall are gathered into it more securely, and so passed on to the lower wall in a manner that does not disturb our sense of vertical balance (see Plate 48). But while this might give a useful account of a great many – especially vernacular – mouldings, it cannot possibly provide us with a universal maxim. Consider, as a counter-example, a fairly typical German rococo church: what could be more balanced and harmonious than the West Front of Anton Jentsch's church at Grüssau? (Plate 49). Yet here the lower entablature advances and retreats perpetually under the thrust of window frames and pilasters. Only a fanatic would say that the effect is ugly or unsettling. It is true, indeed, that the baroque cornice shows a deliberate emancipation from its structural role, turning eventually into a fairly familiar piece of domestic vernacular: the joined window entablature, seen on many a ludicrous Victorian mansion block. But why should this transition from virtual function to domestic ornament be regarded as an inevitable error of taste?

It might be said in reply that the baroque style is a very special one,

PLATE 47 Palazzio Venezia, Rome, courtyard

partly parasitic upon a received idiom which it exploits for dramatic ends. And it might be pointed out even here, that while the approach to virtual structure is unorthodox, the requirements of structure are never openly defied. Even in the interior of the church at Ottobeuren, where the ceiling and the upper walls seem to float free of their supports altogether, there is no absolute *negation* of structural premises: if the roof seems unsupported, it is partly because it seems not to *need* support. And indeed, when the style is carried so far as to defy structural requirements altogether – as in the *Helblinghaus* at Innsbruck and later quasi-rococo excesses of *art nouveau* – we may very well feel that a flaw in taste is beginning to show. The virtue of the true baroque lay in the reconciliation of structural clarity with variety of form. Where ornamentation exists for its own sake alone, and could be discarded without apparent structural change, it seems quite natural to think that an axiom of aesthetic judgement has been disregarded.

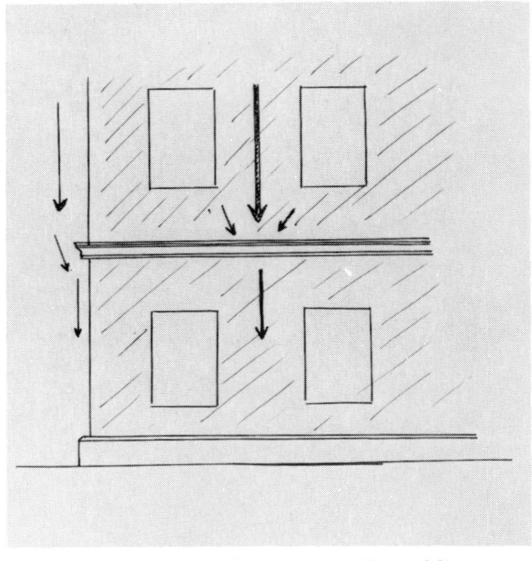

PLATE 48 Virtual structure and mouldings

But of course, the very process of reasoning which might establish this judgement at the same time denies its universal force. Once again we are confronted with a criticism of the individual building, a form of reasoning whose validity depends on the particular transformation of the particular experience. The very dependence that exists here, between judgement and experience, forbids the elevation of any single principle, even one such as this, of virtual structure (which reflects the essential nature of architecture as closely as any principle may), into a universal law of taste. The conclusion of critical reasoning lies in an experience, and experiences, like actions, but unlike beliefs, cannot be logically inconsistent with the arguments that support them; hence they cannot be logically *compelled* by reasoning. Moreover – and this is more important – the experience is open to change in the light of any consideration which might reasonably be brought to bear on it. It is arbitrary to limit the critic's reasoning to considerations of function, even when one has substituted 'virtual function' for the more solid preoccupations of the engineer. For the very arguments which suggest that an experience can be the persuasive outcome of such considerations, suggest that other considerations must be capable of bearing just the same persuasive weight. Anything will be relevant, provided only that it may influence or upset aesthetic attention.

If that is so, however, what becomes of the objectivity of taste? How

PLATE 49 Anton Jentsch: Abbey Church, Grüssau (Krzeszów)

can there be a *valid* critical judgement, when every rule or standard seems beset by the same liability to endless qualifications? It is not enough to say that it is all subjective, and that 'right' and 'wrong' are simply out of place. For as we have noticed, the whole structure of aesthetic judgement belies that facile subjectivism. Indeed, it is precisely because of the intellectual complexity of taste and its deep connection with all the preferences that most matter to us, that we seem condemned to pursue an ideal of objectivity even in the face of the most persistent disappointment. Our pleasure in a building therefore incorporates a sense of its own validity, and seems to possess, on that account, a quasi-scientific aspect. We are drawn into a quest for standards, and when, as may happen, a building strikes us as truly beautiful, or truly hideous, it is impossible at one and the same time both to experience it and to believe that our feeling might be wrongly based. A man feels that he has reason for his preference, even when he can *give* no reason; and here, to have reason is to have a right. It is to believe that others ought to share in or at least acknowledge what one feels; if they do not do so, then they must be blind, insensitive, misled. Serlio, describing an over-wrought Roman architrave, writes that this is a thing which 'not only I would not do, but of which I expressly say that . . . such things ought never to be done'. And he feels able to declare himself so vehemently precisely because he shows, through argument, how the experience of this ornamentation is confused – in other words, by reasoning which so affects the appearance of the architrave that the observer is repelled by it.[24] His reasoning brings about not only dislike, but a sense of the validity of dislike, and a recommendation that others share in it. Nor is this pursuit of the objective the peculiar property of Serlian architecture. It is as much present in the didacticism of Ruskin, Le Corbusier and the Bauhaus, as it is in Serlio, or in the serene circumspection of Alberti, who considered that in matters of aesthetic choice one is dealing not with mere subjective opinion but with a true rational capacity of the mind.[25] And this rational capacity is in every case strangely untiring. There is hardly a critic who will rest content with a discussion of proportion and form, who will not pursue his enquiry to that further and more mysterious area where the 'correct' way of seeing becomes part of the moral life. At this stage it is perhaps enough to give one slightly comic example – Trystan Edwards's defence of his love for the Regency stucco buildings of London. 'Now stucco,' he says, 'is a *polite* substance; a stucco-faced building is apt to express not only politeness but intellectuality . . . it makes no appeal to the false pride of the vulgar rich', and so on,[26] hoping in all this to give reasons that align the judgement of taste with attitudes whose objective validity he regarded as unquestionable.

That is an example of criticism at its most insubstantial. Clearly, we shall have to do better than that if we are to be persuaded of the objectivity of critical argument. We must look deeper into the processes of reasoning which underly criticism and see whether they can really lay claim to the validity that we seem ineluctably disposed to attribute to them. Now the task should not seem a hopeless one. Few people would doubt that it was in some sense objectively wrong of Oscar Pfister, for example, to see the shape of a vulture in the folds of the dress worn by Leonardo's St Anne.[27] In a similar way we make a distinction between experiences of architecture which are expressive of understanding and those which are not. We have seen already in the last chapter that the notion of a 'correct' experience gains easy application to the formal properties of building. It is clearly the very same notion of 'correctness' that is being extended in architectural criticism, and which is being applied in the judgement of taste, but applied outside the limitations of any narrow formal concept. This notion indicates that the experience of architecture is *already* a mode of understanding, and will be justifiable just in so far as our understanding is answerable to objective canons of assessment. And we cannot say, at this juncture, just where those canons will be found, or how far 'understanding' must penetrate – whether, for example, it really must make contact with the feelings and precepts of the moral life – if it is to be given its true content and validity. But our discussion of taste seems to suggest that understanding really will have to penetrate that far; for all attempts at justification end by ascribing to architecture significances of the most abstract and all-embracing kind. It is through the search for a 'meaning' in buildings that the judgement of taste acquires its full elaboration, and it is this 'meaning' which the observer must be brought to 'understand'. For aesthetic judgement, as I have described it, is entirely indispensable. It may have been thought that to speak of 'taste' is to reduce the study of architecture to the self-conscious predilections of the connoisseur, to remove the element of imaginative understanding and creative achievement, to put all the emphasis upon discrimination at the expense of serious involvement in the art of building. But that forced separation of 'taste' and 'imagination' is as dated as it is facile. As soon as we examine the matter, we discover that the exercise of taste, and the imaginative transformation of experience, are in fact one and the same. Critical discrimination requires that transformation, just as imagination itself requires the search for the true standard, the 'correct' experience – in short, the cultivation of the 'appropriate' in all its forms. And to search for the appropriate is to search for a significance in buildings. We must now ask ourselves what that significance might be; we know only that it must be of such a kind that understanding it, and experiencing its expression, are inextricable components in a single intellectual act.

All the same, it might still be thought that, in my desire to present a forceful picture of aesthetic reasoning, I have reversed the natural order of things. I have made it seem as though aesthetic reasoning is the fundamental feature in aesthetic choice, whereas in fact it is more naturally seen as a sophisticated extrapolation. Reasoning here depends for its power on something more basic, which is the aesthetic choice itself. The real fact of the matter lies in the *primitive* expression of aesthetic choice, and that primitive expression subsists without the benefit of reasoned reflection. Indeed, it might be said, that in its normal, everyday, manifestation, aesthetic choice has just such a primitive character, a character of resistance to any reasoning which does not already presuppose it.

I shall try to show that it does not matter that I have reversed the natural order of things, putting the sophisticated expression of aesthetic choice before its more primitive variants. As we consider the practice of aesthetic reasoning we shall in fact find ourselves gradually driven back – not in retreat, but in a state of compromise – over all the territory that I have seized in the name of Reason. And having returned to that core of primitive aesthetic choice, we shall find it sufficiently stripped of its mystery to permit us to advance again to the high point of critical reflection, to re-survey all this territory in the knowledge that the realm of the connoisseur, and the realm of the man who simply 'knows what he likes', are in fact one and the same.

PART II

6

FREUD, MARX AND MEANING

IN THE first part of this book I began by suggesting that aesthetic considerations have a central place in architectural thought and practice. I went on to describe our interest in architecture as a species of imaginative attention, and the experience of architecture as an expression of reasonings and choices derived from the deepest processes of self-conscious reflection. Like all imaginative experience, the experience of architecture aspires to the status of a symbol. It aims to reflect every significance that experience can bear, and to place its object at the focal point of all accepted values. It follows that there can be no such thing as imaginative experience which divorces itself from the practice of criticism. However reluctant a man may be to articulate his experience of buildings, to engage in reasoned discrimination and self-conscious choice, the experience itself inevitably bears the stamp of an evaluation. The cultivation of aesthetic experience, without the corresponding adoption of a critical point of view, is, therefore, nothing more than self-deception.

However, because the aesthetic experience aims, as I tried to show, at a kind of objectivity, it follows that criticism, too, will try to share in that aim. It will involve a pursuit of standards, the attempt to locate examples of the good and the bad, and to derive from those examples a system of principles, or at least a pattern of reasoned reflection, that can be applied beyond them to other works of architecture. Is such an objective criticism possible? If so, what form will it take? I shall try to answer those questions in this second part, and I shall begin from certain attempts at a critical 'method', attempts to formulate the concepts and principles of a generalized critical science. These attempts share one important feature: they try to reach critical standards through the 'deciphering' of architecture, through the discovery of principles through which the 'meaning' of a building is revealed. And there is certainly much sense in that approach. For if the objectivity of aesthetic values is to be established, where else might it reside? As we saw, it is precisely the capacity of imaginative experience to bear a 'meaning' that leads to the possibility of reasoned criticism. And the first and most important form of deciphering that offers itself is that which employs the concepts and methods of psychology, which attempts to find the meaning of architecture in its relation to the facts of mental life. It is that approach which I shall start from.

I shall begin by considering the eighteenth-century theory of the association of ideas, which provided one of the first systematic accounts of the significance of architecture. It is this theory that underlay the 'Gothick' movement, and the prevailing 'sentimentalist' attitude to architectural forms.[1] According to this view the significance of a building is nothing more nor less than the totality of the 'ideas' suggested by it – or at least, to be true to the eighteenth-century spirit, suggested by it to the normal cultivated man. The idealist objection to that view, to put it simply, is that the relation between idea and experience must be internal, whereas on the empiricist view it is external, and therefore no part of aesthetic understanding.[2] The objection is correct, and therefore it is important to see what it means.

It is best to take a simple example. Consider, then, the idea of 'support' or 'security'. Hume, with his genius for locating philosophical problems, wrote of architecture in the following words: 'The rules of architecture require that the top of a pillar should be more slender than its base, and that because such a figure conveys to us the idea of security, which is pleasant.'[3] Let us leave aside the alleged universality of this 'rule' (refuted by items of domestic furniture, and by many of the finest modern bridges), and try to see what *kind* of theory of architectural understanding is implied in it. Consider, then, the three 'post-and-beam' constructions, adapted from Sinclair Gauldie,[4] in Plate 50. One has a sense of these structures as progressively more comfortable, and for a philosopher of Hume's cast of mind, this sense is a matter of an associated idea. The sight of the first structure, much used in modern architecture as a result of the Bauhaus and Le Corbusier, causes the observer to think of a drill piercing a beam, or a pole pushed through some unresisting material. As a result one thinks of the building as a hanging structure, a kind of curtain strung upon an internal frame. (And here, of course, we have a whole *theory* of walls, and a revolutionary conception of how they might be seen.) To speak in Hume's terms, the idea of security, or support, is fully evoked only by the final structure. The abacus affects us as a kind of cushion between the mass supported and the column on which it rests: it creates a still point between the upward thrust of the column and the downward pressure of the wall. (See Plate 51 and the rival conception in Plate 52, where the virtual force of the column continues upwards until its energy is spent.) Clearly, such an account, once allowed, can be extended to the furthest reaches of architectural meaning. The meaning of a building will simply be the totality of the ideas evoked by it – whether they be 'architectural' notions of security and rest, or the complex dreams of poets, critics and historians.

PLATE 50 Three post-and-beam constructions

But the account is too simple. Hume argues thus: the sight of the object causes me to think of certain things, and this thought in its turn causes a feeling of discomfort. And it might at first seem that we can say nothing more helpful than that. Certainly it would be wrong to say that the structure is simply the *object* of my discomfort, in the way that it might be the object of hatred or admiration. I do not feel uncomfortable *about* the structure which I find discomforting, any more than I feel depressed *about* a building that I find depressing (though I *may* feel depressed about the fact that it was built).[5] Invocation of the distinction between cause and object is not in itself enough to explain what is wrong with Hume's causal theory, partly because the notion of an object – as such examples well illustrate – is not a clear one.[6] Nevertheless, the relation between the feeling of discomfort and the experience of the structure is not *merely* causal. For example, my knowledge of the reason why I am made uncomfortable has the sort of authority normally associated with knowledge of an object, rather than knowledge of a cause. (The authority of 'I am afraid of *him*'.) This is not to say that my knowledge is incorrigible, although it is true that in the normal case

PLATE 51 St Katherine's Dockyard, London, Doric column

I am here the best authority. I can be led to revise my opinion of why I feel discomfort. But it is significant that we may not be able to tell whether I have truly revised my opinion rather than come to attach my discomfort to another 'object': we lack criteria whereby to distinguish between these cases. Normally, then, if someone says to me 'I know why you feel discomfort; it is because the column is like a drill piercing the shaft above', then I can reply that the reason is nothing of the kind, and if I am speaking sincerely, there the matter ends.[7]

This last point may be greeted with some scepticism, for it seems to

PLATE 52 Annaberg, St Annen Kirche

render the criticism of architecture superfluous, or at least irrelevant. It seems to suggest that the search for an explanation of beauty (in the sense of an account of the beautiful object which will convey a genuine *understanding* of it) is always and inevitably misguided. For, although it is not true that I know all along what pleases or displeases me, it is at least true that I have privileged knowledge of this fact in the sense that when it is pointed out to me I accept or reject it with complete authority, rather in the manner of a man who has been struggling to find the words that exactly locate his thought and finds himself at last with the sense that '*That* is what I wanted to say'. How then can I learn anything new about the objects of experience? And yet surely I *do* learn something new when I am told that the impression of vital strength and elasticity which I witness in the Parthenon originates in the imperceptible curves of column, architrave and stylobate. This fact makes the building intelligible to me in a way that I might not have predicted, and I do not have to accept this explanation immediately in order to be convinced of its truth. It may need some study if I am to see the dependence which exists between the total effect of the Parthenon, and the feature of *entasis*.

To understand this example of a critical explanation we must first describe a typical rejoinder. Suppose I were to reply to the critic in the following way: 'You tell me that the effect is partly due to the *entasis* of the columns and architrave. I cannot myself notice this feature, but of course I accept your explanation.' Here we would say that the critic has given a psychological explanation of my experience of the building, but he has not really described it, or described the way the building looks. He has said nothing about *what* I appreciate in the building. His account is of the same kind as that of the doctor who says: 'The reason why you feel confused is that you took too many sleeping pills.' (Compare the reply: 'The reason why I feel confused is that you are wearing your wife's hair': which describes the *nature* of my confusion, and not just its cause.)

Suppose, however, that I reply as follows: 'You tell me that the effect is due to the *entasis*, and after looking again I see that you are right – it is indeed this feature that is responsible for the effect of elasticity.' Here I have taken the critic's judgement not as an explanation but as a description, a description of what I *see* in the building. The critic has led me to understand more completely the object of my response. (As when the doctor replies, and I agree, that 'It is not so much the fact that I am wearing my wife's hair which confuses you, as the way it clashes with the colour of my tie.') The critic has led me to a new understanding, but it is not the kind of understanding that is associated with scientific explanation.

But now, precisely because I do not accept the critic's explanation immediately, on the strength of my own immediate knowledge of my experience, it is doubtful that my reaction after accepting the critic's judgement is the same as my reaction before. For my reaction is now directed towards different features: the aspect of the building has changed for me. As criticism the description of the Parthenon does not so much elucidate my reaction as change it: and that is not surprising, for, as we saw, it is the distinguishing mark of aesthetic argument that its conclusion lies in an experience rather than a judgement. Here, the superior understanding of the building induced by criticism is one with the improved way of *seeing* it.

It seems then that when the critic describes the features of the building, and the thoughts about it, which determine my *present* reaction, he must describe something of which I have immediate knowledge. When the critical description is offered, I accept it immediately, on no basis, without additional scrutiny. This is a feature that is characteristic of knowledge of an object, rather than knowledge of a cause. It shows that the understanding which the critic seeks is an understanding of internal, rather than external, features of experience.

There are further reasons for rejecting the theory of the association of ideas. For it fails to explain or characterize precisely what is most important in aesthetic experience, the fact that (in Hume's example) the discomfort felt is not a mere thought, but an experience, and essentially connected with a particular act of attention. It has all the 'imaginative' character of the attention which it qualifies. The discomfort ceases, therefore, with the experience; it has gone the moment I have shut my eyes. If it were a mere association with my perception of the building then it would be impossible to explain this fact: why does not the discomfort last, just for a little while, when I have ceased to look, like the sadness I feel when I see again the unpeopled windows of my childhood home? In *aesthetic* attention, thought, perception and feeling are inseparable; being focused on a common object, they live and die together. The causal chain envisaged by the theory of the association of ideas must give way to a single process, conceptual, perceptual and affective at once.

At first sight it might seem that some such objection ought also to be valid against psychoanalytic theories of architecture, theories which look for the 'meaning' of architectural experience in its unconscious origin. It is well known that Freud, for example, despite his great interest in art, and despite the many suggestive remarks which he made about it, was sceptical of the possibility of a psychoanalytic aesthetics. He felt that, whatever psychoanalysis might say about the unconscious determinants of the creative process, it could have little bearing upon the aesthetic value of the result.[8] The meaning which the psychoanalyst discovers in the creative act is not the same as the meaning which the critic discovers in its outcome. If that is so, then, of course, there cannot be a psychoanalytic 'method' of criticism. But Freud's hesitation (uncharacteristic of this great fabricator of certainties) has not been shared by his disciples. Hannah Segal, in an influential article,[9] writes that:

> it is possible now, in the light of new analytical discoveries, to ask

new questions. Can we isolate in the psychology of the artist the specific factors which enable him to produce a satisfactory work of art? And if we can, will that further our understanding of the aesthetic value of the work of art, and of the aesthetic experience of the audience?

The 'new discoveries' belong to Melanie Klein,[10] who attempted to describe the workings of the human mind in terms of certain infantile 'positions' towards the breast, towards the 'bad breast', which removes and disintegrates, and the 'good breast', which provides and restores. Thus Dr Segal writes that 'all creation is really a re-creation of a once loved and once whole, but now lost and ruined object, a ruined internal world and self', meaning that the artist is engaged in that process of reconciliation and restoration, which is the process of advancement from childish resentment of loss, to mature acceptance of a world where giving and taking, receiving and losing, good and evil, commingle irredeemably. And there is truth in that. But we wish to know whether it can cast any light upon the meaning of aesthetic experience, and specifically, upon the experience of architecture.

The Kleinian school of analysis achieves its 'universality' without any lapse into Jungian mysticism, and without any impetuous adoption of a total theory of the mind. It stays, as psychoanalysis ought to stay, with the individual study of the individual case, and with the therapeutic process which arises out of that. It is interesting to us for another reason; for Kleinian theory has been applied in a systematic way to architecture by Adrian Stokes,[11] and it is through his application that we will be able to assess the bold claims which have been made for it.

For the psychoanalyst, the interesting feature of our experience of architecture is its ineffability. Our feelings towards buildings are both extremely powerful and extremely elusive; and for the psychoanalyst, a feeling eludes description most often when it seeks to *avoid* description – when it is repressed. Architecture operates, therefore, upon the unconscious, and the meaning of architecture is to be found in the order that it imposes there. For Stokes, architecture becomes an instrument in the struggle against fantasy, a struggle on the part of both builder and spectator to overcome envy, resentment and guilt, and to find oneself once more in the presence of the 'good' breast, both accepted and accepting, in a world the value of which one has measured and whose objectivity one has come to recognize. Great architecture awakens profound emotion, and 'profundity' is to be found in the 'depths' (that is, for such is the peculiar axiom of psychoanalysis, in the unconscious). If forms, details, and materials seem charged with emo-

PLATE 53 L. Laurana: Ducal Palace, Urbino, courtyard

tion, this is because of a link with deep and enduring 'fantasies' which define for us the true content of every serious feeling. Thus, if the *cortile* of the Ducal Palace at Urbino (Plate 53) has for us an atmosphere of sublime stillness, then this is not the reflection of any conscious thought of repose that may inhabit those shapes and textures, but rather the outcome of a 'deeper' thought on which all visions of repose

– even the Heaven of Christian belief – are founded, namely, the unconscious thought of the mother's breast.[12] The meaning of architecture lies, therefore, in the unconscious origins of our sentiments towards it. And to describe those sentiments psychoanalytically is at the same time to describe their value. We are, therefore, one step on the way to an account of success in architecture. The traditional vapourings about harmony, proportion appropriateness and the rest can be discarded, since architecture is in essence neither more nor less than a form of therapy for the disintegrated self.

The theory can take two forms: a general and a particular. I shall argue that the first interpretation makes the theory *too* general, and the second must make it too particular, and that in either case the failing comes from not seeing that the meaning of aesthetic experience lies *essentially* in what is conscious. The unconscious determinants of aesthetic response cannot hold the key to the nature and value of aesthetic argument, any more than the unconscious determinants of a love of mathematics can reveal the nature and value of mathematical proof.

In the general version the theory simply re-describes the entire field of architecture, implying that in responding to a building we treat it as a 'representation' (in the psychoanalytic sense) of something else. In Stokes this redescription is interesting in that it incorporates not only elements of psychoanalytic therapy, but also elements of a more traditional view – the view that we perceive the emotional significance of architecture because we spontaneously compare the forms of architecture to the forms and movements of the human body. As Stokes puts it, the house is a womb; but it is also 'our upright bodies built cell by cell'. A ledge is a foot, the knee, the brow. At the same time the smooth wall has a psychoanalytic meaning: it is the 'good breast' that we wish to appropriate as a source of our own goodness – here one remembers Ruskin's reference to 'the warm sleep of sunshine on some smooth, broad, human-like front of marble',[13] a reference that would alert even the sleepiest psychoanalyst. The wall pierced with apertures then becomes the 'bad breast' torn open by vengeful teeth, and the incorporation of those apertures into a carefully modulated façade represents the process of reconciliation between love and hatred, a process through which we all at some time must go. The building as a whole transmutes our longing for 'part objects' by presenting, and inviting us to accept, an image of the whole: the loved and hated attributes united in a seamless representation of the self. And when it is said that beauty is a 'sense of wholeness', this is no longer a mere platitude; Stokes offers to tell us what wholeness consists in.

Such a general account of architectural experience cannot describe the crucial act of attention in which the aesthetic experience resides; in an important sense, therefore, it allows the object of architectural interest to drop out of consideration as irrelevant. The object has become a means to the production of feelings which do not require it. Architecture is valuable at best only instrumentally, as one among many possible methods (psychotherapy being another) to the same basic result. Why then, if the unconscious impulses to which we have referred are the true source of our enjoyment, should we take such costly means of fulfilling them? But suppose that the theory were to propose some feature of architecture which allows to it a special place in the therapeutic process – some feature which gives to the public representation of the breast in architecture a unique consolatory power. It would still not provide us with an account of the particular act of attention that we have in previous chapters sought to describe. For in effect the experience of architecture has been reduced to something archaic, detached entirely from the particular significance of the particular building. Why then should we ever wish to visit a building that we had not seen before? Why should we not remain content with what we already had, queuing for our mother's milk at the gate of the Ducal Palace? The meaning that we seek in architecture is essentially particular, to be discovered case by case: and yet we have been provided with no method for that discovery. Moreover, the meaning that we seek lies in experience: in an important sense it lies on the surface, as the central constituent in aesthetic attention.

Another way of bringing out the same point is to note that 'explanations' of the kind envisaged by Stokes would apply equally to our enjoyment of the impressions of smell, taste and so on, impressions to which, as I have already argued, notions of aesthetic judgement and discrimination do not apply. But it is not at all difficult in these cases to discover a psychoanalytic 'meaning'; there would never be any problem in explaining why some smells are alluring, some repulsive. But in the attempt to explain the 'alluring' quality of architectural forms, Stokes finds himself involved in an obscure doctrine of the 'invitation' in art which leaves all criticism and all aesthetic understanding exactly where it was.

But the theory can be re-stated more persuasively, and more concretely. While psychoanalysis is associated with an unclear and largely metaphorical account of the causality of human consciousness and behaviour, it has an important realization in therapeutic practice. As Wittgenstein pointed out,[14] it is not at all obvious that the aim of therapy is to discover a causal explanation of the subject's state. Psychoanalysis aims at a different kind of understanding, an understanding that is not reducible to explanation, and which has more in common with the critical procedure described earlier in this chapter. For it seems that the 'correct' account of a man's behaviour is one that, in the course of analysis, he can be brought to accept; or, if he does not accept it, this must be, not because he is confused or mistaken, but because he is 'resisting' what he is being told. In other words, the true unconscious determinants of a feeling are not simply its unconscious causes, but rather those causes which can be 'salvaged' for consciousness. Until they can be brought into the sphere of self-ascription (into the realm of conscious experience) the hypothesis of their unconscious reality remains entirely void. The psychoanalyst gets his patient to transform the 'he' of observation into the 'I' of self-knowledge. For until I can lay claim to an experience, and assert of it, not merely that it belongs to an entity which bears my name, but that it is *I* who feel it, then that experience lies outside the province of my self.[15]

But if this account (or something like this account) is correct, the claim of psychoanalysis is to give not an external but an internal description of the architectural experience. This is what the experience really *is*, as is established by the criterion which we all use and accept – by the subject's own immediate knowledge that it is so. It does not matter how that knowledge is *induced*, just so long as it has the right kind of immediacy. The *cortile* of the Ducal Palace is therefore *seen* as the harmonious reconciling of aggression (represented in apertures and mouldings) with the achieved adult persona (the upstanding proportions, the part answering part) and with the perennial yearning for the object of infantile love – the door kept in shadow which will quietly open. The delicate proportions of the columniation turn resistance and loss into a kind of courtesy; they offer us peace not as a mere yielding to demand, but as a mature harmony of once opposing impulses.

I invent the example: but perhaps it could be put in some such way. So construed, however, the criticism of the building is essentially *addressed* to the reader: it is an invitation to see the building as the psychoanalyst sees it. It is now open to the reader to respond that he does not and cannot so see it. The analyst has two replies. Either he will say that this *must* be what the reader sees, because this is the true *explanation* of what he sees – which is simply to reiterate the theory in its generalized form. But that form, as we saw, cannot describe the content of the individual experience, nor the meaning of the individual building. Alternatively, the analyst may try to persuade the reader: now the subject of the analysis is not the building but the individual who responds to it. The psychoanalyst must show that the man who disagrees is really resisting him. The 'interpretation' of the building is taken for granted. If the subject likes it then the real reason for his liking *must* be the one which the analyst gives; the only question is why the man fails to confess to it.

But now the theory is open to refutation. If the object of the analysis is the reader, then what is being reported is a fact – or hypothesis – about *him*, namely, that he sees the building as the analyst says. Suppose, however, that the reader 'resists'. The analyst can now embark on the process of therapy which will bring him to his senses (by showing that, in fact, he is mistaken about his experience and resisting its true description) – in which case the critic's reasoning will not be concerned with the building at all, but with the observer. Alternatively, he can begin to give to the observer particular *reasons* for seeing the building as he recommends. In the first process the method is truly psychoanalytical: but through that very fact it ceases to have critical relevance. The building is being given no meaning that distinguishes it from any other object in the libidinal process; the meaning which attaches to it will be simply a personal fact about the observer. In the second process the method is critical; but the invocation of psychoanalysis is redundant as an account of it. The proposed interpretation uses psychoanalytic concepts; but it is not by psychoanalysis that it is *justified.* Nothing has been said about the *kind* of reasoning that would show – as a fact about Laurana's courtyard – that it ought to be seen in Kleinian terms. Surely, then, we cannot look to psychoanalysis for a theory of the meaning of architectural forms, when such a theory will already be presupposed in any psychoanalytical interpretation.

In fact, the notion of an unconscious experience is an obscure one, and it is often hard to see how far its supporters will be prepared to go in order to affirm its significance. Nevertheless, our description of the aesthetic experience seems to place it firmly among the contents of the conscious mind, expressive, as it is, of imaginative attention. Aesthetic experience is not just significant, but consciously value for its significance, which it gains partly from the reasoning and reflection which surrounds it. This is not to say that there can be no such thing as psychoanalytic criticism of architecture. It may be possible to see some particular building in terms of a psychoanalytic idea, just as one might see it in terms of historical or religious conceptions. And seeing it in that way might lead to a greater enjoyment. Here, despite the psychoanalytic trappings, the enjoyment, like the experience, will be essentially conscious and have its meaning *in* consciousness. For example, I might be persuaded (as Stokes suggests) that there are certain 'fantasies' associated with limestone – fantasies connected with its fossil character, fantasies of life in watery depths.[16] And I may come to think of certain works of quattrocento architecture (such as the

Tempio Malatestiana (S. Francesco) at Rimini) as in some way acquiring their significance in relation to those fantasies. I may think that one should see the finely cut stonework of the Tempio, and of Agostino da Duccio's reliefs, as 'revealing' the 'life' already implicit in the stone, which has been, as it were, trapped there and is now released. In seeing the building in that way I may see, too, a parallel with my own locked or buried feelings; the temple becomes in some sense a *release* of feeling. (And such a suggestion is far from incoherent.) But the process of reasoning which leads to this experience is not psychoanalytic; indeed, it is no different from the process that all forms of criticism observe. An idea is expressed, and then some kind of correspondence is sought between idea and appearance. The ultimate aim is a conscious experience in which the idea is revealed and elaborated. The psychoanalytic interpretation adds no 'method' to the discovery of meaning, and no authority to its result. If we accept the conclusion it is not because a more *fundamental* description of architectural experience is being offered than could be given in terms of *Kunstgeschichte*, say, or old fashioned iconography. The descriptions compete on the same level, and if one of them is accepted it is only because it makes sense (in a way that we have yet clearly to analyse) of the particular building to which it is applied. It cannot acquire any *a priori* precedence, and the fact of being framed in psychoanalytic terms is irrelevant to its acceptability. The aim of interpretation remains the same – a conscious experience of 'meaning' – and the critic is psychoanalysing neither the building, nor its creator, nor even the man who observes it.

Similar doubts must be felt about the possibility of a Marxist 'method' in architectural criticism. Once again we are presented with a theory which claims to show a 'meaning' in every cultural object, and which therefore ought to be as applicable to architecture as to every form of art. And once again, the very generality of these pretensions removes all critical sting: there can no more be a Marxist method in criticism than there can be a Marxist method in mathematics. But to establish the point we shall have to discuss architectural experience in the most basic terms; we must resist the redescriptions which the Marxist will continually seek to offer. For there attaches to both Marxian and Freudian theories a similar charm, the charm of demystification. Both theories claim to reveal the true nature of things, prior to any discussion of their value, thus opening the way to a sense that our existing judgements of value might be entirely ill-founded, or entirely 'ideological' in the Marxist's sense.[17] And both Freudian and Marxist theory locate the true source of human phenomena outside the conscious self, outside the conceptions, ideals and arguments with which we flatter our autonomy; they provide effective weapons against any view which, seemingly impregnable to frontal attack, must necessarily be subverted from beneath. It seems clear, then, that once the Freudian or Marxist is permitted to phrase the question in his own theoretical language, he will obtain the answer that he desires. In criticizing Marxism one will be criticizing a way of describing cultural phenomena, and not just a theory which attempts to explain their significance. Since there has been so little Marxist criticism of architecture and since none of it has been systematic, it might be thought that I shall be tilting at windmills. But there exists a large body of Marxist literary, pictorial, and even musical criticism,[18] and the intellectual imperialism which this criticism exemplifies makes it important to forestall advances. Besides, there are aspects of the Marxist theory of human nature that I shall later wish to apply to architecture; their significance will be clear only when they have been detached from their dogmatic origins.

Now Marxism arises from mingling a theory of human nature derived from Hegel, with a species of economic determinism that has its roots in the empiricist economics of Adam Smith and Ricardo. To a great extent the two facets are separable, and only when we have separated them will we see the value that lies in each. The theory of human nature, to which I shall later return, aims to account for the facts explained by Kleinian analysis, facts concerning the intimate relation between our conception of architecture and our conception of ourselves. The point at issue here, however, is whether Marxist determinism will lead us to a true critical 'method', a procedure for describing the 'meaning' which aesthetic experience provides. The deterministic theory sees all 'cultural' phenomena – by which is meant all art, social activity, language, indeed all that might normally pass under the label of 'consciousness' – as a part of the social 'superstructure', which rises or declines in obedience to the causality of an economic 'base'.[19] The base lies in the class struggle – the struggle for power, influence and wealth – and in the various relations to the means of production which dictate that struggle. The ultimate outcome of the struggle is determined by historical forces which may be wholly independent of the outcrop of 'consciousness'; the superstructure 'represents' the base without seriously or permanently affecting it. The consciousness of a class may, however, have a certain influence upon its economic position, since it can be adapted to represent historical reality in terms which will best satisfy a self-image and fortify a dominant role. Consciousness – in particular bourgeois consciousness – is engaged continually in the manufacture of an 'ideology' with which to 'mystify' the world, by denying the true causality of the world's evolution. The ruling class is the only class which can impose its ideology, and therefore the only class whose ideology is *established.* Other classes, in accepting the ideology of the ruling class, accept as natural what is in fact artificial. Their perception of the world is 'mystified' – not seeing the true causality of things, they are momentarily disposed to accept as inevitable what in fact can be overthrown. Ideology represents the world as 'unhistorical' – by which the Marxist means 'not subject to human agency and change'. The process of 'demystification' is a process of restoring to objects, and in particular to cultural objects, the historical nature of which they have been robbed.

That brief summary cannot possibly do justice to the many recent refinements of the Marxist position. But it will serve to guide the discussion towards the most important of the Marxist concepts, the concepts of ideology and superstructure. Architecture, like any part of the 'superstructure', can become an ideological instrument. Consider, for example, the neo-Gothic factory of the late nineteenth and early twentieth century (such as the Horlicks factory at Slough). Such a building is meant to be seen in a way that is not dictated by – indeed, which is wholly independent of – its social and economic reality. It is designed as a public building, expressive of an agreed social order, with religious and narrative associations which assert the changeless identity of that order, and suggest a validity of form and purpose beyond the particular uses to which it will be put. The Marxist critic will see his principle task here as one of demystification – for clearly, the description that I have given is ideological; it is a description which detaches the building from its economic reality, and situates it in a world of values and predilections which console and consolidate the feelings of a ruling class – values of 'historical continuity', of the 'social order' implicit in a 'public' building, of religious and romantic sentiments designed to subdue the perception of less tolerable things. Critical understanding is reached by throwing the building back into its socio-economic context, and so unmasking the ideological nature of its message. No meaning can be understood except in that way, in terms of the social conditions which gave rise to it. In the present case we will then see that the factory is not public but private, an essential instrument in the entrenchment of private property. Its true ethos is individualistic, at variance with, or at best indifferent to, the 'agreed social order' implicit in its Gothic forms. Its economic reality is that of the Industrial Revolution, and therefore exhibits a radical break with the historical continuity which it pretends to represent, while the romantic and religious associations bespeak only a defunct form of society, a form which the factory itself has most served to destroy. From such a description, we arrive at the true meaning of the building, its meaning as a part of the process of production. And at the same time we can understand exactly what in the building is ideology and what is social truth.

It is wrong to think that the Marxist approach can simply be dismissed, by saying that these speculations are all irrelevant to the visual beauty of a building. For we have seen that there is no such thing as an apprehension of visual beauty which is sealed off from intellectual understanding. The Marxist is proposing a critical method, a way of determining the intellectual content of a building which will also be a way of determining how to see it. He might say, quite reasonably, that if you insist on divorcing something called 'beauty' (and the 'aesthetic experience' which is its psychological correlate) from the kinds of consideration to which he refers, then you will find yourself unable to say why this 'beauty' is important, or why men should cultivate a taste for it. He will be happy to dispense with what you call 'beauty' – and, as the early constructivists declared, good riddance. To dismiss the approach in the interests of a hedonistic aestheticism is of little interest: it saves us from a Marxist aesthetics only by saving the words; it has nothing valuable to say about their meaning.

The essential features of a Marxist aesthetics are these: that aesthetic experience belongs to superstructure, and is therefore intrinsically open to ideological distortion. The true understanding of aesthetic as of any socially constrained experience involves a 'throwing back' of its object into the socio-economic conditions that determined it. In criticism we are led to an understanding which is at once aesthetic and political; there is no problem, for the Marxist, in showing how it is that bad architecture can make us so angry. But having conceded that advantage, we must find that the remaining aspects of the theory are far from satisfactory. This is not the place to criticize the socio-economic determinism upon which it is founded, except to point out how incapable it is of accounting for what Ezra Pound has called 'a live tradition'.[20] It is clear that the principle cause of a building's erection and its style might lie, not in social or economic factors, but in men's apprehension of other cultural products. The 'superstructure' has an intrinsic power to generate and perpetuate itself, independently of the so-called 'base'. Anyone who doubts the point should consider the history of German music, and the enduring soul of German music as Schoenberg and Thomas Mann, in their different ways, attempted to describe it.[21] And there is no better evidence of the autonomous life of the 'superstructure' than architecture itself, in which styles, buildings, towns and cities have risen and perpetuated themselves independently of their fluctuating economic circumstances. Consider, for example, the history of the Doric column, from the Parthenon to St Katherine's dockyard. The fact is that all those aspects of architecture which we assign instinctively to the 'aesthetic' dimension of experience, everything short of the mere quantity of building undertaken, partake of the rich contingency implicit in every social act, and suggest a causality internal to the superstructure, a causality in which tradition and precedent are by far the most important factors. What 'meaning', then, can be revealed by 'throwing back' a building into its economic circumstances? The Marxist who argues that the Gothic factory is a kind of economic lie, ought to say the same of Roman Hellenism, of Renaissance classicism, of the Gothic movement, indeed of every self-conscious approach to architecture, including the true Gothic style itself.

In fact, the economic determinism, even if true, seems to provide us with an access to aesthetic 'meaning' only because of the unhealthy diet of examples upon which Marxism is fed. Marxism is at its best when dealing with the century which made it possible – its vision is confined to that small, as it were parochial, procession, from aristocratic to bourgeois rule, from agrarian to industrial economy, which has dominated the world for a mere two hundred years, and given rise to the quaint myth of a 'classless' society in which the necessary consequences of industrial production will somehow be averted. But can we envisage a full-blooded Marxist criticism of the Gothic cathedral, or of the Renaissance palace? How would the Marxist distinguish the Gothic cathedral from the Romanesque – how would he explain, for example, the arguments about the art of building which occurred in the wake of the first Cistercian style, and the polemics of St Bernard of Clairvaux?[22] Viollet-le-Duc's attempt to give a quasi-Marxist theory of this transition shows, through its historical distortion, and critical naivety, how hopeless is the task.[23] These spiritual conflicts lie in the superstructure and their 'depth' is not to be found by digging beneath it. The Marxist, like the Freudian, is systematically misled by a metaphor of 'depth'. Hence it is that, dealing with these examples, it seems impossible to envisage what a Marxist would say about them.

But to fight the Marxist on this slippery battlefield is unnecessary. There is no way that the theory can issue in aesthetic judgements, and that is alone sufficient to discredit it. For there is a significant obscurity involved in the notion of 'throwing back' when used as a critical instrument. Suppose we were to describe the unique economic conditions of fifteenth-century Florence: how will that affect our critical perception of the Pazzi Chapel? We cannot tell; for we have been given no directions as to how our experience of *this* particular building is to be brought into relation with our knowledge of *those* particular economic circumstances. Once again, there is no critical method, but only a critical hypothesis, which has to be fought for and established case by case. And yet who can doubt that the relation of the Pazzi Chapel to its socio-economic circumstances – a relation which it shares even with the most mediocre of contemporary buildings – is the least significant fact about it, and that all that is seen in it by way of harmony, proportion, dignified and solemn repose, remains unaffected by the knowledge of its economic base?

Now, so far, we have located the realm of aesthetic experience among 'immediate impressions', impressions which are capable of bearing in themselves the meaning which we attribute to their objects. The Marxist, too, must admit that dimension of 'immediate' meaning; for it is this which provides the 'superstructure' with architectural significance, and which qualifies architecture for its peculiar social role. So what account can the Marxist offer of 'immediate meaning'? Surely, none that is new to us. The Marxist method is not a method for deciphering what we see, but rather for relating the results of that decipherment to something else. The validity of the procedure depends upon the truth of Marxist theory as a whole. But even if valid, it has nothing special to add to our understanding of architecture, nothing which it does not claim to add to our understanding of everything. In a crucial sense Marxist theory must leave everything as it is: leave as it is, for example, our description of the nature of aesthetic experience, and our methods for elucidating the 'immediate' meaning which that experience contains. So that even if we accept the conception of an 'ideological' significance, this will provide no critical method, and no standard of aesthetic judgement. Not being aware of the economic base from which most buildings arise we could never know, on the Marxist theory, their aesthetic quality: yet that is something we do know and can know, just so long as we have eyes.

The true Leninist may have a reply to all this, and it is in considering his reply that we find the important grain of truth that is embodied in both the Freudian and the Marxist approach to architectural practice. The Leninist's reply is that which I have already attributed to my hypothetical constructivist.[24] He will simply dismiss these 'aesthetic' intimations and seek for the true meaning of a building elsewhere than in the act of imaginative attention which we direct towards it – in its social and economic reality. But what is that reality? For example, what is the social and economic reality of a house or a factory? Surely, either we must *include* aesthetic values in the description of that reality, or else we must eliminate them; and if we eliminate them, what remains but function? The building's reality is that of a means to a specific end. But we have seen that there is an inadequate notion of rationality involved in the attempt so to consider buildings, as objects whose primary meaning is determined by external aims, and not by the 'residue' of aesthetic value. It is a small step for the Marxist (though one that it is, for liturgical reasons, sometimes difficult to take) to see in that attitude – the attitude which reduces all meaning to means – a symptom of, together with a covert desire to perpetuate, the condition of alienated man.[25] For this condition arises precisely when a man cannot see his surroundings in terms of any aim which he can identify as his and towards which he can direct his labour. It is the condition of seeing himself and his activity as a means to an end, while being deprived of any adequate understanding of the end itself. Since the constructivist programme involves precisely the loss of that sense of the ends of conduct, and a reduction of all activity to a proliferation of means, it must therefore lend itself to this alienated condition, cutting off those who live and work in the resulting buildings from the satisfactions of their 'species life'. And without those satisfactions, according to Marx, no rational being can retain a coherent sense of his own identity. If that is the way in which the meaning of a building can be replaced by something 'deeper', then it is a way that ought not to be open to the Marxist.

If we now consider this aspect of Marxism, the aspect which is borrowed from Hegel's philosophy of mind, we see that there is something important in common to the descriptions of architectural experience offered by the Marxist and the Kleinian analyst. Neither theory can provide a critical method or doctrine, but it is possible that each may be able to say something about the *primitive* aspect of aesthetic choice. As we have acknowledged, there is in aesthetic experience a core of primitive choice, which does not arise from critical reflection but exists as a necessary precondition to criticism. It is natural to seek for a 'deep' description of that core of choice, a description which both explains it and at the same time displays its value. Now it is one of the peculiarities of both psychoanalysis and Marxian determinism that they confound what is deep with what is unconscious. And as we have seen, to step into the realm of the unconscious is to miss the aesthetic experience. But the Hegelian theory does not have to commit that error – characteristically, indeed, it searches for a paradigm of 'depth' in man's own self-understanding, in his way of envisaging self, world and action. And what the Kleinian might present as a truth about the unconscious determinants of experience the Hegelian might equally present as a truth about its surface. Thus we find that Wölfflin, the greatest of Hegelian critics, relied on a theory of what is 'primitive' which closely resembles that of Stokes.[26] What is primitive is the innate connection between our way of perceiving architecture and our way of perceiving the human body. This truth (which has been found, lost, and found again throughout the history of architecture) is one to which we shall have to pay serious attention. The Kleinian – who wishes to explain aesthetic taste through its relation to the libidinal process (as Plato wished to derive beauty as an offshoot of *erōs*) – naturally conceives buildings as representations of the human body. But as Collingwood argued persuasively against Plato,[27] the assimilation of beauty to *erōs* is mistaken. The mistake is to situate the aesthetic response in the realm of appetite, rather than contemplation, and to remove from the object its peculiar intellectual and moral power. The Hegelian and Marxist concept of self-identity may be used to present similar conclusions while avoiding the mistaken premise. For the Hegelian there is a sense in which architecture is to be understood as a physical representation of the self. And that process of representation may involve the symbolization of the human body. When we come to discuss the Hegelian theory, however, it should be remembered that we will have moved out of the realm of explicit critical analysis. In trying to capture what is primitive in aesthetic experience we are also aiming to describe its value. And it may not be possible to proceed from an account of the value of aesthetic experience to a critical method that can be applied case by case. It is for this reason that Wölfflin's criticism bore so little relation to its Hegelian basis. His enquiries into the *Lebensgefühlen* of the several architectural epoques in no way required the premise that a *Lebensgefühl* is a kind of perception of the human body.

But to all that we shall return. For the moment we must conclude that neither Freudian analysis nor Marxist determinism have provided us with a critical 'method'. But they have reinforced our sense of the 'meaning' of architectural forms as somehow 'immediate', involved in the perception of a building, and intrinsic to the object of that perception. But this suggests another answer to our problem. For do not words have meaning precisely in that way, intrinsically, a meaning which is grasped in hearing and understanding them, and which is not reducible to any unconscious origin or to any effect towards which their utterance is a means? It is to the theory of architecture as language that we now must turn.

7
THE LANGUAGE OF ARCHITECTURE

IF IT were true that architecture were a language (or, perhaps, a series of languages), then we should know how to understand every building, and the human significance of architecture would no longer be in question.[1] Moreover, this significance would be seen as an intrinsic property of buildings, and not as some external or fortuitous relation. The Freudian and Marxist approaches to 'meaning' fail partly because they provide no meaning to the architectural experience that is not external to it – that does not consist in some value, feeling or state of consciousness related to the building, not intrinsically, but as cause or effect. Such approaches must remain at one remove from aesthetic understanding. Nor would this surprise us, if it were true that architecture had meaning as language has meaning. For consider the corresponding Freudian and Marxian theories of 'utterance'. Such theories might aim to trace the connection between words and their unconscious, economic or ideological determinants: but that could never tell us what the words literally mean. A Freudian theory must *presuppose* a given meaning: it is because of the literal meaning of the work 'milk' that the word acquires its unconscious significance – not *vice versa*. Hence it is logically impossible to derive the literal meaning from the Freudian meaning. And similarly for Marx: 'thrift' acquires its ideological significance (its significance as a mask for processes of accumulation and exploitation) because of its prior literal meaning, the meaning which causes it to refer to the phenomenon from which the ideological meaning derives. A Marxist account of literal meaning is therefore impossible: nothing about *understanding* language would be revealed by reducing language to its material base.

The analogy also shows how irrelevant to the understanding of architecture is *any* mode of scientific or causal explanation. For consider a theory of psycho-linguistics so exhaustive as to issue in laws which determine the utterance of every sentence. It tells us, for example, just when a man will say 'The grass is green', and just when he will say 'something is green'. In one sense, such a theory gives a complete account of the relation between those sentences, since it gives the causal laws which determine their utterance. But in another sense it is far from complete. For there is a connection between these sentences which is not causal, but which is of the first importance; a connection of meaning. It is that connection which is grasped in understanding the sentences, and a man may have a complete understanding of them while being ignorant of the causal laws which govern their behaviour. He may also have a full knowledge of those laws and yet have no linguistic understanding.

Another way of putting this point involves distinguishing what has been called 'natural' from 'non-natural' meaning.[2] We must distinguish the sense of meaning in 'Clouds mean rain' from that in 'John means that it will rain', or ' "Il va pleuvoir" means that it will rain'. The first of these provides a case of 'natural' meaning – a case of one phenomenon being *a reason to expect* another. One is referring to a natural, causal, external relation between events. It is only by the crudest of metaphors that we could, on this basis, speak of a *language* of clouds; indeed, the metaphor would be so vague as to embrace everything (since there is no phenomenon that does not give some reason to expect another). It is surprising, none the less, that this fact has so often escaped attention. Some have been prepared to say, for example, that there is a *language* of facial expression, simply because expressions are signs of mental states – but this notion of a sign has nothing to do with language. The relation of words to their meaning is not natural but *intended*, and this intention is realized through a necessary body of conventions and rules.[3] These two facts between them serve to discredit all those traditional theories of meaning which speak of the symbol as an 'anticipation' of the object, and which attempt to describe linguistic understanding as a sophisticated variant of the relation of stimulus and response.[4] For example, we may dismiss the influential account of language provided by C. W. Morris and the many theories of architecture which have been derived from it.[5] Such theories define the notion of a 'sign' as a species of 'preparation', standing in a relation to its 'meaning' in a way that presupposes neither intention, nor convention, nor rule. One architectural theorist, for example, fails to discern the essential difference between the way in which tracks in a wood have meaning for a hunter, and the way in which a building has meaning for the man who understands it.[6] But of course, to treat buildings in terms of their 'natural meaning' is a trivial exercise: it is impossible to deny, and unimportant to affirm, that buildings are natural signs – for example, natural signs of their functions – and that the sight of a school may lead one to anticipate some process of education within it.

How do we assess the linguistic analogy? Architecture may resemble language either accidentally or essentially. It might share some or all of those features which go to make language what it is, or it might share only those features which are linguistically dispensable; or again, it might share some of the essential features of language, but only by chance, as it were, and not through the very fact of being architecture. Only in the first case can we expect to derive from the linguistic analogy a theory of understanding architecture. But do we know enough about the nature and function of language to be able to decide such an issue? One problem is that the advocates of 'linguistic', 'semantic', 'semiotic', 'semioligical' and 'structuralist' views of art and architecture all seem to begin from completely different assumptions about the nature of language, and seem equally incapable of settling upon any feature of language which might decide the question. Yet they all claim to have sufficient understanding of language to be able to present a concept of symbolism under which both architecture and language fall. Before considering one or two of these theories, therefore, it will be necessary to say something about the kinds of fact in which the analogy might be based. Simply to speak of architecture as a form of 'symbolism' or 'signification' is clearly not enough.

In fact I have already mentioned two distinguishing features of language which might prove important here, the features of grammar and intention. Buildings, like linguistic utterances, are in all their particulars intentional, and must be seen and understood as such. Moreover, serious architecture has a tendency to govern itself by rules, rules for the combination and distribution of architectural parts. If it is difficult to state the precise significance of these rules, that should not deter us. For precisely the same difficulty arises in understanding the role of conventions and rules in language. In both cases the rules are neither unbreakable nor dispensible, and in both cases they help to determine the meaningfulness of the result. Architecture seems, in fact, to display a kind of 'syntax': the parts of a building seem to be fitted together in such a way that the meaningfulness of the whole will reflect and depend upon the manner of combination of its parts.

Alberti described beauty as consisting in such an organization of parts that nothing can be changed without detriment to the whole,[7] a definition to which we shall have occasion to return. And the classical theory of the Orders, which sought precisely to capture that ideal of beauty, led almost inevitably to a 'grammatical' approach to architecture. The Orders were conceived by Renaissance masters as bodies of mutually dependent constraints; obeying one of these constraints, an architect is forced by its inner logic to obey them all. Thus the use of the Doric Order imposes a strict relation between vertical and horizontal dimensions, it necessitates a certain kind of entablature, and certain window openings. It removes all trace of arbitrariness from the ornamentation, for example, by giving the architect a compelling reason for inserting triglyphs in the freize, for simplifying the mouldings of the column-base, for cultivating in the wall face a certain rugged heaviness; and so on. In this way the Orders serve to control the design of an entire façade, to apply grammatical constraints which enable one corner of a building to limit its most distant counterpart; a false move at any point can mar the integrity of the structure, and destroy the thread of meaningfulness that runs through the details of the whole.[8] The influence of the Orders extends further, even into those parts of a building where they are not so much exhibited as implied: a window-frame may be recognizably Doric, and even a plain wall may have an Ionic articulation, on account of the rhythm of its apertures, the division of its parts, and the ornamentation of the occasional crest or moulding. And while this ideal of grammatical order is most clearly exemplified in classical theory, there are other examples of it; even the most unclassical styles (such as the style introduced by Le Corbusier in his Unité d'Habitation, or that used by Voysey at Bedford Park) will be possessed of a recognizable grammar. The wildest of architects may depend for the significance of his buildings, if not upon obeying, at least upon flouting, compositional rules.

Now of course the Orders leave much undetermined; they can be used more or less strictly; they can be altered and varied with no disastrous results, as in the architecture of the mannerists, of Giulio Romano, Peruzzi and Michelangelo. But until we understand the role of syntax in language, these reservations will not defeat the linguistic analogy. And in so far as we have that understanding, we think of syntax as a series of negative constraints, rules which limit how we may continue what we have once begun to say. And that is precisely the role which we intuitively ascribe to rules in architecture.

It is useful here to consider a pattern of thought, usually known as 'semiology', which purports to decipher the meaning in all social products.[9] Semiology – the general science of signs foretold by

Saussure – propounds a notion of meaning that assimilates language, gesture and art, and which offers to unravel every human phenomenon by bringing it into the sphere of an all-inclusive theory of significance. The school has many aims and many methods; but it is clearly this belief in the generalizability of 'meaning' that we must examine. Semiology starts, then, from the analogy between language and other activities, and uses, in its pursuit of meaning, all the various 'methods' that are available to decipher them: Freudian analysis, Marxism, structuralist anthropology, and the rest.[10] But its intellectual basis is both simpler and more general than its 'methods', and depends upon two straightforward suppositions. First, all human behaviour can be seen as expressive, revealing thoughts, feelings, intentions and so on. Often (as in dreams) behaviour may reveal feelings that are not directly accessible to the subject: and this is a point which is likely to please the semiologist, since it enables him to believe that the meaning discovered by his 'science' may be something that has yet to be recognized, even by those who use and observe the 'signs'. Second, the modes of human expression may be thought of as having a certain 'structure', a 'structure' which is also exhibited in language.[11] It is this 'structuralist' contention which has the most immediate bearing upon our present topic, and which we must therefore begin by considering.

According to Barthes, for example (who in this point follows Saussure),[12] a sentence is a 'system' composed of 'syntagms'. A syntagm is a class of terms which may replace each other without destroying the system – without rendering the sentence 'unacceptable' to speakers of the language. For example, in the sentence 'John loves Mary', 'loves' may be replaced by 'hates' or 'eats', but not by 'if', 'thinks that' or 'swims'. A man who understands language is able to recognize which words can, and which cannot, replace each other in a sentence. He is possessed of certain 'syntactical categories'. Not surprisingly, a similar structure may be noticed in other human activities – for example, in architecture, where (depending on the style) an arch may be followed by another of the same kind, or by a concluding pier, but not by an arch of conflicting size and style, nor by a sequence of broken columns. (Hence the syntactical correctness of the Rue de Rivoli, and the meaningless jumble of the development at the Elephant and Castle.) Or consider another case, explored by Barthes in his *Elements of Semiology*, the case of the menu. A man might order the following: *oeufs bénédictine*, followed by steak and chips, followed by rum baba. That is an 'acceptable' system; in our society the same meal in reverse would be unacceptable. There are comparable cases in architecture. Consider, for example, the 'unacceptability' of a column in which base and capital are exchanged, or a frieze placed where a podium should be. It is true that architecture is a specialized and complex activity, that the violation of rules may be more or less tolerated, and the rules themselves more or less mixed. We might accept the 'mixing' of Orders, or even the mixing of classical and Gothic, as in St Eustache (Plate 3, p. 12). But when critics speak of violated principles, or uncontrolled design, they often use an idea of 'unacceptability' which is not so far from that which we have applied to the menu. It is in that sense, perhaps, that one might wish to argue for the unacceptability of classical window-frames within Gothic arches (as this composition occurs, say, in the architecture of Webb). Let us assume, then, that we can generalize from the case of the menu: writers on the semiology of architecture, from the pedantic Eco to the over-heated contributors to *Konzept* and *Tel Quel*, have certainly given no clear or consistent reason for distinguishing between the cases.[13]

Just as each dish belongs to a 'syntagmatic unity' – it can be replaced by some dishes but not by others – so too do architectural parts. Steak and chips may be replaced by ham salad, but not by a glass of Tokay – for that would be 'unacceptable'; just as it is acceptable (grammatically) to replace an Ionic capital with one of its variants (such as that from Bassae, illustrated in Plate 59, p. 177, or even that used by Michelangelo at the Palazzo dei Conservatori), but not by a capital in the Doric or the Gothic idiom. Which is not to say that there are no architectural *eccentricities*, just as there are eccentricities in food and wine, and flamboyant or slovenly modes of speech. The semiologist will now jump to his conclusion: the menu is a kind of language; architecture too is a kind of language; all such activities have 'meaning' in the way that sentences have meaning, and the meaning can be simply 'deciphered' by those who know the code.

Such a conclusion is, of course, unwarranted. For the 'structures' observed in the menu, or in the classical idiom, are without semantic import. Any activity that is sequential, and which can be judged 'correct' or 'incorrect' will exhibit this structure. (That is simply a necessary truth.) Structure is equivalent to rule. But what follows from that? Consider Barthes's actual interpretation of the menu. Steak and chips is supposed to mean 'Frenchness'.[14] (As the Doric column might 'mean', say, 'manly strength'.) Suppose then that the 'meaning' of *oeufs bénédictine* is 'Roman Catholicism', and that of rum baba 'sensuality' – what now is the meaning of the entire system? Does it mean that French Catholicism is compatible with sensuality? Or that being French is more important than being Catholic? Or being sensual more important than either? There is no way of telling, since while our system may have structure, it has no *grammar*. A grammar is necessary to show how the meanings of the parts determine the meaning of the whole. 'Syntagmatic structure' – being a trivial consequence of rule-guided sequence – shows nothing of the kind.

In fact there are profound differences between linguistic and non-linguistic meaning, differences which semiology has so far proved unable to describe. And one may reasonably suspect that this inability stems precisely from the attempt to give a *general* science of signs. Consider the play on the word 'acceptable'. The sense in which a sentence is acceptable is not the sense in which a menu or an architectural composition might be acceptable, despite the fact that there are in all these cases clear conventions which may be invoked to justify the choice of parts. 'John loves Mary' is an acceptable sentence because it can be used to say something, and it has that use because it can be true or false. In this it may be contrasted with such 'unacceptable' sentences as 'John if Mary'. Acceptability in language is connected to the possibility of truth, and there can be no explanation of linguistic meaning which does not show its relation to truth.[15] Yet it is precisely that relation which semiology ignores, and must ignore if it is to generalize the concept of 'meaning' from language to art and architecture. A man might express his attitudes in all sorts of ways; but when he uses language, then the concepts of truth and falsehood apply to his behaviour. What he says may now correspond, not just to his inner states, but to *reality*. It is this which constitutes the 'aboutness' of language, and its nature as a form of communication, through which people may inform each other about their common world.

It is also through the concept of truth that philosophers have been able to make sense of the idea of a 'grammatical' structure. What distinguishes language is not *just* the relation to truth, but the fact that its syntax *derives* from that relation. It is because the individual words in a sentence refer as they do that the sentence is true or false, and the rules of grammar enable us to derive, from the reference of the words, the conditions for the truth of the sentence. This observation, first made by Frege,[16] has proved, despite its simplicity, to be of the first importance in understanding language. It enables us to see how the conditions for the truth of a sentence can be understood by anyone who knows the meanings of its parts. And if a man knows the conditions for the truth of a sentence he knows what it says, and therefore what it means. This theory of truth provides the cornerstone of a genuine grammar,[17] since it tells us how to derive the meaning of a sentence from the meaning of its parts. It therefore justifies that intuitive division into parts, and shows how the parts fit together – syntax now follows from semantics. And that is why we cannot regard the menu as a linguistic phenomenon: to speak of 'syntax' here is to employ a metaphor. Nor can there be a syntax (since there can be no theory of truth) for clothes, food, or any of the other phenomena to which the semiologist turns his vagrant attention. The fact that he has turned his attention to the study of architecture,[18] should not lead us to suppose that he has anything to say about its meaning. For if the Fregean theory that we have sketched is true (and it now commands wide acceptance) then the whole 'science' of semiology is founded upon a mistake.

It seems then that we have as yet no right to speak of architectural 'syntax'. Until syntax is correlated with semantics – until, that is, it points to a step-by-step elucidation of a meaning – it amounts to no more than intentional regularity. In other words, it imports no true grammar, and can cast no light on the understanding of form. But perhaps we should, after all, be prepared to countenance a genuine semantics of architecture. Eco, for example, in an influential book, has sought to provide something that might seem to deserve that name.[19] He borrows from John Stuart Mill the terms 'denotation' and 'connotation' – roughly a word denotes some object or class of object and connotes some idea or meaning. Eco then concludes that every architectural form denotes a function, and at the same time connotes an idea. Here there is no attempt to talk of truth – the concept of denotation is analysed independently.[20] Understanding architecture on this view is a matter of 'recuperating' from the architectural sign the various meanings which it incorporates; in particular the ideas connoted by it and the function which it denotes. (According to Eco, the Gothic style imports an idea of religiosity, although it will denote different functions according to its use.[21]) To denote a function is not the same as to *possess* a function – to denote a function is to articulate it as a 'message', to make it publicly accessible and publicly intelligible. Denotation, in other words, is a form of symbolic relation; here a building might denote a function which it does not possess (like the spindly buttresses at St Ouen in Rouen, so angrily condemned by Ruskin[22]), or possess a function which it does not denote (like the columns of the RAC club, which in reality serve as drain pipes).

Once again, however, it is proper to be sceptical. The use of these terms – 'denotation' and 'connotation' – does not necessarily import any theory of their application. It is proper to ask whether we have really advanced beyond the idea of 'natural' meaning, of a significance 'suggested' by an object, on account of some non-symbolic relation. The examples we discussed involved causal relations: the natural 'symbol' suggests its cause or effect, and so comes to 'stand for' it. And it did not need Baudelaire to point out that every object is such a 'natural symbol'. Now the relation of a building to a function is not causal but teleological: the function of a building is neither its cause nor its effect but its aim. Nevertheless, it is still a natural feature of a building that it should suggest an aim – not yet a 'linguistic' feature. There are many such examples of teleological 'meaning' in nature. The fish's fin suggests its aim of guiding motion, as the spiral of a creeper suggest its upward tendency. These are examples of non-linguistic meaning for the reason that – once the relation between object and purpose has been comprehended – there is nothing more to be grasped, and certainly nothing of a symbolic kind. There is no content to the suggestion that the fish's fin also *says* something about its function, that it conveys a 'message', or serves as a 'symbol'. A natural object might even suggest a function that it does not possess, as the black nobs on a squid suggest the idea of vision, but have no visual function. It seems then that, if we are to introduce the semantic terms which Eco proposes, some further argument will be necessary. What would this further argument be?

We must return again to the notions of semantic and syntactic structure. Normally, when I say that a word – say 'John' – stands for, or denotes something, I mean more than that the word 'anticipates' or 'suggests' what it denotes (the man John). I mean that the word is so connected with John that it can be used to speak about him, to say things of him, things which might be true or false. In other words, the word *stands for* John because it can represent John in language, taking part in a complete activity of reference, the end of which (in the central case) is to say what is true. That is why such thinkers as Frege wished to see the relation of reference in terms of a contribution made by individual words to the conditions of the truth of sentences. Frege went further, indeed, and asserted that it is *only* in the context of a sentence that a word has reference: nothing is referred to until something is *said*.[23] It is not difficult to sympathize with that view. For it derives from a serious account of the distinction between linguistic and non-linguistic meaning, an account which attempts to show why different abilities are exercised in the use and understanding of each. Knowing how to determine the reference of a word becomes essential to understanding it, since, according to this view, it will be part of knowing what is said by any sentence in which the term occurs. It is, therefore, the systematic connection between reference and truth which enables us to see how a theory of reference is also a theory of understanding. A proper theory of reference will tell us how a man comes to understand, not just individual words, but the totality of what he hears and utters.

According to this view it must surely be little more than a pun to speak of denotation, reference, or whatever, where there is no semantic structure – no path from reference to truth. The denotation of an arch, according to Eco, is its supportive function. But what does the completed building or arcade say about this function? If we cannot answer that question, then we have neither justified the use of the term 'denotation', nor provided any account of why 'denotation' must be understood. Yet the single advantage of the linguistic analogy was that it suggested an account of what it is to understand and appreciate a building. Eco's 'denotation' has yet to acquire any such significance: it is a curious fact, which some may remark on, but which others may with impunity ignore.

Now of course a form may very well suggest a certain function; it may also have connotation in Eco's sense (nearly everything does). But these facts are of little interest until we have provided an analysis of the two relations, of 'denotation' and of 'connotation'. In the case of language the seeming inscrutability of denotation is offset by our understanding of a connection between reference and truth – between referring to something and speaking about it (in a manner that may be true or false). In the case of a building, where we seem to lack that connection, the idea of 'denotation' is little more than an intellectual blank – a word without a concept. We simply do not know what is being said when it is asserted that a building denotes a function; and to describe the relation in linguistic terms, simply because of the quasi-syntactical nature of architectural forms, evinces a confusion.

But the reader is likely to feel that something remains to the linguistic analogy. After all, there may well be something that lies between natural meaning, as we have described it, and linguistic meaning, something which lacks the structure of the latter and yet which expresses intentions, conventions and 'significances' as symbols do. Can we not speak of 'signs' or 'symbols' where there is neither reference, nor assertion, nor truth? We shall see that there are indeed other forms of symbolism, and that art is one of their principal repositories. But first we must give a proper account of those language-like features of architecture which made the analogy plausible.

Perhaps the most important feature is the preponderance in architecture of conventions and rules. What is important is not the obedience to rules – for this obedience is and must be qualified – but rather the manifest bearing of these rules on anything that we can understand as architectural *significance*. Consider, for example, that most criticized (and for the most part unjustly criticized) of architectural genres, the Edwardian baroque, manifest in Norman Shaw's façade to the Piccadilly Hotel (1905–6) (Plate 54). Here we find details lifted wholesale from a tradition that was once understood, and treated with as much respect as might be considered appropriate to the detail of the façade of a modern building. One might say that, whatever the fault of the building, it is not a fault of *vocabulary*: these columns, cornices, mouldings, window frames and oeillets are all derived from the same extended classical 'language' and could be expected to occur together. But there *is* something wrong in the way in which they are combined. The details are in some way out of control: there is no

PLATE 54 R. Norman Shaw: Piccadilly Hotel, London, façade

overall conception into which they fit, nothing which seems to give reason to their existence. And one might well speak here of a disobedience to rule. For example, the columniated screen of the Piccadilly Hotel hides nothing, gives shelter to nothing, supports nothing, is massively oversized, finds no echo elsewhere in the building, and stands out as a mere excrescence, irrelevant to the rest of the structure to which it is by accident attached. The whole façade, one might say, is

PLATE 55 Andrea Palladio: Il Redentore, Venice, screen

syntactically disjoint. And one might compare it with Palladio's beautiful composition at the Redentore (Plate 55), where the screen, which serves the purpose of dividing the monastic from the laical sections of the choir, seems to continue an order established in the church as a whole, and follows a rule of composition that can be readily understood from all the details of the nave. In the Edwardian example, by contrast, the classical reference has become grotesque: the details are

PLATE 56 Andrea Palladio: Palazzo Valmarana, Vicenza

so disordered that they can play no part in our understanding of the building, just as the building as a whole can give no proper meaning to its parts.

It is interesting to reflect upon the idea of a *significant* departure from rule – of a departure that *requires* the existence of a pre-established order. The type of significance that arises here cannot be embraced by any linguistic or semantic theory; it remains, nevertheless, at the heart of all serious experience of architecture. To see this, is to see both how

PLATE 57 Andrea Palladio: Palazzo Valmarana, from *I Quattro Libri*

near and how far is the 'language' of architecture from anything that could be properly called a syntax. Consider, then, the Palazzo Valmarana – one of Palladio's finest Vicenzan houses (Plates 56 and 57). Here, in an elegant and powerfully ordered façade, we find a striking departure from rule (a departure which shocked Sir William Chambers[24]). The Colossal Order of the façade – reminiscent of Michelangelo at his most robust – is suddenly shifted at the corners, precisely where the effect of strength would normally be required, giving way to a humorous combination of frail pilasters and langorous Atlantides, and altering the sizes and positions of the apertures even so far as at one point to break through the entablature. The effect is not incongruous, but on the contrary, lively and delightful, achieving an unexpected harmony between the imposing Palazzo and the unpretentious architecture to either side. If the Palazzo did not impress us with a sense of rule-guided order, we should not be struck by this departure from rule, nor extract from it the meaning which it bears – the meaning, as one might put it, of a civilized accommodatingness, of an absolute lack of vulgar self-acclaim. The departure becomes meaningful because of the order against which it is set. It is in the context of rules and conventions that such 'free gestures' are able to convey expressive intentions.

This example is by no means an unusual one. On the contrary, it typifies the entire history of western architecture. While architects have always been motivated by a search for rule, they have discovered rules only to depart from them. From the moment of their re-establishment, the classical Orders served as a foil for experiment, rather than as an inflexible body of precepts, and while there have been buildings whose perfection reflects an unswerving obedience to order and to rule, their perfection is not for that reason of a different kind from the perfection of an expressive departure. Bramante's Tempietto and Michelangelo's Vestibule to the Laurentian Library are equally beautiful, and beautiful in a similar way, despite the fact that the one breaks the rules which the other follows, and achieves its perfection precisely by exhibiting that it does so.

It seems, then, that the meaningfulness of architectural forms cannot be explained merely through the obedience to rule, and that the importance of rules is misrepresented by the linguistic analogy. Nevertheless, there is more to the analogy than is suggested by the mannerist examples. It is important to see that the kind of 'meaningfulness' which we have discerned in the façade of the Palazzo Valmarana is a quality which may attach not just to the whole of an architectural composition, but also to its parts, and that there is often a dependence of meaning between part and whole and between whole and part which is not unlike the semantic dependences observable in language. Thus one of the principal faults in architecture is that already observed in the Piccadilly Hotel, the fault of misunderstanding composition because one has failed to observe that details have implications, and cannot be combined in just any way without producing nonsense. The details themselves *impose* a possibility of organization. This is true not only of those styles – such as the baroque – which abound in ornamental parts, and which arise from a complicated history of embellishment. It is also true even of the barest effects of architectural modernism. The details of the early Bauhaus language are now familiar enough – the careful brickwork, the glass-wrapped corners, the clean edges, concrete string courses, and rounded door-jambs. But how rarely are those details used with any sense of organization, and how often in defiance of the modest but effective grammar which Gropius and his early associates laid down. The rejection of ornament was, for Gropius, a stylistic principle, a *form* of ornament, and had little to do with the ungrammatical anti-architecture which has claimed descent from him, and which marked the first serious attempt by architects to abolish the principles of their art.

As a result of this we can know that it will never be possible to separate the quality of a building from that of its detailing, and that a disposition of badly worked details, however finely patterned, may well be meaningless in comparison to the same disposition where the details are properly executed. A superficial analysis might suggest that the same *kind* of meaningfulness attaches to the façade of a building like the Palazzo Grimani in Venice as to the façade of Scott's station at St Pancras. In either case there are rhythms established and conventions obeyed in the combination of parts, and the success in each case is a success of composition. But it is possible to argue (whether rightly is not in point) that the crudeness of detailing in Scott's building – its heavy machine-made quality – means that the composition of the façade does nothing but transfer to the whole the vacuity of its parts. It is for some such reason that one should be suspicious of claims, made on behalf of the Corbusian style, that it provides a true modern equivalent of classicism. Regularity is not enough, and the repetitiousness of The Unité d'Habitation can amount to an architectural style only if the details themselves are made into living parts of it; and that means that they must lose the childish, lumpish quality of moulded matter and begin to carry the articulation of a human act. The Palazzo Grimani derives its sedate harmony, its joyful, restful character, precisely from the fact that the lively meaningfulness of its detail is spread by the operation of a structural 'grammar' over the entire façade.

This mutual dependence between part and whole, and the sense that a 'significance' might arise from its operation, is the single most language-like feature of architecture, and any theory which aims to do justice to the facts, and aims to provide some analysis of architectural meaning, must take it into consideration. It is this which accounts for the special place of Ruskin and Viollet-le-Duc among writers on architecture. For their express aim was to show how the significance of a building arises from and depends upon the understanding of its parts. And the same consciousness of architectural 'grammar' motivated Pugin, who (like Viollet-le-Duc) attempted to give a functionalist turn to the ideas of the Gothic revival, purely in order to arrive at some notion of a *valid* detail, some way of determining the *implications* of the separate architectural parts.

But in considering the criticism of such writers, we soon come to realize that what is being discussed is not language but style. Pugin was reacting against the view[25] that the sole aesthetic value is to be found in emotional and narrative associations, associations which may well outlive the perception of a building, in the way that the associations of Culloden linger in the mind long after one has left the scene. Pugin was at pains to point out that such associations cannot possibly figure as a guide to the architect, or as a serious standard of taste, and (as we saw) his argument is persuasive. For it needs a standard of taste to create a style, and until there is a style there can be no associations to endow it with meaning. Now Pugin chose to express himself in functionalist terms, arguing that the valid detail is the detail that is structurally significant, bearing or creating some load, like the Gothic arch and pinnacle. But his insight is independent of that. It is the insight that there can be no style without the sense of architectural 'grammar', of parts fitting to parts, and of parts dominated by a whole conception.

At this point we must leave the linguistic analogy. For 'style' connotates an order which is not the order of 'syntax'. A style creates harmony where no syntax could apply. An incomplete sentence will be meaningless: for syntax imports meaning only to what is entire; syntax is the slave of semantics; there can be syntactic unity only in that which is semantically whole. But an incomplete building can manifest stylistic unity and all the meaning which derives from that. Alberti's façade to the Palazzo Rucellai, for example, which represents one of the great stylistic achievements of the early Renaissance, is not meaningless because of its incompleted state. The order and serenity for which it is admired is there in the unfinished fragment. If stylistic regularity amounted to a form of 'syntax' then we should have to dismiss the façade as architectural gibberish. And again, style operates in surprising ways. It can have a purely additive function, allowing the architect to go on adding part to part (as he might add bays to a wall) in the certainty that he will never arrive at nonsense. As an example, consider the series of Gothic traceries pierced in the West façade of Peterborough Cathedral (Plate 58). This is not nonsense, however difficult it might be to see it under the aspect of a syntactic rule. The traceries, in obeying similar stylistic constraints, can be combined successfully despite their contrasting shapes, and despite the fact that there is no successful composition (other than that of the outermost shell) which is achieved thereby. The result is not 'meaningful' – not at least, in the manner of the Palazzo Valmarana; but nor is it nonsense. All we can say is that, despite the difficulties which the architect had to face, a stylistic unity derives from them.

A further point that deserves mention is the radical difference between the two enterprises of combining languages and combining

PLATE 58 Peterborough Cathedral, West Front

styles. The latter is an act of creative endeavour, which shows something more than the understanding of the several styles. If I understand French and English then I can without difficulty complete in French what I have begun in English: the sense of what I am saying will automatically carry over from one language to another. (If this were not so then it is hard to imagine how our mediaeval literature could have begun.) But it is an achievement, for example, to continue a Gothic building in the style of the baroque. Hawksmoor succeeded in doing so in his West Towers to Westminster Abbey, but even there it is possible to see the towers as a detached adjunct to the Abbey, rather than an integrated conclusion to its longitudinal movement. And consider the enormous difference that exists between a self-consciously 'mixed' language (as in macaronic verses: 'A celuy que pluys eyme en mounde,/Of all tho that I have founde,/Carissima . . .'), and a selfconsciously 'mixed' architectural style. In the Ashmolean Museum, Cockerell combines Roman half-columns, Greek capitals, Palladian windows, Vignolesque cornices, Greek frets and mouldings, baroque pediments and Michelangiolesque window frames, together with many an original invention of his own, all in one of the most harmonious of English buildings. This remarkable stylistic achievement defies description. Certainly it shows order, development, significance. But it is not the significance of linguistic utterance, nor the order of syntactic rule. Every 'rule' that the architect applies he applies only to amend or disobey it. And yet, in some indescribable way, a style emerges from the synthesis, and each detail serves to emphasize the lively serenity of the conception (Plate 59).

Such an example shows how very far are all artistic enterprises (including architecture) from normal linguistic activity. Perhaps one motive for the semantic and semiological theories of art that have become so fashionable is the desire to find a single concept or set of concepts under which all the arts may be brought together. But, even in the case of literature – for which a semiological account might seem to be particularly suitable – it is doubtful that 'aesthetic' values and significances can be described in semantic terms. Even here the creation of aesthetic significance depends, in the last analysis, on the discovery of 'correct' and 'appropriate' details, and we cannot assimilate this idea of correctness to a semantic rule. The ability of the poet is the ability to choose between words *despite* their identical semantic properties, to choose, for example, the word *sans* instead of the word *without*, as in a famous Shakespearian example. It is the ability to choose between words with, as Frege would put it, the same sense but different tone. And we cannot assimilate 'tone' to any semantic category. A word acquires its tone as a consequence of its use and of the rules which govern it. Tone cannot therefore be the *subject* of a rule.

It is for this reason that we must distinguish, even in literature, between style and linguistic competence. A style might be imitated, but it is already an aesthetic achievement, not available to any language user irrespective of his creative powers. Therefore style is learned by a quite different education from that involved in learning language. And in the case of architecture, style is acquired visually, without the aid of any translation or dictionary. Perhaps the strangest thing of all in the theory that architecture is a language is the proneness

PLATE 59 C. R. Cockerell: Ashmolean Museum, Oxford, detail of façade

of those who best understand architecture to deny that it is. What is it that they are denying? Naturally, they are denying the presence of 'semantic structure'.

But there are forms of what are loosely called 'symbolism' which are not linguistic. Consider, for example, codified signs, such as road signs and heraldic blazons. Such forms exhibit only a fragmentary grammar, and only a partial 'reference' to the world. It is doubtful that a 'general science of signs' could be extended to include them – not at least without providing a theory to distinguish codes from languages.

Nevertheless, they have some kind of symbolic function; they 'stand for' something, and in doing so make information available to the observer. Furthermore, there are forms of symbolic 'utterance' which neither exhibit grammar nor contain definite information, and yet which, for various reasons, we might still wish to consider to be forms of symbolism. We shall be able to understand these forms of symbolism, however, only if we disregard the linguistic analogy. As we have seen, it is an obscure and uncertain analogy, and contains no theoretical insight that would enable us to apply it in an illuminating way to architecture. Let us, then, explore these other forms of 'symbolism' without the supposition of any 'general science of signs'.

8

EXPRESSION AND ABSTRACTION

THE ARGUMENTS that I have given for saying that architecture is not a language could be applied *mutatis mutandis* to the representational medium of painting and to the expressive medium of music.[1] Yet 'representation' and 'expression' might also be thought of as modes of symbolism – at least if we allow a wide extension to that term. Indeed, it is through understanding representation and expression that we shall be able to grasp what is meant by this generalized talk of 'symbolism'. And we must discover whether either of these properties belong to architecture.

It is usual to describe architecture as an 'abstract' art. This is meant to imply some contrast with the 'representational' arts of poetry, fiction and painting. What is this contrast? We know that there is *some* difference – and a difference of the greatest importance – between works like *Middlemarch* and *Le Déjeuner sur l'Herbe* on the one hand, and works like *The Art of Fugue* and the abstracts of Mondrian on the other. But a precise description of the difference has proved difficult,[2] partly because philosophers have attended not to what is in common to the various modes of representation, but to what distinguishes them. (A notable exception is Nelson Goodman, who describes the common feature in representation as 'denotation', a species of reference. And by so generalizing the concept of reference as to cover the entire field of linguistic and artistic symbolism, he attempts to prove the position against which I have already argued, that there is an important sense of language in which all art is language. But it seems to me that Goodman reaches this conclusion by generalizing the notion of reference to the point of triviality.[3])

To put it very simply, a representational work of art expresses *thoughts* about a *subject*. By 'thought' I mean roughtly what the modern logician means: the content of a declarative sentence, that which might be true or false.[4] Of course, it is not always the truth or falsehood of the thought that is of interest to us in aesthetic judgement. But it is in this relation to 'truth' – the relation definitive of thought – that representation consists.

Examples should serve to illustrate the point. Among the thoughts that give rise to my interest in *King Lear*, and which give a reason for that interest, are thoughts about Lear. These thoughts are communicated by the play and are common property to all who understand it. Something similar occurs in the appreciation of a painting. Even in the most minimal depiction – say, of an apple on a cloth – appreciation depends upon determinate thoughts that could be expressed in language without reference to the picture; for example: 'Here is an apple; the apple rests on a cloth; the cloth is chequered and folded at the edge', and so on. Of course there is much to a picture that is not so translateable; there is a content that is not so much *stated* as *shown*, and it is partly in order to separate the two kinds of content that I shall deploy the distinction between representation and expression. Representation, as I shall define it, is essentially propositional. (The definition is of course stipulative; but its purpose will soon be shown.) It follows that a man understands a representational work of art only if he gains some awareness of what it represents, and some awareness of what is said about the subject. His awareness may be incomplete, but it must be adequate. He may not see Masaccio's *Tribute Money* as a representation of the scene from the Gospel; but to understand it as a representation he should at least see the fresco as a group of gesturing men. If he does not see the fresco in some such way – say because he can appreciate it only as an abstract arrangement of colours and lines – then he does not understand it.

The point is important. For it shows that the question whether architecture is a representational art is not a question about the intrinsic properties and structure of architecture, but a question about how we do and ought to *understand* it. It is not enought to show, for example, that a given building *copies* the shape of something – of the Holy Cross, say, or (more profanely) of a hamburger. For representation and imitation are quite different things. The question is really how this act of 'copying' should affect our architectural understanding. And that in its turn is a question of how we should experience the building; for there is no adequate idea of aesthetic understanding which does not show its relation to experience.

Of course, it is certainly true that, in the first instance, Raphael's St George (Plate 60) represents something because of an intentional resemblance between the painting and its subject. But, as many

PLATE 60 Raphael: St George

philosophers have pointed out, resemblance – even intentional resemblance – is here just not enough.[5] For it is simply not possible to understand a painting like Raphael's St George while being indifferent to, or ignorant of, its representational quality – of its 'reference' to a subject. To suggest such a thing is to suggest that the Raphael could be understood as a work of purely abstract art. And yet one could notice the resemblance, and not be aware of any 'reference', as one may, like

Freud, notice a resemblance between the folds in St Anne's dress and a vulture, while knowing that Leonardo's painting contains no representation of a vulture.

Here someone might claim that at least a *partial* understanding of the painting could be achieved by studying it as a piece of abstract art. One may understand, he will say, the composition of the painting, the

PLATE 61 Palazzo Zuccari, Rome

balance of tensions between ascending and descending lines, the sequence of spatial planes, and so on, and in none of this need one have an awareness of the subject. But such a reply is wholly misguided. For it seems to suggest that these important aesthetic qualities of the Raphael – composition, balance, spatial rhythm – are quite independent of the representation; whereas that is not so. For example, we perceive the balance between the upward thrust of the horse's hind legs and the downward pressure of the lance only because we see the two lines as filled with the forces of the things depicted – of the horse's muscles and the horseman's lance. Take away the representation and the balance, too, would dissolve. And the same goes for the composition. Alter the representational meaning of the horse (close its eye, for example, or attach a bangle to its hoof) and the composition would be utterly destroyed. Nothing here is comprehensible until the representation is grasped.

It follows that there is a distinction between representation and imitation. Clearly there is much imitation in architecture; the hamburger-shaped restaurant is only an extreme and ridiculous example of something which is wholly respectable; another such example is that of the window designed to look like a face, illustrated in Plate 61. These examples are grotesque because they show imitation taken to the point where it must either become genuine representation or else be wholly outlandish, a kind of monstrous joke. Because architectural understanding forbids the first of those, imitation on this scale leads naturally to the second. The monstrousness stems from the fact that we are confronted not by a representation but by a mask – the building is *masquerading* as something. Michelangelo's David is not a piece of stone masquerading as a human form; its relation to the human form exhausts its aesthetic identity. Here representation is complete; the stone has been transformed into a living thing. Representation in architecture cannot be complete: the building remains essentially *other* than the mask which it tries to wear. An excellent illustration is the bridge that Boullée designed for the Seine at Paris, the piers of which are formed in the shape of boats (Plate 62). Here the

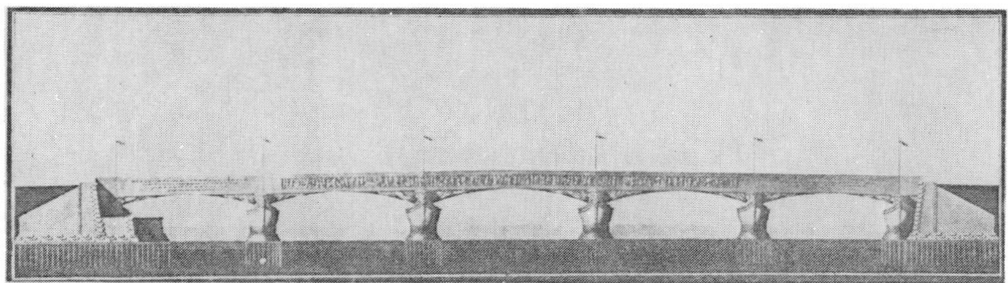

PLATE 62 Etienne-Louis Boullée: project for bridge over the Seine

representation could in no way be brought to completion. At best this has the aspect of a bridge *resting* on boats, but no boat could ever support quite so much masonry or remain unmoved in a fast-flowing stream. The effect of stillness and security which a bridge demands is here abolished, and the attempt at representation militates directly against architectural values.

On the other hand, the imitations of leaves and garlands, of beads and buttons, even of human figures in the shape of Atlantides or Caryatids, are familiar objects of architectural use. So when does imitation amount to representation? The obvious answer is that it becomes representational when knowledge of the thing imitated is an essential part of true architectural understanding. And it seems reasonable to suggest that this is rarely so. We can understand and effectively employ the shell cartouche, for example, while missing its imitative reference, just as we may attribute an architectural significance to the Doric triglyph even though uncertain whether it began life

PLATE 63a and b Leaf moulding from Rouen Cathedral

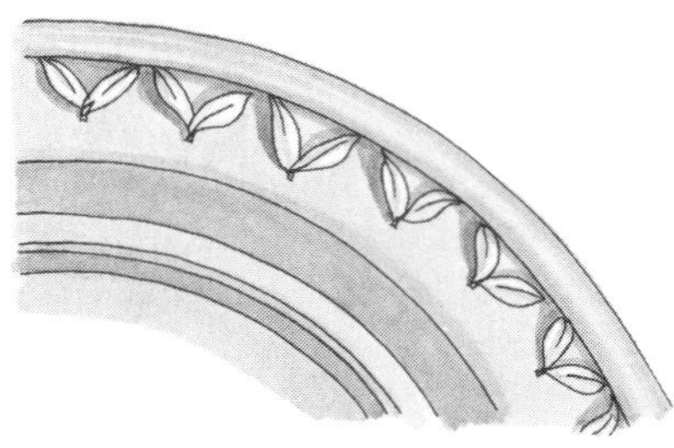

as an imitation of wooden beam-ends or of some other thing. Imitation can be part of the genesis of architectural pattern without being part of its analysis.

Other examples suggest a more serious analogy with the representational arts – examples like the Caryatid, like the allusive imitation of sails in the Sydney Opera House, and of vegetation in the late Gothic vault, or like the more direct imitation of vegetation in Gothic mouldings (see Plate 63a and b). For it is certainly not absurd to suggest that these forms cannot be understood unless the reference to their subject is appreciated: until the resemblance is seen, there will be no understanding. This is perhaps less true of the manifold allusions in the forms of a Gothic vault, than it is of leaf moulding, the architectural significance of which cannot be described without reference to what it 'represents'. It is only *as* imitation that the delicacy of line and intricacy of pattern are perceivable. What gives to this pattern its fineness and coherence is precisely the perceived relationship to certain natural forms. And the same is true of almost all that passes for genuine ornament in architecture, from the most slavishly imitative sculpture to the boldest arabesque. This process of imitation may well be essential to the architectural treatment of stone, if not of stucco, brick and concrete. Even the most sublime and enveloping architectural effects may depend for their impressiveness upon an understanding of minute imitative forms – as in the flowering of the stonework in the Cathedral of Rouen. In a similar way one must appreciate the gradual breaking of the stone into expressive sculpture as one ascends the Corinthian Order from base to frieze – the culmination in direct sculptural representation is not an arbitrary addition, but a proper expression of the intrinsic life of stone as the Order gradually unveils it. Here the architectural effect depends upon seeing an ascent towards representation, a slow thoughtful passage from mere imitation to developed narrative.

But we should hesitate to pass from such examples to the conclusion that architecture may be a representational art, in just the manner of painting or sculpture. For representation, being the expression of thought, contains an essentially 'narrative' element, an elaboration of a story or description. The representational painting does not only present a subject, it also describes and explores it, just as a passage of prose might describe and explore its subject. Representational art requires the *development* of thought. And here one might, I think, properly distinguish the ornamental reference from the narrative reference. The building does not so much describe a subject as profit from it: it profits from our prior familiarity with a certain form in order to render itself intelligible to the human eye. When description *is* present – as in the Greek frieze – then we have fully-fledged sculpture, and while this may indeed be part of an architectural effect, it is not in essence architecture, any more than are frescoes painted on the outer stucco of a house.

This distinction between the ornamental and the representational use of imitation can be understood from a simple example. Between the capitals of the lower order on the façade of S. Caterina de' Funari (Plate 64), garlands are imitated. It appears as if these garlands were strung across from one capital to the next. If this were a case of representation then we would in effect have to understand this ornament as a representation of a sequence of garlands swung between columns (the pilaster being itself a 'representation' of a column). But we cannot so see it. This is obvious just as soon as we turn to the central bay, above the door, where, since there is no pilaster to support them, the garlands are continued in the same rhythm, but with no apparent points of fixture. To see this as representation would be to see one end of a garland of flowers as fixed to a point of air – an absurd conception. (A similar effect can be observed in many Renaissance buildings, for example, in the garden façade of the Villa Medici.) Nearly all architectural imitation is in this sense ornamental, and depends for its effectiveness on no developed representational thought. Of course, it does not matter much how we use the *word* 'representation': what matters is that we should not assimilate the various phenomena too hastily, for fear of arriving at a distorted picture of architectural understanding.

Why, then, should we define representation as I have defined it? Briefly, the answer is this: we need to make a distinction between two kinds of aesthetic interest. In either case there is one central object of interest, beyond which attention does not wander. But in one type of aesthetic interest you do not think only of the work of art; or rather, in thinking of the work of art, you may also be thinking of something else, of its subject. Here attention is focused on the work, even though, in some sense, thought is not. This happens when your thoughts are not

PLATE 64 Giacomo della Porta: S. Caterina de' Funari, Rome, façade

about the work of art, but nevertheless derive from it, and remain within the work's control. Here thought is not mere association, but on the contrary, is both conveyed and developed by the work to which you attend. The true subject of thought is the subject of the work. In reflecting on Aeneas and his adventures, however, you may also be attending to the *Aeneid* – and there are not *two* acts of attention here involved. That is why it is right to say that the *Aeneid* is a representation of the adventures of Aeneas. The subject of a representational work of art is also the subject of the thoughts of the man who sees or reads it with understanding; to enjoy the work is therefore to reflect upon its subject. There we see the importance of such an aesthetic interest, in which the thought of a subject remains entirely within the control of a work of art. We see too why we should wish to distinguish the quite different kind of aesthetic interest in which attention to the work of art is *not* bound up with an interest in its subject, and why we should wish to say that 'understanding' the work is a different matter in either case. And however much we may be persuaded that, in some cases, a *knowledge* of a 'subject' might be important to architectural understanding, it is hard to argue that architectural understanding can be itself a mode of *interest* in a subject. Here lies the principal reason for saying that architecture is, after all, an abstract art.

The remarks of the last paragraph help to explain why so many philosophers since Hegel have attempted, in their various ways, to distinguish representation from expression.[6] Even in the second kind of aesthetic interest – where there is no narrative or anecdotal element – it is possible that our enjoyment of the work will involve us in thoughts about other things. But such thoughts have no narrative or descriptive character; they are much more like ostension than statement, consisting in reference to or reminiscence of things which are not described. A funeral monument may seem to carry some reference to grief, say, to eternity, or to transience; or to something one knows not what. Characteristic of such reference is the frequent difficulty one has in putting the 'thoughts' conveyed by the work of art into words. A man may feel that *something* is being said, for example by Michelangelo's tombs in the Medici Chapel (Plate 65), but be quite unable to say what it is. But this inability is in no way a sign that he has not understood the tombs, either in their sculptural or in their architectural significance. Here we may wish to speak not of representation, but rather of expression. Characteristic of expression is the presence of 'reference' without predication: sadness is expressed by the sculpture but nothing is said about sadness; eternity is made present in Michelangelo's brooding figures, but it is not described there.[7]

In this notion of expression, therefore, we seem to be approaching that ideal of 'reference' without description (reference without semantic structure) which the semiologists look for in their over-generalized 'science' of signs. Here we have the residual core of the contention that architecture is a language. Moreover, we also seem to have access to the 'immediacy' of architectural meaning. If 'expression' in architecture has anything to do with the expression of a face or gesture, then we are referring to something that is the object of immediate reaction – we do not *infer* the expression from the features of the face, or see it as something independent which the face serves to convey. The 'expression' on a face is part of its appearance, and to try to subtract the face from its expression would be like trying to separate the Cheshire cat from its grin.

It is important, then, to know exactly what we mean in describing the 'expressive' qualities of architectural forms. The first thing to notice is that expression can be – and in the case of architecture usually is –

PLATE 65 Michelangelo: Medici tombs, S. Lorenzo, Florence, new sacristy

impersonal. That is to say, it need not involve the expression of any personal feeling or any other state of mind (whether real or imagined) on the part of the architect. Of course, a work of art *may* be expressive because it is an outpouring of personal emotion. But that is only *one* way of being expressive, and those aesthetic theories which attempt to make it into the principal way misunderstand the concept with which they have to deal. (For one thing, most outpourings of emotion are inexpressive: expressiveness, unlike self-expression, requires distance and discipline.)

There is a further failing in such theories, however, which deserves more consideration. For impersonality can mean two rather distinct things, either the impersonality of expressive sculpture, or that of expressive architecture, and as I indicated in chapter 1, these derive from different sources. Even when we have distinguished, as we must, between artistic expression and self-expression, we must further distinguish that kind of aesthetic expression which has to be *seen* as personal (the brand exemplified in lyric poetry, lieder, and, above all, dramatic monologue), from that which must be seen as abstract and detached. In the latter case we do not attribute, even in imagination, an *emotion* to a *subject*, for there is no subject to imagine, and rarely any emotion to attribute. Expression is more like a display of atmosphere, an abstract presentation of character. The distinction is not sharp, but I think it is real, and can be understood by comparing architecture with music.

Suppose I hear a piece of expressive music, and hear it as expressing grief. This perception is tied up with thoughts of personal suffering and personal release. I hear sighs and sobs, I imagine loss, and I hear the music as a response to loss. It is as though my perception were governed by the thought: 'If I were to suffer such loss, it is *thus* that I would feel'; and in that thought of a shared emotion there may be inexpressible consoling power. There is an enormous amount to be said about the 'depth' of this experience of shared emotion. But perhaps it should be apparent that the experience of 'expression' in architecture is not like that. As I remarked at the outset, architecture is a public activity; it aims at an objectivity and a public accessibility which might be absent from works of music and poetry without detriment to their aesthetic value. A building is essentially a public object, to be looked at, lived in and walked past at all times, in all conditions and in all humours. The observer is not normally putting himself in a special frame of mind when he passes or even when he enters a building, nor does he regard it, as he might a book, a painting or a sculpture, as an object of private and personal attention. There is surely, therefore, something inherently anti-architectural about the view – sometimes known as expressionism[8] – which sees architecture as the middle term in a process of personal communication, the process of passing emotion (that is to say, imagined emotion) from artist to public. To meet with an expressionist building in one's daily life is like being constantly button-holed by a self-vaunting bore, who urgently wishes you to know what *he* feels, and yet who feels just the same every day. It is thus with the architecture of Rudolf Steiner, than which little in the world of architecture exemplifies greater confusion of thought or greater depravity of emotion. Expressionism becomes plausible only as architecture approaches the ideal of sculpture, beginning then to make quasi-sculptural demands, as may be done, for example, in the design of a monument. Expressionism provides an intelligible motive for a 'building' like Tokuchika Miki's famous 'Tower of Peace' at Hiroshima, but considered as architecture this tower is utterly grotesque.

Now there are ambiguous structures, lying between the world of sculpture and the world of architecture, structures like the trophic column, which seem both to defy architectural interpretation and yet also to lend themselves to architectural design – indeed, Fischer von Erlach, in a striking composition, succeeded in representing two trophic columns as integral to a church façade (see Plate 66). But it is

PLATE 66 J. B. Fischer von Erlach: Karlskirche, Vienna

clear that even this great architect had some difficulty in achieving the unity which we observe, and barely avoided fully reducing the columns to minarets or towers. Moreover it is interesting to note that Fischer's use of quasi-sculptural elements derives from a complex iconological meaning, and that the architect was working with a monumental purpose throughout.[9] And when an architect has this monumental purpose, he will find it difficult to give his work expression of a personal kind. Even a funerary monument, if it is to have architectural significance, must lay claim to a public, rather than a private feeling: which is why it must be a *monument*. The architectural expression of grief attributes to its object a public importance that he may not deserve: it treats the individual life and individual loss as a symbol of some national or religious sentiment: as in the pretentious monument to Victor Emmanuel II in Rome, the grey slabs of the Lenin mausoleum, or the achieved tranquillity of the Taj Mahal. In all these cases expression has been divorced from personal emotion and become one with the values – values involved in the public representation of human life – implicit in all architectural labour. The florid pomposity of the Victor Emmanuel monument, like the oppressive lifelessness of the Lenin mausoleum, speak not of grief nor of any other personal anguish, but rather of the social order and its self-image. Even Hans Poelzig, the arch-expressionist, was aware of this public nature of architectural symbolism, and devoted much of his time to the projection of unexecuted memorials to great dead men. In fact Poelzig is probably best known (or at least best liked) for his background sets to expressionist films, in particular to Paul Wegerner's *Der Golem* (Plate 67). Here we find the true *telos* of expressionist conceptions in architecture. For here the audience is necessarily a theatre audience, prepared to treat the background as part of an unreal world in which they do not live and of which they can only be spectators. 'Building' is subsidiary to dramatic expression. As architecture, these stage-sets are characterless; but they lend themselves to dramatic expression, however absurd they might appear in a public street.

PLATE 67 Hans Poelzig: film set for *Der Golem*

Nevertheless, there is an important feature of buildings that has great bearing on their expressive character, and which we must here bear in mind – the division between exterior and interior display. To enter a building is to change from a façade to a surround, from public to private, and unless the building is itself a public building, it is not inapposite for the interior to make quite special – even quasi-sculptural demands on its visitor. A man who enters a church, a crypt, or a memorial prepares himself for what he will find there. It is quite possible for the interior of a funerary chapel, for example, to demand appreciation in terms that are more nearly sculptural than architectural. In Michelangelo's Medici Chapel, there is no question of a public use, no question of functional, ceremonial or domestic purpose. The Chapel marks out a consciously *inner* space; it is almost a hollow sculpture. It is not the open space of a public hall, or the private space of a domestic hearth: for both those – the private and the public – are forms of what is outer, forms of objectively realized life. In the Medici Chapel architectural features are used with a peculiar *innigkeit*, symbolic of the inner life precisely because they have been borrowed and de-natured from their objective forms. Consider, for example the restless articulation of the walls, as this is revealed in the ground plan (Plate 68), the constant advancing and retreating of vertical planes, so inimical to the classical language which the artist borrows here, but so perfect as a frame to the sombre statuary. Consider too the doors, crowded into the corners, with their fine mouldings continued round on four sides, so that the chapel must be entered with a sudden drop of the foot, making the visitor fall with an arresting movement into the hollow of the floor; and the much admired niche frames of the aediculae above the doors, which take in an area of the gable (Plate 69), showing the determined interpenetration of all structural and decorative parts, and a partial defiance of any purely architectural meaning. The personal expression here is that of sculpture: the demands of architecture have been refined almost entirely away – the Medici Chapel is not so much architecture as a monumental frame, a frame carried round into a complete space like a four-sided niche.

The example shows that architecture may have expressive uses which bring it into direct relation with sculptural values. And it is not only in funerary monuments that these uses are displayed. Bernini's idea of the unified *concetto* – in which architecture, lighting, material, ornament and sculpture are combined in an essentially dramatic display of feeling – exhibits the same continuity between public and private expression. But, when truly 'inner', the architecture becomes dramatic scenery, an elaborate articulated frame, which finds its true meaning in some representational centre – the classic example being

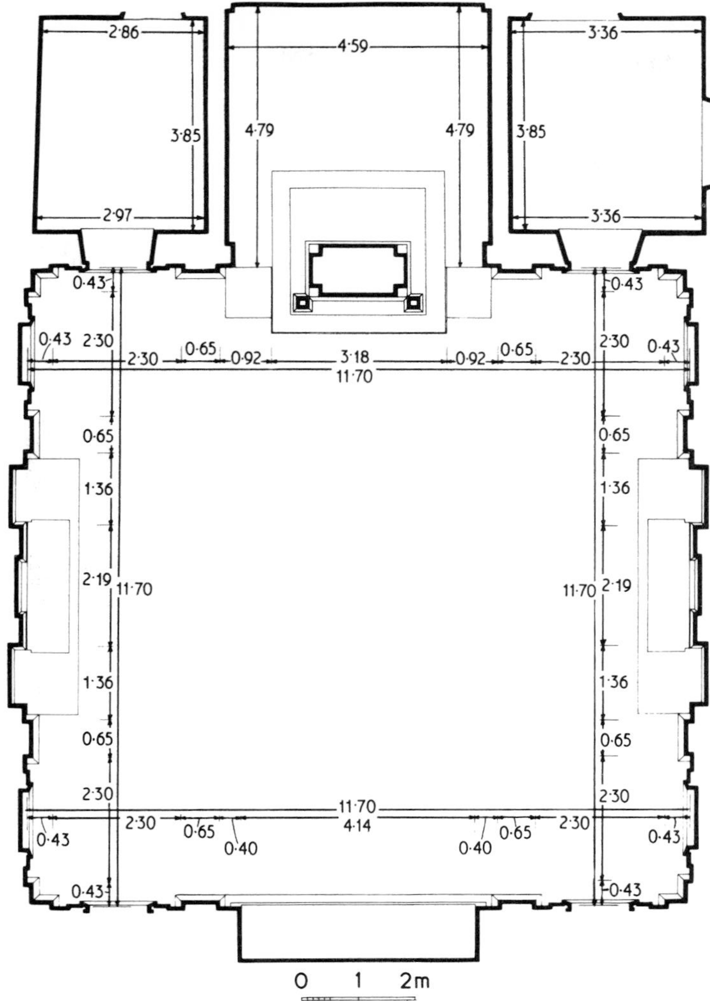

PLATE 68 Michelangelo: Medici Chapel, Florence, ground plan

the elaborate frame of the Cornaro Chapel, which displays Bernini's sculpture of the ecstatic St Teresa, bathed in unearthly light (Plate 70). The effect of this remarkable composition has been described by Sir Nicholas Pevsner in the following words:

> The chapel . . . is faced with dark marbles, their gleaming surfaces of amber, gold, and pink reflecting the light in ever-changing

PLATE 69 Michelangelo: Medici Chapel, Florence, gable aedicule

patterns. In the middle of the wall in front of the entrance is the altar of the saint. It is flanked by heavy coupled columns and pilasters with a broken pediment, placed on the slant so that they come foward towards us and then recede to focus our attention on the centre of the altar, where one would expect to find a painting, but where there is a niche with a sculptural group, treated like a picture and giving an illusion of reality that is as startling today as it was three hundred years ago. Everything in the chapel contributes to this *peinture vivante* illusion. Along the walls on the right and the left there are also niches opened into the chapel walls, and there Bernini has portrayed in marble, behind balconies, members of the Cornaro family, the donors of the chapel, watching with us the miraculous scene, precisely as though they were in the boxes, and we in the stalls of a theatre.[10]

PLATE 70 G. L. Bernini: Cornaro Chapel, S. Maria della Vittoria, Rome

A world of such monuments, of theatrical illusions, inward-looking spaces, agitated or mournful surrounds, would be visually intolerable. Architecture may stretch to this, but in essence it is different. (The architecture in Bernini's chapel is almost as unreal as the people: it is not so much built as represented.) All the same, we cannot conclude that architecture, even as commonly understood, has no expressive character. All that we are entitled to conclude is that the expressive character of architecture is not subjective – it does not lie in the imaginative rendering of individual feeling. Buildings have expression as faces do; their individuality is not that of a particular feeling which they express, but of their public aspect. It may be that the term 'expression' is not the best one to refer to this public aspect – no particular word seems forced on us here (a fact worth noting, since it suggests that the phenomena have yet to be clearly identified). Nevertheless, the intimacy of the connection between a building and its 'character' is very like the intimacy of those relations which are normally called 'expression' – and this suffices to justify the transfer of the term. A building does not so much express an emotion, as wear a certain expression: it has expression in what has been called (perhaps somewhat misleadingly) an 'intransitive' sense.[11] That is to say, we regard the building as 'imbued with character', and this 'character' is not only immediate – part of the way the building looks – but also observable in principle by anyone. The attribution of 'character' is so little separable from our experience of architecture that Vitruvius – in attempting to explain the feminine character of the Corinthian column – referred to a legendary account of its discovery, perhaps assuming, in the manner of Hume, that it is the memory of this legend that is stirred whenever such a column is seen.[12]

Buildings may look feminine; they may also look tranquil, upright, bullying, amused. The Georgian townhouse has a graceful and convivial expression, the baroque palace is stately, proud but genial, the high-rise block is cold and estranged. These judgements are not to be taken in a literal sense; a building cannot *be* convivial or proud, as a man can. Nor do we mean simply to speak of a resemblance. Resemblances are not important to us, in the way that expressive character is important; besides, there is no serious resemblance between a Georgian town house and a polite or convivial man.[13] Rather, we are using language indirectly, to locate the character of our experience of architecture: the way buildings look, sound and feel to us. We say that the building has a tranquil look, or even that it 'looks tranquillity', as in the following passage from *The Mourning Bride*:

> . . . . this tall pile
> Whose ancient pillars raise their marble heads
> To bear aloft its arch'd and ponderous roof,
> By its own weight made steadfast and immovable,
> Looking tranquillity! . . .

Clearly it is unhelpful, in elucidating the thought of this passage, to say that Congreve means that the building looks as thought it is tranquil. That would be like saying that sad music sounds as though it is sad, even though *sad* is something that it can never literally be. The tranquillity, like the sadness, belongs uniquely to an appearance – this is how we *see* the building. Here then, we seem to be approaching more nearly that ideal of an 'immediate meaning' which our analysis of aesthetic judgement suggested to us.

Once again, however, we have to face the problem of how we establish the relation between the experience of the building and the meaning that it bears for us. If expressive character is not a matter of *personal* expression, then what we are noticing here is not some relation between the appearance of a building and the emotions of its architect, even though such relations – as everyday experience amply evinces – can be part of the immediate perception of our world. (One sees a man's grief *in* his face. And this 'immediacy' in our perceptions of the mental life of others is clearly part of what we *transfer* to our experience of architecture; but the two experiences, and the thoughts involved in them, are not, for all that, the same.) It seems that we have here, once again, that primitive 'fusion' of concept and experience – a fusion which depends on no specific belief or judgement – which we saw to be characteristic of imaginative attention. So we must avoid the temptation to think of the recognition of this intimate relation between experience and concept in terms of the association of ideas, or in terms of some detachable 'feeling' which is aroused by the building.

It is at this point that we can begin to return to the discussion of taste that I broke off at the end of chapter 5. In concluding that chapter I pointed out that I had emphasized the place of critical reasoning and deliberation, but said little about what is primitive in aesthetic choice. Again, in considering various 'explanatory' theories of aesthetic judgement, in particular the theories associated with Marx and Freud, I argued that while they could provide no account of critical reasoning, they seemed to offer some rudimentary explanation of the primitive aspect of aesthetic choice. For here reasoning is not in question; the best we can do is to look for some sufficient description of the facts. We have now been forced back into a consideration of what is primitive; for it is at the primitive level that the concept of 'expression' must first be understood.

We must begin by rejecting (as we have already implicitly rejected) the theory that we can elucidate the concept of expression through some notion of 'association' or 'arousal'. Consider the following theory: tranquil things, or sad things, or noble things, all arouse in us certain feelings, and when one of these feelings is aroused in us by a building we will describe it accordingly as tranquil, noble or sad. What we really *mean* is that the building arouses certain feelings in us. Hesselgren, for example, compares two interiors, one with a plate of sticky cakes, the other with a loaf of rough brown bread, and remarks that the visual perception of one interior is 'accompanied by' a feeling similar to that which accompanies the perception of the cakes, and that the sight of the other gives the 'same feeling of harshness' as the sight of the bread.[14] It is not difficult to see why that is wrong: there is no description of the 'feeling' that is 'given' by these interiors except in terms of the experience of seeing them. Here what one means by 'feeling' is an act of attention, which has its life in the particular experience and cannot be said to survive it. To speak of two objects as arousing a 'similar feeling' is to speak as though they were treated as a means to that end (as one could describe heroin and cocaine as means to the same end of self-forgetfulness). The aesthetic object is unlike a drug in that the 'feeling' which it arouses is wholly exhausted by the act of attention of which it is the object. We could no more illuminate the nature of our experience of an 'oatmeal' room by saying that it is the means to an 'oatmeal' feeling, than we could illuminate our experience of comedy by saying that it is a means to amusement. In either case, what we mean by the 'feeling', has to be described in terms of the particular pattern of attention to the particular kind of thing.

Nevertheless, aesthetic experience is not always, and not even normally, as primitive as these examples suggest. As we have already indicated, there is a process of reflection and comparison which might have the 'experience of expression' as its conclusion. In other words, we must not make the experience of expression so primitive that it seems incapable of rational justification. On the contrary, as soon as we speak of expression the concept of justification seems immediately to take root. Consider the 'exciting, ecstatic and intoxicating' that figure in Wölfflin's description of the baroque.[15] These terms do not report a psychological effect – at least not when they are used in support of an aesthetic judgement. They convey that a certain way of seeing the buildings is appropriate, no matter how any particular observer reacts. One might argue that Wölfflin was wrong to see the baroque style in such a way, that it should be seen more in terms of lively adaptability than of intoxicating grandeur: it would not then be possible for Wölfflin to reply that that was how *he* saw it – not without giving up the argument. The building is not just the cause of these reactions; it is their object, and since they spring from the act of imaginative attention to form and detail, the question of their appropriateness arises not just by accident, but essentially, and cannot be laid aside.

Consider, then, the question 'why?', used of these expressive features. It makes sense to ask why a building is exciting, and the question is asking for a reason and not a cause. In so far as one can speak of a building as 'arousing' certain feelings, and in so far as these feelings are considered integral to an aesthetic response, they seek to root themselves in the aesthetic object. What I mean by an 'oatmeal' feeling could be explained only by pointing to this kind of thing, and to the features of it which particularly engage my attention. In this process of 'rooting' feeling, I am also representing it as 'appropriate' to its object. Recognizing a sugary or an oatmeal look is, first of all, a matter of immediate impression; but it is at once something more than that. One may advance from this impression to perceiving the detailed correspondence among visual parts. I justify this attribution of an oatmeal character by describing not just the fleeting impression of a room, but also the correspondence of textures, colours, forms. I may attempt to articulate a certain underlying moral idea (an idea of healthy simplicity, of unassuming cleanliness) which might show itself in everything, from the grain of the floorboards and the texture of the bedspread, to the colours, subject-matter, framing and position of a picture on the wall. It is no mere whim to make these judgements, to learn to see objects as it were decked out in the moral character of other things and so to see these other things – whether they be oatmeal or courage, cakes or despair – as symbolically displayed in an architectural appearance. It may be difficult to express all the values implicit in an oatmeal look, but it is certainly true that these values are far more important than is often recognized. Knowing how to perceive an oatmeal look, how to recognize the totality of its visual and emotional implications, is simply one part of knowing how to dress, how to furnish, how to decorate, how to charm, how to realize a self or identify an appearance, in other words, it is a small but important part of knowing how to live. It is not surprising that the phenomenon appears to partake of everything that is most primitive, as well as everything that is most considered, in human choice.

It seems then, that we cannot admit the primitive recognition of expressive character into aesthetics, without at the same time allowing the question 'why?' – construed as a request for reasons – in its wake. And if I produce reasons for my way of seeing, I think of these reasons as reasons for others as well as for myself. Even when I suppose that I am explaining myself, my reasons will seem apt to me only if they seem to put me in the right. Moreover, I justify my reaction in a particular way: the endpoint of reasoning is always an experience, a way of seeing: it is partly because we justify our description of a building in terms of its appearance that the description ceases to be a mere 'association' – for by this process, it gains its *content* from the experience. But of course the existence of such a process of justification is not in itself sufficient to explain the attachment of thought to experience. As I earlier argued, this 'attachment' cannot be explained; it is what is 'given'. Consider the well-known phenomenon of the 'ambiguous expression'. A building might have an ambiguous character. At one moment it seems threatening and claustrophobic, at the next moment quiet and solemn. (This is true, I think, of Borromini's cloister at S. Carlo alle Quattro Fontane (Plate 71.) Each of these characters may be

PLATE 71 Francesco Borromini: cloister of S. Carlino, Rome

thought to be appropriate, but only one of them, at any moment will be *seen*. It follows that there is always something more to the experience of meaning than the process of justification that might be provided for it. Justification can never *constitute* the reaction or experience which it supports. Fully to accept the process of reasoning that might be given for seeing Borromini's cloister as threatening is to accept not just an argument but a way of seeing.

Once again we are likely to be struck by the inscrutability of this relation between meaning and aesthetic experience. We have eliminated from the stakes every theory that claims to diagnose meaning; we are left with a meaning that is so immediate, so much a part of what we see, than no mere diagnosis will suffice to describe its nature. At the same time we are clearly on the brink of understanding architecture, its value and its success. To explore this phenomenon of expression is therefore the task that lies before us. But because we have found ourselves confronted with the primitive part of aesthetic choice, we shall have to neglect questions of analysis and concentrate instead on the *genesis* of aesthetic judgement. Gradually, during the remainder of this book, I shall let analysis reassert itself, and so bring the argument to a close.

We are to begin, then, from what is most primitive. Imagine that a man wishes to build a door and that he stands back while another traces its possible outline against a wall (the example is Wittgenstein's[16]). His response will be something like 'Too high! Too low! Now, that's right!' (the use of the word 'right' here is what is most significant). This is a primitive example of aesthetic choice, unmediated by extraneous reflections, a choice which is wholly abstract and divorced even from ideas of meaning and expression. We suppose that the demands of utility are already satisfied: a choice still remains to be made among indefinitely many forms. It can be explained, perhaps, but it has, initially at least, no further basis. Nevertheless it is intrinsic to preferences of this kind – founded as they are in an act of self-conscious attention – that they should seek justification. It will be in place to confront our builder with the question 'Why?' – 'Why is the door too high?' In searching for an answer he will perhaps make comparisons with other doors; he will produce precedents and examples. And he is likely to extract from this stock of precedents some system of principles, some repeatable set of answers to the recurrent problems of construction – to the problem posed by his desire to do what will 'look right'. Imperceptibly, and inevitably, he will develop standards that will guide his choices; in doing so he will acquire the beginnings of a style. But his work will be open to criticism; it is not a private performance for the benefit of himself alone. He will need to persuade his fellows to accept the product of his labour, and he must therefore seek for reasons which have an authority transcending the appeal of individual preference. A style is not the invention of one man only, and has value only when it is recognizably 'right' to others besides oneself. Only then does a style fulfil its role of giving order to otherwise nebulous choices, of situating primitive preferences in a framework of enduring possibilities. Style ennobles choices, giving them a significance that otherwise they lack. Only in exceptional circumstances can an artist entirely create his own style, and even then he ignores established practice at his peril: where there is a 'free' choice of styles there is no longer any style, and therefore no true freedom.

But this brings us back to the linguistic analogy, at the point where we left it. For the argument – which establishes not the indispensability of style but only its naturalness, and its central role in the articulation of aesthetic choice – has an important corollorary. It shows that there is after all a perfectly legitimate connection, even in the case of an abstract art, between convention (in the form of style) and meaning. Thinkers such as Sir Ernst Gombrich and those influenced by him, have explained style in quasi-semantic terms.[17] Convention, by limiting choice, makes it possible to 'read' the meaning in the choices that are made. But on such an account, style ought to be no more than superfluous ornament until subordinate to representational aims. That is clearly wrong, even in the case of those representational arts to which the theory directly applies. Style is simply the natural crystallization of all aesthetic endeavour, and, if it makes a contribution to 'meaning', it is in virtue of its independent nature, a nature that is as clearly visible in abstract as it is in representational art. And it *does* make a contribution, as our example shows. For style serves to 'root' the meanings which are suggested to the aesthetic understanding, to attach them to the appearance from which they are derived.

Now, in the judgement of taste, aesthetic preference may be brought into relation with ideas whose content is not only visual. For our builder the dimension that he chooses might come to have a 'comfortable' look; it is so executed as to embody a value, and this value might find its correlates throughout his experience; it is not specifically 'aesthetic' in its meaning. Now we can see the acquisition of taste in the following way, as built up from successive layers of sensuous and intellectual choice. Certain forms appeal to us – we choose them in preference to others – and this phenomenon is primitive in the sense that there is initially no reason why we do this, even though, as we have seen, the experience that determines our preference is, like the preference itself, one for which reasons can be meaningfully adduced. We begin to search for such reasons, and in the course of doing so endow our chosen forms with meaning. We then come to *see* those forms differently, rather as a man may hear the inflections of a foreign language differently once he has learned to associate them with a certain meaning. The process may be repeated, further reasons may be found, and a new way of seeing emerge. The result may be the discovery of a style, not as a body of rigid rules, but rather as the creation of an architectural 'vocabulary', the endpoint of which is to render an appearance, not only comfortable to the uninstructed, but also 'intelligible' to the instructed eye. The language can itself be supported by reasons, which in their turn require further reasons, until finally the process peters out, as Vitruvius's explanations peter out, in the reference to religion, history, morality or myth.

The outcome of this development is a sense of the 'validity' of certain architectural forms, a sense which communicates itself as a visual experience. Certain forms look right, and looking right they reassure us of the values that seem implicit in them. Architecture is simply one activity among many in which this phenomenon of taste finds expression. Now there is a temptation to see the exercise of taste as *simplifying* the visual problem of the architect, by laying down rules that reduce the number of alternatives. I suggest, on the contrary, that we should see taste as a means of complicating rather than simplifying our visual choices, through the accumulation of a sense of 'fitness'. If strict rules are initially important in this process, it is because until something is fixed and lawlike nothing looks right or wrong, except in an uninteresting way. In general, children doodling lack any developed conception of form; their products tend to naive and streamlined shapes without true conception of detail (except in so far as detail is conceived as representational) – we see rockets on the move, or fluid masses of transparent glue. It is possible never to emerge from this infantile state of visual preference, to remain wedded to a kind of visual 'pleasure principle', with no ability to separate the outer object and the inner fantasy. As I shall argue, the exercise of taste achieves objectivity by endowing the world of materials with demands of its own: the architect's materials do not then simply accommodate themselves to his independent conception but help to form that conception. The architect must learn to see his materials (to borrow a Kantian phrase) not as means only but as ends. He must see them not just as the vehicle of his will but also as partly autonomous beings, already redolent of human aims. It is not surprising, then, if taste leads to the creation of a repertory of forms. It is only when such a repertory has developed that our sense of the 'appropriate' or 'fitting' detail can achieve full expression.

If that account of the genesis of taste is right, then it would seem that there could be no such thing as an aesthetic sense which did not involve at the same time an apprehension of expressive qualities, a 'reading' of objects in terms of concepts which have their true application in the description of human life. It is inevitable that the primitive movement of aesthetic taste, the desire to choose and build according to a perception of what is 'right', should lead towards the recognition of expressive meaning. Even in the aesthetic appreciation of nature we attribute character to what we see: caves appear majestic or gloomy, cliffs seem robust or hostile, trees, parks and alleys appear friendly, relaxed, harmonious. But – while these exhibit the same imaginative transference that I have described – they belong to a fairly primitive level of aesthetic experience. At the same time, the very tendency that would lead from the primitive choice to the recognition of character, points onward to the incorporation into aesthetic experience of all those further intellectual influences whereby aesthetic choice is elevated to the level of rational understanding. It seems then that the primitive choice and the critical judgement are parts of a continuous spectrum, and just as the second provides reason for the first, so does the first prefigure and justify the second.

In illustration of this transition from lower to higher levels of aesthetic understanding it is valuable to contrast two notions of aesthetic expression. I have so far used the term expression rather loosely, to cover those cases in which an object is seen decked out in a character that is not its own. In this sense one recognizes expression in hearing a piece of music as frenzied or melancholy. But there is a distinction between hearing something as melancholy and hearing it as an expression of melancholy. We do not speak of landscapes as expressive in the way that works of art (or at least the higher forms of art) are expressive. This is because landscapes cannot be seen as articulating or exploring the concepts which attach to them. Our experience of them does not involve the *pursuit* of meaning; there is, here, none of the deliberate infusion of matter with the demands of our moral life, the deliberate endowment of an object with the burden of a message, that we see in art. When we have expression on this higher level, it is as though forms and materials have taken the life out of the artist's hands, as though they speak to us with that borrowed life, and refuse to accomodate themselves to the fantasies either of artist or public. If we speak of *meaning*, rather than mere 'character', this is partly because of the detailed correspondence between visible form and moral significance – the kind of correspondence noted in discussing the example of the Oratory in chapter 5. It is this detailed correspondence which enables us to see a building as constituting a kind of elaboration or articulation of a character or concept. A state of mind seems to be explored by the building, and the building itself, far from being a mere husk which may be discarded, as it were, when the meaning is extracted from it,[18] becomes the central object of the act of attention in which meaning is grasped. The experience of Chartres is the apprehension of a divine light penetrating all things, of matter made permeable to Soul, of a universal harmony which transforms every stone from its material roughness into a minute symbol of the intellectual love of God. But to understand that meaning – understand it fully, in all its elaboration – nothing short of a visit to Chartres will suffice, and no mere description can compensate for the radiant experience in which the meaning is embodied. However intellectual the content of aesthetic experience, it is the experience which remains the important thing.

For this reason, we should not think that, if we are to understand expressive architecture, we must be able to name or describe the character that is presented by it. If there is knowledge here it is what philosophers have called 'knowledge by acquaintance' – a sudden 'familiarity' with something to which one may, indeed, be reluctant to attach a name.[19] The critic's reference to meaning is no more than *aid*, a way of drawing the observer's attention towards the full complexity of what he sees. The observer has to see what is there, and respond to it appropriately: it is irrelevant that he should also be able to attach names, either to the building or to its meaning. Aesthetic understanding is a *practical* matter; it consists not in theoretical knowledge, but in the organization of perception and feeling. To grasp the expressive character of a building is to *feel* its significance, to know what its character is like, to feel the inward resonance of an idea or way of life, and, on the strength of that, to know how to recognize and respond to its other manifestations. One does not learn *about* mediaeval theology from Chartres: but one does learn what it is *like* to believe in it, what it is like to see and feel the world as the people of Chartres once saw and felt it. The man who cannot so 'enter into' the character of a building will never be at home with the higher forms of architecture, however articulate he may be in describing what he sees. He will be like the man who is able coldly to attach names to the feelings which he reads in the faces of his fellows, but who has no knowledge what to do in response to them, how to behave appropriately, how to feel in return. To understand expression in art requires sympathy; it is a matter that is fully as practical as the moral sense itself.

We understand a building only if our experience is persuasive for us: only if it occupies a place in which we can feel its relation to the workings of the moral life. But what is that place? We must answer the question, if we are to give a full characterization of the significance of buildings. From what I have said in this chapter it would seem that the central operation in all aesthetic taste, whether in its primitive or intellectual form, is the sense of detail. It is through the operation of this sense that forms and materials become objective, pregnant with demands and meanings which both constrain and liberate the architect, constrain him towards style and liberate him from fantasy. It is through the sense of detail that architectural meanings become 'rooted' in experience, and in the apt use of detail that even the most unreflective builder feels confident in what he does. In the next chapter I shall describe this sense, and show its centrality in all architectural practice and criticism. In the course of doing so I shall suggest an account of the meaning of certain aesthetic terms, and a theory of the structure of critical reasoning.

9
THE SENSE OF DETAIL

To take an aesthetic interest in a building is to attend to it in all its completeness, to see it, not in terms of narrow or predetermined functions, but in terms of every visual significance that it will bear. This act of aesthetic attention is not a rare or sophisticated thing, a detached gesture of connoisseurship, requiring some special attitude of 'standing back', of 'disinterestedness', or 'abstraction'.[1] Like any act of attention, it can exist more or less intensely, more or less completely, at any moment, and in any frame of mind. To divorce it from practical life, to consider it as something outside all considerations of function, utility and value, is to misrepresent its nature. But whatever degree of aesthetic attention is exercised, it will aim to embrace the significance and interdependence of every part and aspect of what is seen. The sense of detail is therefore an indispensable component in aesthetic attention, being fundamental both to the elementary act of aesthetic choice and also to the sophisticated process of critical reflection whereby meaning is 'rooted' in experience. In exploring this sense of detail we shall be approaching the actual workings of architectural understanding, not only in its self-reflective, but also in its primitive form.

It is right to begin, however, on a note of scepticism. Someone might complain that there is no such 'sense of detail' figuring as a separate or separable part of the architect's intellectual equipment. For what is a 'detail'? Is an urn a detail? Is a patera a detail, an intaglio, the pressed pattern of a wooden mould? What is a detail if not itself a small, but completed, form? So how does one understand a detail? In terms of the further details which compose it? Clearly such a process might never end, and to emphasize the sense of detail at the cost of comprehensive understanding is to run the risk of making architecture wholly unintelligible. By contrast, to explain detail in terms of its contribution to a completed form, and so to place the sense of the whole before the sense of its parts, seems to suggest a less paradoxical account of aesthetic attention. Now there will be no endless pursuit of minutiae, no 'infinite regress' of eye-boggling observations, but a relaxed contemplation of the finished whole. Returning again to the analogy with language, it is surely more reasonable to regard the 'unit of meaning' as the completed building, and the details as gaining whatever significance they have from the totalities into which they can be combined.[2] Certainly, there is nothing more meaningless or repulsive in architecture than detail used at random, outside the control of any governing conception or design. (Consider that version of the Spanish baroque known, after the three brothers who were its chief exponents, as the Churrigueresque, seen at its most fantastic in the Charterhouse at Granada, Plate 72.)

There are two reasons for ignoring this scepticism. First, it mislocates the issue. It is no part of my claim that the sense of detail is the whole of aesthetic understanding, or that it can be fully described apart from the activity of which it forms a part. We are to explore the sense of detail, not only because it has been wrongly described in architectural theory, but also because it exhibits the connection between aesthetic and practical judgement. Second, the very analogy with language that might seem to demote the sense of detail, could also be used to elevate it over everything else. It is true that, in language, the sentence is the unit of meaning – it is through the complete sentence that something is *said*. But it is also true that the meaning of a sentence is determined by the meaning of the words which compose it. It is because sentences have meaning that words do; and it is because words have meaning that significant sentences can be composed from them. It seems then that we can trace linguistic meaning down to 'significant detail'. And the process is finite: there is a point beyond which meaning expires. That, indeed, is how we distinguish words from the sounds which compose them. In architecture, too, the pursuit of meaning comes to an end. There are genuine 'units' of architectural meaning – the classical and Gothic mouldings, the types of building stone, the unadorned vertical, and so on; in one sense these are like words in a language, for their significance cannot be derived from the significance of their parts. There is no reason to think that, in exploring

PLATE 72 Luis de Areválo and F. M. Vasquez: Charterhouse, Granada, detail of sacristy

detail, we are being driven further and further along an infinite path. If there is anything left to the linguistic analogy, then detail and form must be complementary.

As we have seen, architecture is not a language, and the relation between whole and part can be neither semantically nor syntactically defined. Nevertheless, there is a long tradition of thought which sees the relation between whole and part as providing the essence of architectural success. Alberti, for example, considered the beauty of a building to reside in a 'harmony (*concinnitas*) of parts, fitted together with just reflection, in such a way that nothing could be added, diminished or altered but for the worse.'[3] Hence there is no appreciation of the beauty of a building that does not involve an awareness and understanding of its parts.

As a *definition* of beauty, Alberti's remarks are far from satisfactory. The phrase 'for the worse' naturally invites the question 'worse in what respect?' and if the answer is 'in respect of beauty' then the account is circular. Besides, is the 'organic' conception of beauty that underlies Alberti's definition really so very persuasive? The Doge's Palace in Venice could certainly be altered for the better, by bringing the windows on the lagoon into line, as could Bramante's Tempietto, the lantern of which (due to subsequent interference with Bramante's hemispherical plan) is certainly too high. Yet these buildings are among our touchstones of architectural beauty. Similarly, a charming or lively detail can exist in conjunction with the most mediocre of forms and still be beautiful; consider the frieze and crown which Borromini added to the dull little church of S. Giovanni in Oleo (Plate 73).

In fact, Alberti was referring not to some definable property of beauty, but rather to the sense of beauty, and the thoughts and perceptions involved in the exercise of that sense. It may be that we *could* alter the Doge's Palace for the better; but to *see* it as beautiful, even in its present state, is to see an adequate correspondence of part to part, a harmony of detail, a visual completion that is *felt* as intrinsically correct. The concept of beauty is thus absorbed into a certain pattern of reasoning, whose terms are at once intellectual and visual. As Alberti seemed to recognize, definitions in this area are unlikely to succeed. What is important is to investigate, as we have done, the mental phenomena of aesthetic perception, and the reasoning intrinsic to it. As we have already suggested (again following Alberti) a proper account of aesthetic reasoning will put concepts like the 'appropriate' at its intellectual centre. But such concepts elude explicit definition. They seem to bear in themselves the subjectivity of their user, and indeed we might be tempted to seek for their true meaning, not in the properties of the object, but in the state of mind of the man who observes it. At the same time, they contain an intimation of objectivity: the *sense* of the appropriate seems to point always to a form of reasoning through which it becomes rooted in the object. And it would be impossible to conceive what that reasoning might be if we felt that the essence of architecture lay elsewhere than in the dependence of part on part.

PLATE 73 S. Giovanni in Oleo, Rome

Once we recognize that (and we have already suggested arguments that point towards its truth), then we seem forced also towards the view (implicit in Alberti's classicism) that the understanding and execution of detail must constitute a basic feature in all architectural practice, and that a style which claimed to treat detail merely as the means to the end of 'form' would have misunderstood the nature of the aesthetic sense, and hence the aesthetic nature of form itself. It is well known, indeed, that men tolerate all kinds of ill-thought-out or unbalanced compositions, provided that the parts themselves are lively, sympathetic and intelligible; while the most perfect 'proportions' achieved with cheap or ugly details will always be offensive. In a sense this goes to destroy the absolute force of Alberti's ideal. At least, it goes to show that Alberti's 'beauty' is only the perfect form of something that can be appreciated as well in its lesser as in its greater manifestations. In all manifestations, the sense of detail will be prominent in architectural understanding. The Georgian house is loved as much for the mouldings of its sash windows, for its brickwork and doorframe, for its iron railings and area steps, as for the grace of its proportions. As I have argued, there is no true concept of proportion which can be divorced from that of the details which embody it. Compare the two plans for Downing College in Plates 74 and 75, one by L. W. Wyatt, the other by Porden, both following a traditional Palladian motif, with an emphatic centre and two connected wings. Both are undeniably 'well-proportioned'. And yet in the one composition (that which depends on classical detailing), the shapes are low, settled, compressed; while in the other (the 'Gothic' design) the entire emphasis is vertical and the shapes modified in answer to it. It is impossible to extract from these examples some ideal of proportion which might be understood without seeing how classical detail constrains and answers classical detail, and how similarly Gothic detail constrains and answers its kind.

There is another reason for emphasizing detail in architecture, a reason that is as important practically as it is philosophically elusive. This is that detail may be the only thing which an architect can enforce. The ground plan and elevation of a building are usually affected (if not dictated) by factors beyond the architect's control – by the shape of a site or the needs of a client – while details remain within his jurisdiction. It is through studying detail that the architect can learn to impart grace and humanity to the most unusual, troublesome or disorderly conglomeration. Consider the oddly placed baroque window in Plate 76, or the disorderly rooftops of the Wolverhampton Brewery: neither of these could be spoken of as beautiful compositions, but they have grace and charm nevertheless.

It is a disheartening feature of much modern architecture that it lacks this flair for detail. Indeed, modern architects have often shown a hostility towards everything that could be conceived under the aspect of 'ornament'; out of this hostility arose not only the stripped classicism favoured by totalitarian regimes, but also the ideal of architecture as a kind of *Gesamtkunstwerk*, which can be aesthetically serious only if the total conception remains within the architect's control. Serious building seems to demand an untouched space, like Brasilia or Chandigarh; if the space is not available it is produced by a work of clearance, such as preceded the great exhibitions, the 'festival' of Britain,

PLATE 74 L. W. Wyatt: project for Downing College, Cambridge

PLATE 75 William Porden: project for Downing College, Cambridge

and the building of the Barbican. It is not the street that matters but the 'site', and the site itself is often forced into unnatural regularities, or filled out with regular blocks which leave unsightly voids of pavement, ugly projections of wall, or some desultory patch of earth where a stark little sapling struggles to grow. This is not to condemn 'exhibition architecture' as inappropriate to the life of everyday. Some of the finest detailing that the modern movement has witnessed was displayed in the immaculate lines and cruciform columns of the German pavilion at the Barcelona exhibition. Its architect, Mies van der Rohe, is one of the few who have devoted their energies to the task of transferring the

PLATE 76 Window in Piazza S. Eustachio, Rome

sense of visual aptness to buildings (such as the famous Seagram Building) whose scale might at first seem to defy its proper application. Nevertheless, it is a singular fact that the baroque architects, who have so often been admired for the changes which they effected in the canons of space, proportion and form, acted without the aid of any massive clearance, fitting their churches and palaces into cramped corners and curving streets, or placing their buildings, like the churches of Wren, as landmarks to punctuate the unbroken line of the vernacular buildings which they were to grace. The changes in form and proportion achieved by these architects were arrived at through the transformation of detail, through the shape and cut of balustrades, cornices, niches and columns, indeed, through the complete re-articulation of architectural parts. This respect for detail enabled the baroque architects to work satisfactorily in any space available. Their love of detail was so great that Guarini, for example, accompanied his published designs not merely with an illustration of the completed façade, but with fragments of moulding, represented with equal emphasis, out of a conviction that the experience of the whole could be envisaged only from a sense of the visual intricacy of its parts.[4]

Some might object that there is something peculiar to the classical tradition, in that it attempts to crystallize the sense of detail in a received 'vocabulary' of forms. And it is this which enabled the baroque 'language' to present its formal variations with such assurance, while at the same time forestalling any sense of arbitrary ornament or inarticulate parts. But it is misleading here to speak without qualification of a 'vocabulary', and misleading to identify it as the recurrent feature of all 'classical' styles. Perret, who regarded himself as a classicist (on account of his fervent addiction to column and entablature), used no 'vocabulary' of detail. If he lacked a sense of detail, however, it was not for that reason. Nevertheless, it is useful to begin with a baroque example, if only to reiterate our previous warnings against the linguistic analogy, and against the doctrines which seek for the essence of architecture in space and form. I shall begin with an example from high art: later I shall try to say something about the sense of detail in vernacular building.

Consider, then, the conventional classical detail of the shell – the placing of a scallop in the cove of a niche. This is to be found in Roman architecture, and has, from the very beginning of the Renaissance, been an essential element of classical 'vocabulary'.[5] Plate 77 shows an example from Bramante's Tempietto, an example which is fine partly on account of its situation behind stout Doric columns, and its harmonious relation to their strong ascending lines. We find it difficult now to see what a remarkable achievement is represented in this

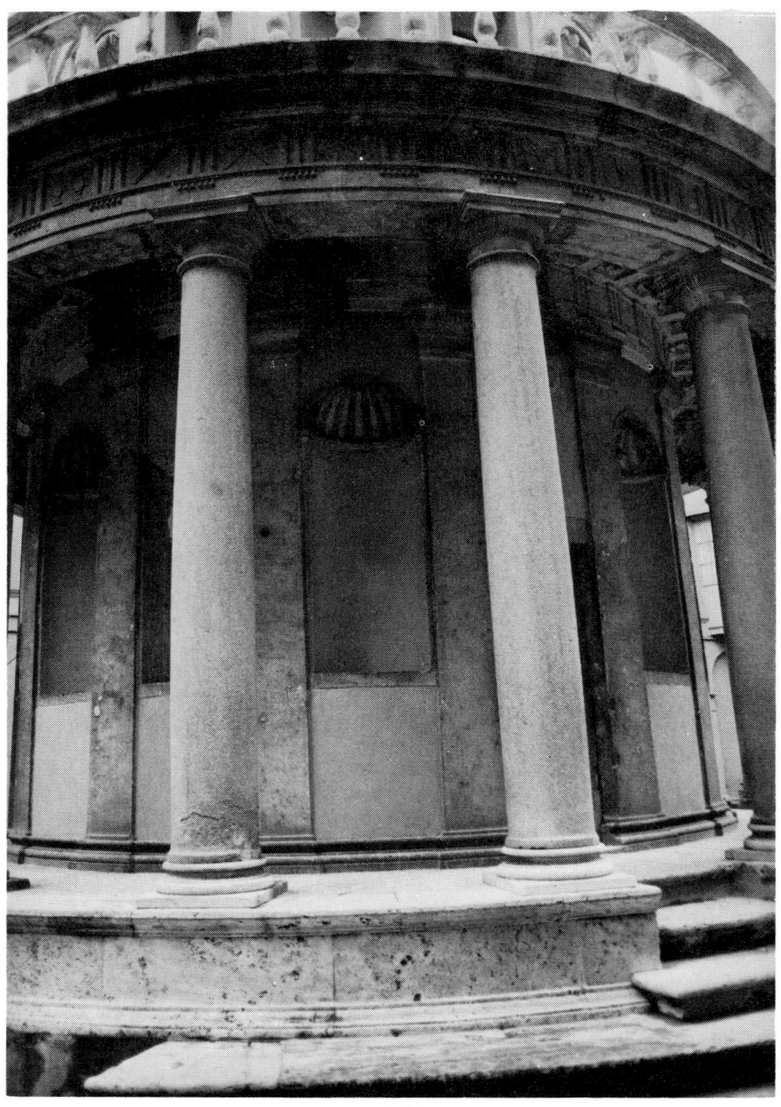

PLATE 77 Bramante: Tempietto, Rome, niche

detail. It is comparable to the discovery of the perfect word for something that we have long been struggling to describe. A form has been achieved which has the significance of a standard, and this opens up new possibilities of meaning. Against the norm created by this detail, we can judge the significance of deviations, for example, of the ingenious varieties of shell niche in the architecture of Borromini (Plates 78 and 79). In the first of these we see just the same juxtaposition against strong ascending lines (in a form which was later used by Wren in the Drum of St Paul's). But the niche has now come forward into the wall space, it has acquired an entablature which follows its form, making it appear as an articulation of the wall rather than a niche cut into it, and at the same time borrowing the form of the full altar surround, as this is seen in the Pantheon. The shell has acquired a flame-like quality which fills the space with movement and light. And yet, if we did not still remember the classical arrangement, and so see the hollow as a crowned niche, as a repository for statues, as a place of rest, the tension between that meaning and the achieved vitality would altogether escape us. Borromini's forms achieve their intelligibility precisely because, in departing from a norm, they at the same time affirm it.

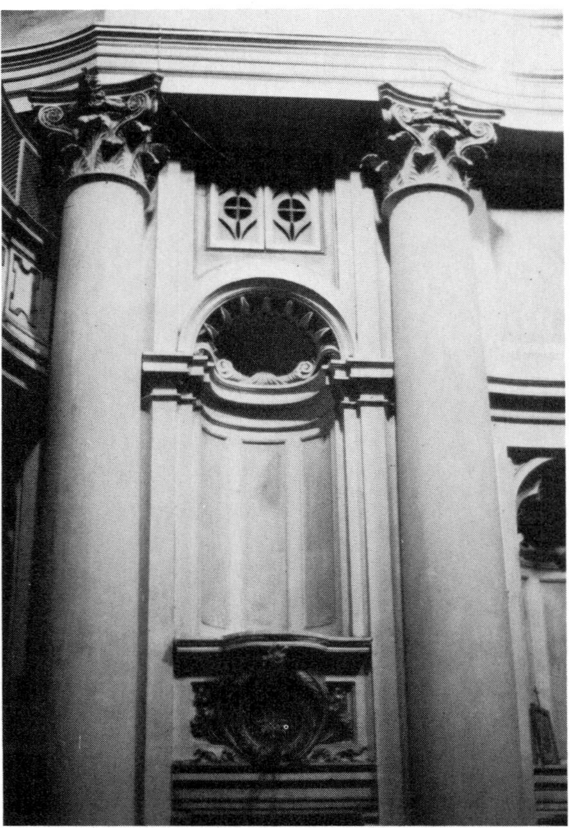

PLATE 78 · F. Borromini: S. Carlino, Rome, niche

PLATE 79 F. Borromini: S. Carlino, Rome, niche

This first example leads us to a point of immense critical and philosophical significance. Wölfflin, in his justly famous analysis of the baroque idiom, described it as 'painterly', meaning to refer to its mobile, fluid, textural quality. But it is not the fluid aspect of a Borromini façade that pleases. Rather, it is Borromini's *way of arriving* at this form, through the progressive development of pierced and moulded parts, each redolent of the constraints of the classical language (see Plates 80 and 81). Wölfflin's words suggest, not this kind of minute articulacy, in which the whole architectural movement develops from the vitality of each individual part, but a kind of imposed fluidity of form, a fluidity which requires not so much the presence of a 'vocabulary' as its absence. Such a style of building, in which everything is moulded into stylized fluid shapes – the style of Gaudì at the Casa Mila, or of Mendelsohn at the Einstein Tower – is one which addresses

PLATE 80 F. Borromini: S. Carlino, Rome, façade

itself to very different interests, interests in which the sense of detail may well be absent or subdued. It is not here that 'meaning' is likely to root itself; enjoyment may perforce remain at the primitive level characteristic of our preferences among colours, our preference for smooth against rough, for straight lines against squiggles. To say that

PLATE 81 F. Borromini: S. Carlino, Rome, façade

is not to disparage the 'concrete baroque'; it is to say something about the *kind* of aesthetic judgement to which it might naturally lend itself.

Equally misleading in this respect, and illustrative of a fundamental fallacy that infects many discussions of modern architecture, a fallacy derived from the persistent inattention to the nature of architectural detail, is Giedion's comparison of the forms of the baroque with the forms of the modern movement. For example, Giedion compares Le Corbusier's plan for Algiers with Lansdown Crescent in Bath (though he might better have compared it with Aalto's Baker House), basing his comparison on the similarity of the overall 'mould' of the forms.[6] As a result, the pomposity of Le Corbusier's conception (the swelling masses of which could have been built only by destroying vast sections of the existing city and altering the outline of both landscape and bay) quite escapes him. He cannot see that, for the modest and considerate Georgian architect, the undulating shape arose out of intricate and detailed attention to the individual house, that it consisted of elements each of which is fully intelligible in terms of a recognized visual tradition, so that the final effect seems more discovered than imposed. The 'harmony' of the Georgian terrace is not that of Hogarth's 'Serpentine Line'. It is more like the *concinnitas* of Alberti, a gentle correspondence of answering parts, a harmony which is perceived because we can 'read' the details. It is through the reading of details that we may come to see one feature of a building as providing an adequate visual reason for another feature, and it is only then that we can have any experience of the unity and coherence of the whole. The context in which this is possible is an *achievement*. It cannot be assumed as the property of every architect at every period of history, even if, until now, it has been so common. Le Corbusier's plan, despite its unbroken lines and its impressive sweep, set beside the achieved form of Lansdown Crescent, seems arrogant, and otherworldly.

The baroque examples illustrate another point which is of great importance. Our way of seeing detail may be inseparable from an apprehension of the activity whereby it was produced. Consider the well-known sculptor's distinction between carving and modelling, and the corresponding distinction between carved and modelled form – distinctions vividly described and elaborated in Kleinian terms by Adrian Stokes.[7] In its most simple version this distinction records the fact that the way in which a form is produced may persist as a characteristic of the form's appearance. As such it is by no means exclusive or exhaustive. There are many processes of shaping – carving, modelling, moulding, chipping, slicing – and all may persist as a felt characteristic of the resulting form. The moulded form, for example, is one that bears an impression: it has been pressed or poured into shape, and whatever roughness it displays results either from the material used or from the mould which once confined it – consider the grain of wooden boards so often impressed on the grey surfaces of modern buildings. The carved form, however does not bear an impression: it would be more correct to say that it exhibits an activity: an activity of cutting, as in the Corinthian capital or the fluted column, or of shaping, as in the slates of a roof, the Tuscan column or the classical 'flight' of stone steps (not to be confused with the 'hover' of moulded steps).

These distinctions are difficult to describe precisely and are by no means absolute. In one sense it is trivially true that the moulded surface, like the carved surface, exhibits activity; there is an activity involved in the production of every shape, even in the production of the fibre-glass bodies of modern yachts. But every sailor sees the difference between the moulded and the constructed hull, and feels in the one the memorial of an activity that he cannot see in the other. To say that this perception has no place either in the love of boats, or in the judgement of their beauty, would be to show no understanding of aesthetics.

The interesting fact then, is not that shapes can be formed in several ways, but that we perceive the results so differently. However small may be the *geometrical* difference between carved and moulded form, from the point of view of perception, in particular of the imaginative perception characteristic of the experience of architecture, the difference will be absolute. In the moulded form what we perceive (in the normal case) is the result, and the finest moulded forms, such as the dome of the Pantheon and the sails of the Sydney Opera House, owe their quality to the rhythm and movement implicit in that result. In the carved form what we appreciate is not the result but the process – or rather, the process as it is *revealed*. The distinction is a fine one, but in aesthetics it is the fine distinctions that matter. The carved form has a peculiar life, and bears on its surface the mark of human labour. It is this mark which transforms the stones of the Gothic cathedral from inert masses into centres of vitality. The Gothic cathedral is, therefore, able to risk the greatest possible height and scale, while never approaching the downcasting inhumanity of the modern skyscraper. Consider the mouldings at Rouen, discussed by Ruskin[8] (Plate 82). The observer cannot see these mouldings simply as shapes, as a sequence of nicely paralleled lines, which might have been pressed into clay or plaster, but which happen to have been cut from stone. Or if he tries to see them in that way, the sense of their intrinsic orderliness will begin to dissolve. This sense comes when the cut of the stone becomes integral to the act of attention, so that the form seems inseparable from the way in which it is achieved. Seen in that way, the moulding gives life to the stone, and imparts to it a lightness and articulation that are truly architectural. It is only by virtue of such a perception that it is possible, for example, to see the Gothic style as Worringer saw it, as the 'spiritualization' of stone.[9] There is no doubt that our perceptions in this particular are capable of a peculiar vividness. Consider the fluted

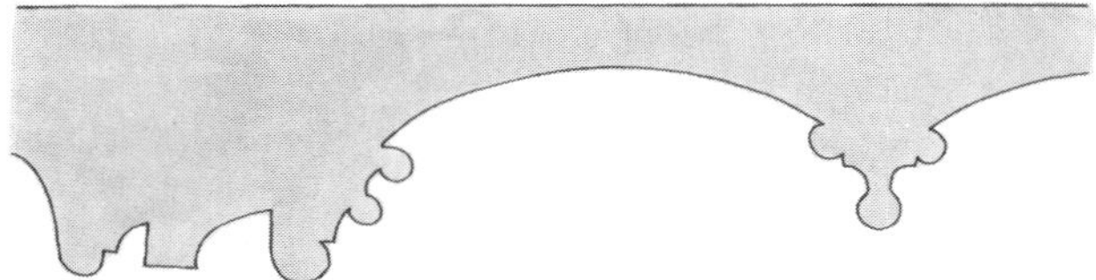

PLATE 82 Section of moulding from Rouen Cathedral

Doric columns of the Parthenon, now chipped and battered to the point where it might seem strange that they should preserve any of their intended clarity of outline. Yet so precise is the workmanship that their carved appearance survives; from whatever distance they are observed, these columns are seen as crisp and sharp, with a freshness that no damage has served to diminish.

It should perhaps be emphasized that this distinction, between carving and moulding, may qualify an experience in defiance of belief. The perception of a form *as* carved is distinct from the perception that it *is* carved, and may coexist with the observation of the form as moulded out of stucco or cast in ferroconcrete (*vide* the crisp stucco mouldings of St Ivo, Plate 14 p. 50). Conversely there are carved forms which wear an inalienably modelled appearance, like the carved brick pilasters and cornices which the Romans (or more probably the Etruscans) introduced into architecture, and which have survived as an effective element in vernacular constructions.

This sculptural distinction is a special case of the more general distinction, which we have already seen exemplified in baroque detailing, between forms imposed and forms discovered, between forms which seem to borrow their nature from some constraining force, and forms achieved through the discovery and articulation of their parts. As we noticed, the curving shapes of a Borromini façade result from the arrangement of considered details, each derived from the classical language, and each marked out by a precision of form that gives power and splendour to the composition. Now the general distinction, between forms arrived at and forms imposed, is likely to be noticed by psychological theories of architecture (theories like that of Adrian Stokes). But perhaps it is in terms of the Hegelian theory of human nature that it is best described. Certainly the Hegelian would wish to argue (for reasons that I shall spell out in the next chapter) that there is a fundamental difference between our attitude to objects which bear the imprint of human labour and our attitude to objects which do not. The machine-made object is the result of human intention; it may not be, for all that, the expression of a human act. If it is seen merely as machine-made, then it must appear to some extent alien to us, seeming to derive its being from a source that we may not identify in ourselves. At least one can say that the carved form is *near* to us, in the way in which a machine-made form may not be; it seems already to be identified with the movement of human life. And the same is true of any form that has the character of being 'discovered' as I have tried to describe this. That is part of what Ruskin had in mind in holding up before the architect his 'Lamp of Life'; in describing the modest adaptability of the true baroque style, its humanizing use of detail, and its pursuit of an intelligible reason for every part, I do no more than praise the architectural manner which Ruskin most supposed to be in want of his Lamp's illumination. At the same time it should be recognized that I have given no critical principle, no irrebuttable reason for preferring some forms against others, or for rejecting in advance the extensive use of pre-cast, moulded, and machine-made parts.

In fact I have so far used the word 'detail' in a somewhat imprecise sense. If there is to be any philosophical description of its significance, it will be necessary to widen the examples I have given in order to include everything that is less than an architectural whole. The mould of a cornice, and the carving of a capital are details; so too are the positioning of mullions, the shaping of corners, the nature of materials. The purpose of the baroque examples was to show how stylistic development may be comprehensible only as a transformation of significant parts. It is through this transformation that new values become rooted in experience. But the process of 'rooting' may attach itself to any detail, irrespective of whether the architect is possessed of a classical 'vocabulary' of forms.

The activity of the builder consists in designing an effective façade and interior, often to fit a site the dimensions of which are predetermined, and with the aim of accommodating his work to the surrounding scene. The proper understanding of detail is the principal capacity that might equip him for this task. Architecture is in this respect no different from the art of clothing. The tailor has a small measure of freedom in his choice of form, of size, of weight and material. But his freedom in these respects is limited by factors outside his own surveyance, and the principal exercise of aesthetic judgement must remain, for him, in the apt and telling choice of parts. His art resides in a study of textures, colours, patterns, and of the appropriate relations among the various sartorial textures and forms. In clothing, as in building, the search for an organizing principle, for an order implicit in detail, leads automatically to the development of style. Without style and without detail, there would be no such thing as decorative art.

It should not be thought, however, that the importance we have ascribed to detail stems only from the *applied* nature of architecture. Naturally, any applied art encounters unforeseen problems, which can be given aesthetic character only when seen under the aspect of ornament. (Suppose one has to furnish a room the dimensions of which have not been chosen, or to embellish a garden wall whose position is dictated not by taste but by law.) In this sense the ideal of an architecture without ornament is a chimaera. For what is ornament? Ornament is nothing more than detail which can be enjoyed and appreciated independently of any dominant aesthetic whole. Without such detail there can be no *application* of art to problems which are not already aesthetic.

Nevertheless, there *are* aesthetic problems in architecture, problems which are, from the artistic point of view, 'self-imposed'. The purity of an art-form is a matter of degree, and it is true that even in the 'purest' of architectural tasks (for example, in the construction of a church in an unconstrained locality, like the church at Todi) there are few merely 'aesthetic' problems. The solution of an architectural problem always involves a synthesis of aesthetic and engineering abilities, the kind of synthesis which is seen at its most magnificent in the great domes of Sancta Sophia, St Peter's and the cathedral of Florence. Nevertheless, even in architecture, there is a relative 'purity', and it is from the 'pure' examples that much aesthetic detail gains its sense. In a wholly pure art (an art conceived in the manner that Stravinsky conceived music[10]), all problems are self-imposed. A large part of art will then consist, not in the solution but in the creation of problems – since there can be no artistic freedom before there is artistic constraint. Consider for example, the self-imposed constraints in music which go under the label of 'form'. Bach did not *have* to compose the canonical sequence of the *Goldberg Variations* in such a way as to incorporate a successively increasing interval between the parts. But he chose to do so, and in creating that problem for himself, he made it possible to delight us by its solution. Here the creation and solution of problems is essential to the aesthetic task. It is this which engages and rewards our attention. In architecture the creation of such problems may seem to have an artificial air. However, that is not so; often the case exactly resembles that of music. Indeed, if architecture did not exhibit any of the deliberate problem-setting that is characteristic of the purer arts, it would be hard to see how many cherished details could have arisen.

PLATE 83 Brunelleschi: Pazzi Chapel, Florence, interior corner

The most obvious illustration of this is the 'problem of the corner', which has obsessed architects from the Greeks to the present day, and perhaps no-one more than Alberti.[11] Brunelleschi, in learning to take a pilaster around a corner, both created and solved a striking aesthetic problem (Plate 83). Instead of doubling the pilaster, as Sangallo does at S. Maria dei Carceri, an effect which leads to an overemphatic corner and destroys the lightness and serenity which are the chief characteristics of the Brunelleschian order, he almost completely buries one of the elements in the wall, leaving only the smallest projecting fragment; in some corners, where proportion requires it, he uses nothing more than two such residual strips. The success of the solution (a solution adopted and refined by many later architects, for example by Gibbs at St Mary le Strand) is measured in terms of constraints that are internal to the problem. It was not necessary for Brunelleschi to adopt his pilaster order, but the delight of it comes precisely from the details to which it gives rise. I add two later examples of self-imposed 'corner problems', the one (Palladio at S. Giorgio Maggiore, Plate 84), because of its brilliant complexity, the other (Mies at the Seagram Building, Plate 85), because it shows that it is not only classicism that generates detail in this way.

Our discussion of the sense of detail has been discursive. But it enables us to return to the notion which we have invoked as central to aesthetic judgement – the notion of the appropriate. If Alberti had meant his conception of the 'parts' of a building to include all that we have

PLATE 84 Andrea Palladio: S. Giorgio Maggiore, Venice, corner of organ loft

included under the head of 'detail', then we must surely agree with his description of the aesthetic sense, as aiming at a right and proper fitting together of the parts of a building. Each part must be bound to the others in some relation of 'appropriateness', a relation which enables us to see the existence of one part as providing a reason for the existence of another. We can now approach this thought more closely.

In the example given to illustrate the genesis of taste, and to show its inevitable association with 'expressive' meaning, we remarked on the initial *primitiveness* of aesthetic choice. Some forms, shapes and colours

PLATE 85 Mies van der Rohe: Seagram Building, New York, external corner

look right; others do not. But we also noticed an inherent tendency to transcend the primitive, to proceed to a reasoned reflection on the nature and significance of architectural choice. The reflections thus engaged in transfigure the appearance of their object, and so confirm themselves as part of imaginative understanding.

Now it is clear from Alberti's account that 'beauty' interested him far less than the idea of the 'appropriate' (*aptus, decens, commodus, proprius*)[12] and his definition of the former can be seen as an extension of his concept of the latter. It is not difficult to see what he had in mind. It is the notion of the 'appropriate' that sums up the process of reasoned 'fitting together' which is the primary intellectual gesture in any decorative art. And if it is important for an architect to have a style, it is partly because it enables him to employ this concept to better effect and, as it were, more concretely. Style is not the accumulation of detail, but its fitting deployment. This (which might at first seem to be a simple truth about 'classicism') is in fact definitive of style, and we shall not understand style until we see how intimately are all its workings penetrated by 'appropriate detail'. Consider the so-called 'international style' (the style which Gropius defended to Dr Goebbels as uniquely German in its synthesis of classical and Gothic forms[13]). This too contains its characteristic details – metal fenestration, wrapped corners, sharp horizontals, delicate verticals – but it is no more an accumulation of these details than the classical style is an accumulation of Vitruvian parts. It is possible that its affected disdain for ornament has made the style difficult to employ effectively in constrained locations. But its claim to be an autonomous aesthetic force (and one which can be seen at work not only in the factories of the Bauhaus and the houses of Maxwell Fry but also much later, for example in the works of Venturi and Rauch) rests largely on its creation of details that can be seen not merely to coexist but also to answer one another, as part answers part in the classical style.

What, then, does it mean to say that a detail is appropriate? We should notice first of all that this judgement is not exclusive: other details might have been equally appropriate. What is appropriate is not necessarily what is best. Our sense of the appropriate develops through recognizing multiple choices and through seeking a potential order among them.[14] It does not aim at rule-governed punctilio, but at easy flexibility, at a sense of what is sensible, fitting, apt. This flexibility, as we have noticed, hampers analysis: the concept of the 'appropriate', like other concepts which articulate aesthetic response, eludes explicit definition. Nevertheless it is possible to give a sense of what it means, by filling in the background of expectations, customs and attitudes against which it is deployed.

We must recognize at once that the concept of the 'appropriate' is of universal application, and that it would be wrong to confine it to some specifically 'aesthetic' usage from which its sense derives. We speak of what is appropriate in every sphere of rational conduct: appropriate behaviour, appropriate feelings, appropriate gestures, appropriate dress, food, wine, décor. Nor should this permeation of the practical surprise us. For in nothing that we do can our aim serve to determine the manner of its execution. Even in an activity which is bent as completely as possible to the realization of a given end – and such activities are few enough – there will be many equally effective means to it. It follows that there is something incomplete in the reasoning ability of a man who does not reflect on the various ways of going about what he has to do; who does not attempt, not just to do it, but to do it appropriately.

Nevertheless, someone might still try to analyse the concept of the appropriate in terms of the relation of means to end. He might say that, in determining what is appropriate, a man considers what he does, not only in relation to the immediate aim, but in relation to the totality of aims which may be furthered or thwarted by his action. For example, the sense of appropriate behaviour at table is dictated by the desire not to offend or alienate one's neighbours, the desire not to splash food and drink on one's face and clothes, the desire to eat and digest without pain, pathos or eructation. To evolve a canon of the 'appropriate' behaviour is, it might be said, simply to steer a course through varied disasters, to achieve an 'Optimal solution' to varied aims. This view hearkens back to the design theorist's approach to architecture, as a kind of 'problem-solving'; but, as we saw in chapter 2, that approach reflects no serious understanding of practical reason. The greater part of our aims cannot be stated in advance of their realization, and the attempt to find a 'solution', in terms of means to end, will usually involve the arbitrary limitation of the problem it is proposed to solve. This must be so in those activities which reflect the 'aesthetics of everyday life', activities like tailoring, decorating and building, which – because we have to live in the most intimate contact with their products – cannot be separated from the *Weltanschauungen* of those who engage with them. In these areas, the notion of the appropriate develops beyond what can be comprehended in the relation of means to end, and comes to stand rather as an intimation of ends that cannot all be stated, as an indication, in concrete immediate terms, of aims and satisfactions which – because the occasion for their expression has only now arisen – can be revealed in no other way. For consider the judgement of the appropriate as this develops in the field of manners. There is no doubt that here a man at first learns simply to understand and use certain conventions, conventions which may vary between groups and communities, but which have in common the aim of creating settled expectations, against the background of which the true freedom of social intercourse may develop.[15] But a man who remains punctiliously ruled by those conventions, who shows no ability to adapt or reject them, to look on them with humour or irony, in particular, no ability to do what is appropriate in those circumstances where convention denies its help, such a man is, socially speaking, a disaster. And it is impossible to cure him of his ineptitude simply by reminding him of some overriding aim – say, that of always pleasing others and himself. For he must also learn when it is appropriate to displease others and to displease himself. How else is he supposed to respond to rudeness, injustice and abuse? To acquire the art of the appropriate, he must learn to see in his own behaviour the intimations of a success to which he cannot coherently devote himself before he is already on the verge of achieving it. The art of manners is the art of seeing what is apt before knowing exactly what success will consist in.

To illustrate the point I shall take an example that may at first seem somewhat flippant, but which in fact has an important heuristic purpose, the example of holding a fork. In Japan, where such things have been regarded for centuries as the culmination of all aesthetic endeavour, and where the masters of the tea ceremony have been revered as artists of the highest order,[16] it would scarcely be considered outrageous to elucidate the nature of art through a consideration of table manners. We do not share the tragic outlook which makes such an emphasis possible; nevertheless, even for us, the phenomena of manners have what we are inclined to call an 'aesthetic' meaning. The important thing, it might be said, is to do what you and your neighbours find decorous. But to say that is already to concede that there might be something serious involved in the matter. For consider how a particular way of holding a fork might be justified. Our desire to describe this as an aesthetic matter derives from the fact that, in the first instance, a practice will be justified in terms of how it looks: it looks nicer that way. But reasoning will stop there only accidentally; the question why it looks nicer at once arises, and there is no proper answer that does not go to the heart of a social problem. It looks nicer because it results in more harmonious or more elegant movement, because it brings the food not directly to the mouth but with a sideways motion that requires no stretching of the jaws. And that is naturally more pleasant to see; for a wide open, frontally attacking mouth has a careless, greedy, egocentric look, a look which is in some way discreditable. And so on. Clearly this process of reasoning stops short of nothing that is morally significant. To argue in this way about the 'decorous' quality of a certain gesture is to use concepts that derive their significance from their application throughout the realm of moral life. The concept of the decorous – the *decus* which Cicero placed at the heart of moral virtue[17] – is but another concept through which the world of personal choice is transcended into that of moral understanding. (Dignity might be the highest of a man's ideals, and Horace was in no way detracting from the sublimity of patriotic self-sacrifice when he described it as *dulce et decorum*.)

What we notice in this example is the fact that, once one begins to reason in terms of an appropriate appearance, it is impossible to confine one's reasoning to conceptions that have a uniquely 'aesthetic' sense. Indeed, it is doubtful that there are such things as 'aesthetic' terms – terms whose meaning is given simply by their use in aesthetic judgement. This point was implicitly recognized by Alberti, each of whose many articulations of aesthetic judgement employs terms which derive their meaning from a wider usage, indeed from the whole structure of practical reasoning. Even the *concinnitas* upon which he put so much aesthetic emphasis had, for him, a significance that was primarily moral. He had probably derived the term from Cicero's *Orator*, where it denotes a kind of sweetness and persuasiveness of sound, and used it in several early works, in particular in the *Della Famiglia*, to refer to the harmony and grace intrinsic to civilized behaviour. It is this moral significance that Alberti sought to transfer to the aesthetic sphere. By thus always using terms which take their meaning from a wider usage he was simply following – as the concept of the 'appropriate' compels us to follow – the path from aesthetic taste to practical reason, from the sense of how things should look to the judgement of how they should be.[18] The sense of the appropriate exists as an embodiment of moral thought, as a perception in the immediate here and now, of aims and values that lie buried in distant and barely accessible regions of existence. In a very real sense, the cultivation of the aesthetic values intrinsic to good manners – the cultivation of 'visual decorum' – is part of a process of bringing order to the otherwise nebulous choices of individual life. Through the sense of the 'appropriate' a man may herald in the immediate present those aims in his life which are not immediately statable. The pursuit of the appropriate appearance is, therefore, an ineliminable part of knowing what to do, in those activities for which, because of their complexity, no single aim can be enunciated. And architecture is such an activity. Here too, then, the sense of the appropriate is a part of being engaged in the task completely, of being constantly on the verge of transcending the immediacy of present impulse, of perceiving from afar the reality of distant aims. To apply that sense is to transform an inert body of 'problems' into a comprehensive practical task.

My examples of the sense of detail have been taken from high art, partly in order to illustrate the presence in architecture of those autonomous problems which characterize the highest forms of aesthetic endeavour. But, as I began by saying, the sense of detail has an additional importance in architecture on account of the applied nature of the art. Consider the vernacular architecture that surrounds us. Is it really surprising that, despite its irregularities, disproportions and clumsy ornament, the vernacular architecture of the seventeenth century remains so pleasing, while that of the twentieth century (or at least the twentieth century of collectivist propaganda) seems so often hostile, alien, indicative of a world at variance with individual fulfilment? Suppose, for example, that one were to construct a wall, in 'brutalist' fashion, with no detailing whatsoever. All that matters is that it should be of sufficent height and length, and sufficient strength to withstand predicted blows. One forgets material, using poured grey concrete, or rough breeze-blocks. Most people would say of such a wall that it gives no rest to the eye, that it invites no contemplation, even that it repels the gaze. Any question of the appropriateness of part to part is avoided, and the appropriateness of the material would seem impossible to describe, unless as means to an end.

Suppose now that the builder attempts to articulate his wall, to display its shape and form as things arrived at, as the products of an activity whose rules, precedents, aims and examples, can be seen as implicit in the separate parts. The railway wall in Plates 86a and 86b

PLATE 86a and b Westbourne Park Villas, London, railway wall

provides a simple example of such vernacular articulation. Its precedents are partly classical – the successive buttresses are also half-formed pilasters, the swelled base is a vestigial pedestal, the cast concrete coping a partial cornice. The buttresses have strong quoins of hard-baked blue brick, matching the base, while the interstices are soft, matt, pink brick, scuffed and pitted with use. The wall follows the street, but in its own rhythm, the vestigial 'Order' constraining it to rise and fall stepwise, thus attractively counterpointing the scarcely visible curvature of the pavement. The buttresses answer each other, each leading the eye onward between points of rest. The backward curve of the upper wall gives an effective emphasis to the 'cornice' and enhances the apparent weight of the whole. The pleasure that is naturally felt in passing such a wall in not simply the recognition of sound construction or workmanship. It is a sense of the natural fittingness of part to part, of an achieved articulation which, because of its amenability to the aesthetic question, casts the wall in human form. As our account of the 'appropriate' suggests, the correspondence of part with part is also a correspondence of outer and inner, of building and observer. The judgement of the appropriate has its origin in us. It serves, even in these vernacular examples, to transfer to the object the demands and values of the man who studies it. The properly detailed wall has an accumulation of moral character, it wears a sympathetic expression, and unlike the brutalist invention with which I have compared it, it inhabits the same world as the man who passes it.

None of this is to suggest anything like a *rule* of taste – only a prejudice in favour of comprehensible detail. Of course, the vernacular

PLATE 87 Quirinal Hill, Rome, wall

example shows forms borrowed and adapted from established traditions of ornament and there is no doubt that these traditions made it easy for the builder to envisage the effect of his finished structure. It is indeed one of the strongest features of the classical tradition that it lends itself to the articulation of spaces, and can be used to render even windowless walls tense with human significance (see Plate 87). At times the effect may be less serene than painful, as in Hawksmoor's daring composition shown in Plate 88, brave, soldierly and as full of fettered strength as a Michelangelo captive. It may be that we have lost

PLATE 88 Nicholas Hawksmoor: St Mary Woolnoth, London

the rich tradition which made such an expression possible, which made it possible to transfer every variety of human character to the inanimate face of walls or windows. But the *search* for meaning in architecture, whether in the vernacular or in the highest art, will always require that sense of the appropirate, manifest, as we have seen, in the fitting correspondence of part with part.

This is all very well, it will be said, but have you not left out of consideration a great many factors which are central to aesthetic judgement – factors like balance, proportion, line and unity? Simply to concentrate on the sense of the 'appropriate' is hardly to provide an account, either of the meaning of these terms, or of our reason for being interested in the qualities which they denote. This objection is a serious one, if only because it brings us back to the central and recurrent problem in the philosophy of art. The reader will have noticed that, apart from making critical remarks about a suggestion of Alberti's, I have offered no definition of 'beauty', nor of 'proportion', nor indeed of any other 'aesthetic' term. This ommission has been deliberate: for I have tried to dispense with the notion of an 'aesthetic' term, and to expound aesthetic judgement by exploring the state of mind, and the mode of reasoning, in which it is based. Until that is done, no 'definition' of aesthetic terms will be other than empty or partisan, other than an apology for some particular, possibly dispensable canon of taste, without power to cast light on the nature of aesthetic judgement. I have described a process of reasoned reflection, by means of which an immediate experience becomes the 'sign' or herald of social, intellectual and moral values. My concern has been to describe that process of reflection while assigning no particular role to the individual concepts employed in it. And, as I have suggested, the concepts used in aesthetic judgement have a peculiarly detached and 'fluid' quality, deriving their meaning primarily from some non-aesthetic use, and seeming to float free of any settled basis for their application.[19] Kant even held that they are not really concepts at all, that the aesthetic judgement is 'free from concepts', and therefore that a term like 'beauty' refers to no identifiable feature of the objects to which it is applied.[20] Whether or not we agree with Kant, we must at least beware of providing definitions and analyses, when the form of judgement with which we are dealing has as its aim not theoretical knowledge but the transformation of experience. Concepts like the appropriate and the beautiful float freely in this process of aesthetic argument, serving to direct our attention now to this thing, now to that; they take their sense, not from the objects to which they are applied, but from the state of mind which they serve to articulate.

Nevertheless, we can still say something in reply to the objection. Our exploration of detail has put at the heart of aesthetic judgement a certain sense of the question 'why?' – why this, here? – where the request is for a reason that refers to the way a thing *looks*. Now if we were to ask for an account of the meaning of 'proportion', say, it would be precisely in terms of this question that we should frame it. The classical, neo-classical, revivalist and Corbusian 'definitions' of proportion were not definitions but rather canons of procedures. The mathematical theory of proportion, for example, did not, in any of its neo-Platonic variants, purport to say what the word 'proportion' *means*, but only to give a rule or procedure for achieving proportionate parts. And, as we saw, that rule could claim no universal validity, precisely because it fell short of exhausting the meaning of the term. Essentially, what is meant by proportion can be understood as we have understood the concept of the appropriate. Proportion is exhibited by a building whose parts – judged in terms of their shape and size rather than in terms of their ornamentation – provide adequate visual reason for one another. The 'unbalanced' proportion is the one which provokes the question 'why?' – why this shape, why so tall, so wide, so long? The need to formulate a visual answer to that question might indeed lead to the development of a *canon* of proportion – and in doing so it will play a vital part in the development of style. (Our example of the builder fully explains this.) But there is never any need, in the practice of aesthetic judgement, to say what proportion 'really means', in the sense of pinning down the term to some one property or set of properties which provide its true aesthetic sense. Its sense is given by a certain comprehensive role in the practice of aesthetic argument, and cannot be understood, any more than the concept of the appropriate can be understood, except in the light of a theory which shows the relation between aesthetic reasons and ordinary practical judgement. It is such a theory that I have tried to present. The suggestions of this paragraph ought to make clear that the understanding of proportion and the understanding of detail are far from being rivals in the pursuit of aesthetic meaning: on the contrary, they are complementary aspects of a single process, and neither makes sense except in terms of the reasoning with which that process is imbued.

The reader should evince no surprise, therefore, if he is offered no definition of 'beauty', or if the enterprise of defining 'beauty' is made to seem so unimportant. It seems to me that we should do better to forget about all that. To accord to beauty its traditional emphasis is not only to elevate it above a cluster of aesthetic terms, all of which deserve equal prominence; it is also to suggest that our problem is one of meaning, rather that one of the philosophy of mind. It is in studying the state of mind that underlies aesthetic judgement that we notice the priority of detail, and the predominance of the concept of the 'appropriate' in all aesthetic choice. It is these which determine the aesthetic application of the question 'why?'. The architect may lack the talent or the confidence to face up to that question – he might resort to all kinds of cheap expedients, such as the arrangement of windows in a 'random' sequence, the deliberate condensing or retracting of all approachable parts, in order to avoid its corrosive operation. But such a retreat from style is as valueless as it is futile: there is no possibility of escape from the imaginative eye, and the universal, irrebuttable significance of our question will lead the eye inevitably onwards, to the point of satisfaction or disgust. It is not surprising, therefore, that the aesthetic sense seems constrained to pursue some ideal of objectivity, or that it spills over at every point into the questions of morality that 'aestheticism' has traditionally sought to avoid.

But what now of this objectivity, and this morality? Is the first obtainable, the second describable? I shall try to say something in answer to those questions; ultimately, I shall argue, they are not two questions, but one.

10 CONCLUSION: ARCHITECTURE AND MORALITY

WE FIND ourselves confronting the most difficult of all questions in philosophical aesthetics, the question of the objectivity of critical judgement. Is there a right and wrong in architecture? If so, how is it determined? Often this question is approached in a naive spirit, in full confidence that the distinction between the objective and the subjective is as clear as it seems to be exhaustive. If our discussion of taste has produced no other conviction, it must at least have produced the conviction that this confidence is unwarranted. In one sense, it seems, aesthetic judgement is subjective – for it consists in the attempt to articulate an individual experience. But in another sense it is objective, for it aims to *justify* that experience, through presenting reasons that are valid for others besides oneself.

However, a judgement can aim at objectivity without achieving it, and the crucial point, the point upon which the validity of all critical argument must hang, is whether that achievement is possible here. Now it is important to separate objectivity from truth. Critical judgement is a form of practical reasoning, it consists in upholding or criticizing an experience, in terms of the appropriateness or inappropriateness of its object. Such reasoning is practical because its conclusion is not something believed but something felt.[1] It would be misleading, therefore, to say that critical judgement aims to show the truth of something; practical reasoning tells us not what to think, but what to feel or do. But it may still be objective. This point was made forcefully by Kant, in his two great works on ethics and aesthetics.[2] Kant held, for example, that moral judgements are imperatives – hence they cannot be true or false. What they describe, if anything, is not the real world in which we live but the ideal world at which we aim (the Kingdom of Ends). Despite that, he argued, a moral judgement is objective, since it is possible to uphold it as valid for all rational beings, irrespective of their particular constitution, circumstances or desire. There is a valid way of supporting moral judgement – validity amounts to the fact that there are judgements which can be rejected only through misunderstanding them. The Kantian theory is a bold one, and I have suggested only its outline: a full investigation would have to make clear what is meant by standards without truth: can one deny the place of truth in moral reasoning, for example, and still rely at least on the elementary standard of consistency? But the theory is of interest in presenting a general idea of objectivity; it suggests how the idea of objectivity might be expressed in those realms of human thought that are not in any ordinary sense 'scientific'.

Could we, then, introduce such a notion of objectivity into aesthetic argument? Many philosophers – including Kant – have thought that we cannot, precisely because the endpoint of such argument is always an experience. A critical argument is accepted only persuasively, as it were, only when the opponent has been brought to share the experience of the man with whom he disputes.[3] Certainly, this intimate relation to experience already suggests that no critical conclusion can be reached by the application of a rule; each case is possessed of a certain uniqueness and must be argued for without detriment to its autonomy. But if there are no rules for aesthetic judgement there can be no rules for building, and so no architectural laws, besides those of function and stability. How then can we speak of objectivity?

It is certainly true, as we have seen, that the attempts to give universal laws of building have been peculiarly desultory, and there is never the slightest difficulty in upsetting the critical judgements which derive from them. But the absence of universal laws is not in itself tantamount to subjectivity. It may nevertheless be possible that a given form of architecture, and given works of architecture, are better fitted as objects of aesthetic interest than their rivals. For we might be able to show, in respect of these forms and examples, that there is a right way of seeing them, and that, in so seeing them, the aesthetic impulse is in some way satisfied. It is worth again considering the comparison with moral judgements. On some views morality consists in a set of rules of conduct, and the philosophical problem is simply how these rules might be justified.[4] This legalistic approach to morality is not one that records very accurately the real reflections of moral men, most of whom would be reluctant to specify absolute rules of conduct, even if they find no difficulty in recognizing acts which merit praise or blame. And the ability to recognize right actions partly stems from an ability to recognize good men – to recognize moral virtue *in* action, to recognize that a particular action expresses dispositions that one should emulate or praise, dispositions towards which one 'warms' in the manner uniquely characteristic of moral beings. If this thought is true – and there is certainly a long tradition of moral philosophers from Aristotle on who have agreed with it – then we can understand what is right and wrong not because we possess some catalogue of rules, but because we understand the motives and feelings of the man of virtue. Understanding the virtuous man we can, when the occasion arises, imagine what *he* would do. But the ensuing precept, even if reached thus indirectly, and in defiance of any universal law, may still be objective. It will be as objective as the notion of virtue from which it stems, and if it can be shown (as Aristotle tried to show) that our ideal of virtue is not arbitrary but on the contrary imposed on us by the very nature of rational choice, then all moral judgements will be in some measure objective. All moral judgements would derive their validity from reasoning which no man can reasonably reject.[5]

There is a comparable indirect approach to objectivity in aesthetics. We might try – like the Freudians and Hegelians considered in chapter 6 – to give some very general account of the value of aesthetic experience, and from that account derive an imaginative understanding of the kind of architecture, and the kind of outlook on architecture, which would best reward aesthetic attention. Our reasoning might be wholly objective, in the sense that it might depend on considerations which no rational man would be at liberty to reject. It is unlikely that we will derive from this procedure any fixed body of rules or precepts. But we will have a clearer notion of what an objective aesthetics might amount to, and if we can divorce our idea of validity from the rigid canons of a particular architectural theory, then so much the better.

We are to consider, then, the value of aesthetic experience – the relation between the aesthetic and the moral at its most abstract level. It has been my contention throughout this work that aesthetic understanding, in the sense of the imaginative contemplation of an object for its own sake, is an important part of everyday life, and that, however dispensable may be thought the higher or more personal forms of art – however conceivable it might be that there should be men without taste in music, painting, or the use of words – it is inconceivable that there should be rational beings from whom the aesthetic impulse is wholly absent. In so far as there is – as I have urged that there is – an aesthetics of everyday life, all men must to some extent engage in it, or, if they fail to do so, have a defective understanding of the world. In every task, however functional, there are infinite ways of proceeding. All our choices are extracted from a chaos of functionally equivalent alternatives, and in all choices which affect, not just present purposes, but also distant (and perhaps unstateable) aspirations, it is the non-utilitarian residue that is paramount. To build well is to find the appropriate form, and that means the form which answers to what endures, not what expires. The appropriate form ministers, as I have argued, not just to present purposes, but to a sense of ourselves as creatures with identities transcending the sum of present purpose and desire. And if the appropriate form is the one that looks right a man must, if he is to be able to reason fully about practical matters, acquire the sense of visual validity. This is as true of building as it is of furnishing, clothes and manners. The sense of visual validity is a sense which every man has reason to acquire, and in acquiring it, I shall argue, he will see his activities as part of an order greater than himself; he will think of himself as responding to imperatives which have their origin in a rational and objective point of view.

Now practical reason aims at practical knowledge – at knowing what to do and feel – just as theoretical reason aims at theoretical knowledge, knowing what to think or believe.[6] Theoretical knowledge consists in the reliable apprehension of the truth, and therefore must adopt truth as its proper aim. Practical knowledge, since it does not deal primarily with beliefs, but with actions and feelings, stands in need of some proper substitute for truth, some ideal of success in action (or emotion) which may constitute the aim and reward of practical reasoning. Such an ideal (the ideal of happiness) must – if my arguments have any force – allow a prominent place to the aesthetic understanding, since without taste a man will often remain in partial ignorance of what to do – even though he may have a simpler and more direct approach to practical problems, and might be tempted even to misconstrue his simplicity and directness as a higher form of knowledge. But the argument so far developed is insufficient; to put it convincingly will require the adumbration of philosophy of a practical reason, and that, in its turn, will be impossible without an exposition of the concept of the self. It is of some interest, nevertheless, to see how the argument might be presented in its full philosophical elaboration.

I have argued that the judgement of the 'appropriate' plays a part in bringing together, in the immediate action, purposes and values which it may be impossible now to state or pursue, but which are connected, all the same, with the possibility of satisfaction. I pointed out in chapter 2 that it is impossible to explain what is involved in sartorial choice without taking account of the fact that here aesthetic taste is central.

Taste, I went on to argue, unites in its object all the unstateable aims which determine satisfaction, and transforms the confusion of utilitarian reasoning into the apprehension of a serious end. Aesthetic judgement fills the world with intimations of value – and this is perhaps part of what Kant had in mind in arguing that in aesthetic attention the object is always seen as in some sense 'purposeful', though without specific purpose.[7] In the choice of clothes, as in all other areas where appearance counts, a man will naturally try to herald his adopted character in his present choice – otherwise reason engages only with transient satisfactions.

Now there is a temptation to think that aesthetic understanding, being contemplative, must also be passive, a kind of loss of the self in experience, to the detriment of activity. On the contrary, the aesthetic task precisely involves making experience itself into something active. All that I have *now*, apart from the present purposes which caused me to build, clothe or decorate, is the *experience* of what I make. To engage now with those parts of my life which are not of immediate practical interest, to absorb into the present choice the full reality of a life which stretches into distant moral space, I must lift that experience out of the immediate and transform it into a sign of something universal. Hence my need, as a rational creature, for a concept of the appropriate, a concept that can be applied directly to experience so as to transform it into a sign of permanent values.

As an example, consider the two forks illustrated in Plate 89, one of a contemporary Swedish design, the other of the 'fiddle-pattern' that has been more or less traditional ever since the classical language was rediscovered and adapted to the needs of daily life. Someone might praise the 'clean', 'functional' lines of the first, in comparison with the 'ornate' or 'heavy' quality of the second; he might give these comments as part of the reason for a preference. The judgement, which seems at first to be merely utilitarian, turns out on inspection to be entirely aesthetic. For the function of a fork, in so far as it can be confined to an explicit aim, is to raise food from plate to mouth. The first fork, as is well enough known, is less well adapted to that end. Its short, fattened prongs hold the food less securely than the narrow prongs of its rival, its thin stem slips in the hand, and its tactile sense is of something to be put down rather than held. By contrast, the carefully modelled base of the second fork fits the palm of the hand; its collar makes it easier to steady, and

PLATE 89 Two forks

removes the risk of slipping onto the food. Everything about the classical fork is manifestly 'comfortable' and even its weight adds to the utility, enabling it to balance properly and rest more securely on the edge of a plate. The ideal of 'functionality' displayed by the Swedish fork is an *aesthetic* ideal; but it is an ideal that fails to translate itself from visual into practical values. The search for a pure line, redolent of unfussy function, leads to a childishness of outline, a streamlined, unstable fluidity of form, ill-adapted either to the uses of the table or to the demands of the aesthetic sense. The classical fork, proportioned like a column, with base and capital, and with a frieze of prongs, partakes of a language rich in implications. There is no difficulty in repeating these forms, in finding knife and spoon to go with the fork, in integrating all three into a visual ideal of the covered table. The eye rests with satisfaction on the furled cusp of its handle; all its uses seem present in the form, and no hesitation can be felt in translating them into action. The two forks bear the insignia of contrasting life-styles – the pursuit of uncluttered function (not as a fact but as a symbol) and the leisured movement which despite its superficial contempt for function arrives rather more naturally at its aim. In choosing between the forms on aesthetic grounds one will also declare allegiance to one or other style of life; the true critical judgement must therefore involve the kind of comparison of life-style that I have been making. It is absurd to think that there could be an education of the aesthetic sense in these things which was not also on education of practical reason – that did not attempt to give some account, however sketchy, of satisfactions which are not simply matters of visual choice.

Now let us consider what happens when aesthetic considerations are ignored – when even the medicinal aesthetics of Scandinavia is displaced as a luxury or irrelevance. Consider, for example, the construction of roads, in particular of the 'inner relief roads' and 'ring roads' which have become familiar objects of the urban environment. There is no doubt that roads have a single dominant purpose. They enable men to move at their convenience from one point to another. But the phrase 'at their convenience' immediately suggests that this 'purpose' is far from transparent. It is clear that, whatever satisfaction attended the travelling from one point to another before the building of the road must attend it – and in greater measure – afterwards. The pursuit of an aim is reasonable only in proportion to the satisfaction of attaining it. To produce a state of affairs which is found less satisfactory than that which preceded it is necessarily irrational. (This, perhaps, is one of those basic principles of practical reason which all men would be constrained to recognize as objectively valid.) It could be said, on this ground, that the inner roads at Coventry are unreasonable in a way that the Sistine Roads in Rome (for example) are not, even though they each have the same ostensible aim, which is ease of movement.

Sixtus V aimed at an easy access to the holy places, to the great basilicas, and wished to create a proper path for ceremonial processions. Yet he – and his architect Fontana – regarded visual coherence and visual harmony as an essential ingredient in that aim. The new streets were to be faced by strong and splendid buildings, adorned with statues, obelisks and fountains, flanked by doors and windows, cornices and porticoes, of a kind acceptable to contemporary taste.[8] These streets have succeeded not only in preserving the mystery and sanctity of the holy places, but also the interest and charm of the journey to them, and the incidental rewards of pilgrimage. They have proved adaptable beyond the partial extinction of their original aim, and the journey through them remains satisfactory even in an age without religion. By contrast it is impossible to envisage any satisfaction remaining in the journey across Coventry, once the particular employment of the particular individuals who are forced to make it is extinguished. The total energetic absorption of the motorway-builder in the single end of speed,[9] since it proceeds without any true concept of 'convenience', leads to a loss of any knowledge why speed is important – why it is better that men should live in a world of ceaseless rapid movement than in a world where they are satisfied to remain forever where they are. If, on the other hand, the motorway-builders had been concerned – like the planners of Los Angeles – with the *aesthetic* of speed, seeking to create, as valid objects of visual communication, roads, tracks, junction and flyovers all expressive of an *idea* of rapid movement, whatever their actual use, then necessarily their sense of what they are doing changes from the mindless pursuit of function to the deliberate cultivation of a style of life. The builders of such roads were clearly motivated by a sense of what it would be like to live with the products of their labour; some wider practical intimation – however mistaken it might prove to be in its underlying view of human nature – informed their calculations.

This knowledge of what it will be like to fulfil one's aim is essential to the reasoned pursuit of it, and it is a form of knowledge that is both intrinsically practical (unlike the theoretical knowledge of means to end) and also incipiently aesthetic. To know what something is like in advance of the experience of it, is to have an imaginative apprehension of that experience. The ability to participate imaginatively in future experiences is one of the aims of aesthetic education, and it is only by the cultivation of present discrimination, and the present sense of what is appropriate, that it can be properly achieved. It is this aesthetic education which has enabled men to build structures and streets that have remained agreeable beyond the expiry of their ephemeral purposes.

The way now lies open to a further argument. For the utilitarian approach to architecture will now have to answer the objections which have been levelled at the utilitarian approach to morals and politics. In particular, it will have to confront the radical and devastating critique of individualism as this was presented by such thinkers as Hegel, Bradley and Marx.[10] It is important to understand the basis of that critique, since it will explain more clearly what is meant by the indispensability of aesthetic taste.

In the sections of the *Critique of Pure Reason* known as the 'Transcendental Deduction' and the 'Paralogisms', Kant had argued against the Cartesian view of the self – the view of the self as a simple, immaterial substance – and also against the empiricist theory of the self as nothing more than a 'bundle' of impressions, beliefs and desires. He argued, against the latter view, that there is indeed a unity which constitutes the self, in addition to the sum of its mental states, but, against Descartes, he held this unity to be 'transcendental', a presupposition of self-knowledge rather than a conclusion of it, and therefore strictly empty of any content, and incapable of giving grounds for the inference made by Descartes, the inference to an immaterial and simple soul. At several points Kant suggested that the true content of this 'transcendental unity' lies in practical knowledge – I know myself in action, but *what* I know cannot be reformulated as a kind of proposition, belief or judgement. The knowledge of myself as a unity is inseparable from a certain *stance* towards the world, the stance, as one might put it, of 'taking responsibility' for the acts, feelings, perceptions and so on which I designate as mine.[11]

This idea was of immediate interest to succeeding philosophers, leading at once to the Hegelian theory of self-realization. According to the Hegelian theory self-knowledge, far from being the effect of private introspection, is in fact a form of publicly accessible activity, the activity of creating and engaging in a public world, and of coming to experience oneself as part of such a world, as one rational being among many.[12] According to this view there can be no self-knowledge in a private world, and no self-knowledge in a world that does not bear the mark of human action. The theory has immediate consequences for the philosophy of practical reason, for it is clear that happiness – the complete satisfaction of a rational being – is possible only if it coexists with sufficient self-consciousness, with a consciousness able to look on itself and on the world and say: it is well with me. Happiness requires, therefore, the realization of the self; and, if the Hegelian view is correct, self-realization is possible only in a world which bears the marks of human action. An immediate outcome of that thought was the Marxist theory of alienated labour, of man so treated by his environment that, finding himself nowhere outside of himself, he could find himself nowhere within. In a very real sense, it was suggested, the alienated man must *lack* a self – at least in some degree. (And it is an essential advance in Hegel's thought that the possession of a self might indeed be a matter of degree, that the unity of self-consciousness might be 'transcendental' without being entire – a thought which is finally being understood and discussed by analytical philosophers.[13]) The alienated man literally does not know what he is doing or feeling in his daily labour, for he can bring his activity under no description that makes it a meaningful object of endeavour. Lacking such a description he sees his activity as exacted *from* him, rather than as originating *in* him. His activity is that of a body in the grip of a machine, not of a rational agent acting out a sense of value. In his own eyes he is what he conceives himself to be in the eyes of the world – a means, not an end; an organism, not a man. And the cure of his self-alienation must also therefore be a cure of his world, of the world which forces such an image upon him. Only by transforming the world into the visible and tangible record of things rationally pursued, can a man find place for himself there: without that place there will be no self to furnish it.

There is much in these doctrines of philosophical truth – although to extract it all is beyond the scope of the present work. Even with this simple sketch in mind, however, we can reasonably suggest that it is precisely on account of its impoverished conception of the self, and its failure to recognize the force of those idealist reflections, that the empiricist and utilitarian philosophy which we have been covertly rejecting throughout this work has made so little progress in understanding the moral life, and in understanding that peculiar appendage to the moral life which we have labelled aesthetic. It cannot suffice to describe human beings as bundles of desires, and their satisfaction as nothing more than the fulfilment of as many of those desires as are compatible with the contented continuance of the species. For the satisfaction of a self-conscious being cannot be described in the same terms as the satisfaction of an animal, and a philosophy which repeatedly deprives itself of the vocabulary with which the distinction can be made deprives itself also of any serious understanding of its subject.[14] We distinguish the satisfaction of a desire from the satisfaction of a person, a state which involves both permanence and permeation.

The fact of self-conscious reflection must be part of any intelligible conception of human life. We do not merely *have* our desires and aims, we also *know* that we have them, and, in knowing them we attempt to achieve some objective understanding of their origin and value. A self-conscious being is able to view himself as one of a kind, and must so view himself if he is to have any firm idea of what would be satisfactory – which desire should be encouraged, which suppressed. His very happiness lies, therefore, in the possibility of self-conscious deliberation and reflection, and in so far as there is a coherent ideal of human freedom, an ideal of something other than the mere loss of self in the pursuit of this or that desire, it consists in the responsibility which a man may assume for his own self-realization, for the adoption in himself of those desires and aims to which he ascribes enduring value. On the simple utilitarian model, freedom consists in the ability to satisfy one's desires,[15] whatever their origin and value – and it is with this sterile concept of freedom that the individualistic notion of the self cloaks its deep inadequacy. As soon as a man asks himself which of his many desires he should proceed to satisfy, he at once comes up with conclusions proper to self-conscious reflection – conclusions as to which aim it is right to pursue, and which it is wrong. Clearly, for that to be possible, there must be a concept of self as something over and above the totality of existing desires. The judgement of self-conscious reflection is not of the form: do this, for it is the means to what you want, but rather: want this, for that is where satisfaction lies. A being who can make that judgement must be in a position to see himself from outside, as it were, to reflect that a certain state is desirable, another not. Involved in this process of self-conscious reflection is a stance towards the world that is essentially anti-individualistic, a stance which involves seeing oneself as one of a kind, with fulfilments and satisfactions which can be described only in terms of values that transcend the sphere of individual impulse. Values indicate what is worthwhile, not just for me, here, now, but for anyone. They compel me to turn back on myself those attitudes of admiration and contempt which are learned and transferred from my concourse with others.

On this view of self-consciousness, the possession of a self is no simple matter. It is not reducible to the presence or absence of some Cartesian soul, nor is it identical with the use of symbols, or language, or with any other specific form of behaviour. The self, in the Hegelian theory, is construed as a complex form of social *activity*, and exists precisely to the extent of its own self-discovery; happiness and freedom lie in that process. Whether the notion of 'self' is the most appropriate to use here is not so important as it might seem: what matters is that we should recognize that something indispensable to individual well-being is left out of consideration by the utilitarian theory of mentality, and this thing is not wholly natural (not given to man in a 'state of nature') but at least partly acquired.

Now an important feature in this activity of self-discovery is the agent's sense of his own continuity in time. Ever since Locke's reflections on personal identity,[16] philosophers have been prone to see deep connections between self-knowledge, and the knowledge of oneself as temporally extended. In Kant and Hegel this idea is vital to the very notion of self-conscious experience. We can now see why their doctrines might contain some element of truth. For on the empiricist view of the self, practical reasoning is in danger of becoming no more than a matter of discovering the means to the fulfilment of present desires. It is only *those* desires which determine what is reasonable for the agent, for of his future desires he can have no systematic knowledge, and of his past desires he knows only whether they were satisfied or not. This is the picture of a self, as it were, locked in the present, and it is hard to see by what principle such an agent can conceive his present self and his future self as one and the same, when the aims and interests of the one remain so inscrutable to the other. To take fully into account his future continuity a man must be able, for example, to reflect on a state of affairs that he does not desire and be able to determine that it is all the same desirable: he must be able to take into account, in his present decisions, matters which have little or nothing to do with his present desires.[17]

Self-realization requires then that the agent have some real sense, in the present, of his continuity into the future. His future satisfactions must in some way enter into his present calculations, even though they are not the objects of present desire. Until he has achieved that rational balance between himself at one time and himself at another, he lives as it were expended in the present moment. But what makes this achievement possible? On the idealist view art, and the aesthetic impulse, play an important part in the process of 'spreading oneself' on the objective world. The view gains support from our reflections on the art of building. The process of 'self-realization', of breaking from the prison of immediate desire, is a kind of passage from subject to object, a making public and objective of what is otherwise private and confused. But a man can set his feet on the ladder of self-realization only when he has some perception of its reliability, and this cannot be achieved by subjective fiat. He must first find himself at home in the world, with values and ambitions that are shared. We must be able to perceive the ends of his activity not in himself but outside himself, as proper aims in a public world, endowed with a validity greater than the validity of mere 'authentic' choice. Consider, for example, the passion of erotic desire, an impulse which has its life in the immediate present and which, conceived on the animal level, possesses an urgency that will not be denied. The idealist – and not only the idealist if

Shakespeare's famous sonnet on this theme is to be believed[18] – would regard the pursuit of erotic desire, in its untempered natural state, as a restless loss of self, a constant shifting from one impulse to the next, with no satisfaction beyond the momentary gratification of desire, and no reflection on its larger significance or value – all that Shakespeare meant in referring to 'the expense of spirit in a waste of shame'. In human society this restless pursuit of gratification is translated into elaborate forms and rituals – forms of dance, song, courtship and marriage – which, precisely because they originate from shared values and conceptions, address themselves not to momentary passion but to the apprehension of an enduring self. The individual is presented with a picture of self-fulfilment which imposes itself in despite of the urgency of present impulse, and therefore in a sense gives to him a freedom which, in the surrender to impulse, is denied. He is presented with an intimation of passions that transcend his present motives; his choice is not of gratification only, but of something more properly described as a way of being, a form of life. The institutions of courtship (and the kind of self-reflection which they require) transform passion into a kind of rational enterprise, through which the subject is in some measure distanced from his present need, and comes to see his self-fulfilment as equally involved. It is through such forms and conventions that love becomes, in the Platonic sense, a form of knowledge – knowledge of the self and the other, as creatures with a fulfilment that surpasses the fulfilment of desire.

The example is characteristic of the process of self-realization, and it indicates the way in which the serious choice of a future may be impossible without the passage from private to public, from impulse to ceremony, from individual to social norm, that the idealist places at the heart of the moral order. To give the full reason for accepting the necessity of that passage is here not possible. But such reflections as I have been able to indicate must surely point to the philosophical weakness of individualism, and of the utilitarian morality which derives from it.

But now, of course, we can give added sense to the view that aesthetic judgement is an indispensable factor in everyday life. The process of self-realization is possible only when the world responds to my activity, when it reflects back to me an image of my true fulfilment. The aesthetic sense, as we have described it, is precisely devoted to the task of endowing the world with an order and meaning of that kind. Not only the man who builds but the man who lives with the product, must see the building in relation to himself, as an objective part of a process of *interaction* with the world; in that process his humanity may be either rebutted or confirmed. Every man has a need to see the world around him in terms of the wider demands of his rational nature; if he cannot do so he must stand towards it in an 'alienated' relation, a relation based on the sense that the public order resists the meanings with which his own activity seeks to fill it. Now a *merely* functional building does not lend itself to the imposition of a public meaning. It stands in the world like an individualistic ego, pursuing its own aim in defiance of, or indifference to, the aims of others. And that is how the observer will see and understand it – it has no more life or reality than the individual purposes which gave rise to it, and contains no intimation of an objective world of values beyond the pursuit of limited desires. In seeing it under that aspect – as a manifestation of architectural individualism – the observer will see the building as alien to himself. On the other hand, a building which answers to his aesthetic sense, which extends to him an invitation to understand and identify, such a building provides him at the same time with an intimation of a public order, of a world responsive to objective values, a world in which the individual is realized and not merely gratified. Not finding himself surrounded by such buildings, buildings which bear the imprint of that search for the 'appropriate' which is the hallmark of the reasoned pursuit of ends, a man must see his world as strange to him and hostile. While he may identify in this world the individual aims of individual people, he can find no trace of anything larger than their sum. Inevitably, he will be forced to see himself in such terms, as one individual among others, fighting in the jungle of gratification, with little sense of what he will thereby achieve.

As an example, consider the street. Our aesthetic understanding of the street embraces a relation between interior and exterior, between content and façade. Here we see buildings, as we see people, with both a public and a private side. There is the part which faces outward to the world, and there is the part within, the domestic, private, idiosyncratic part. Public buildings, like public people, have a self each corner of which may be invaded, at least by those with the right connections. Domestic buildings may be impenetrable, like the dark doorway of the Nubian Arab. In all cases the street must reflect the desire for a common public order, the façade being a recognition of that order; nowhere is this more apparent than in the streets and terraces of our Georgian towns, and in the human irregularities of the true baroque. Even the rampant burgeoning of the 'individual' manner in the Victorian age, in which fancy-dress Gothic, Palladian classical, what one might call 'Greeced baroque', and all the other mixtures of a thousand-and-one decorative traditions, competed for eminence in the free market of display, even that glorious eclecticism did not extinguish the desire for a public alignment, a polite jostling forward onto a common street, in a manner finely exemplified by much of Fleet Street and Chancery Lane. It is this, too, which explains Pugin's sense of outrage at the false façade, which he regarded (not seeing the many subtleties of the relationship between inner and outer, maintaining as he did a morbidly Cartesian sense of both) merely as a built hypocrisy. And it is this which explains the desolation that is felt at the realization of the maddest of all Utopian schemes, the open-planned housing complex, where streets are replaced by empty spaces from which towers arise, towers bearing neither the mark of a communal order, nor any visible record of the individual house, and demonstrating in their every aspect the triumph of that collective individualism from which both community and individual are abolished. No less disturbing is the attitude which sees streets as mere conduits through a '*cité radieuse*', upon which buildings turn their backs, or (since they usually are conceived without any 'backs' to turn), against which buildings stand like indomitable cliffs of shining glass, spectacular, luminous and cold. It is surely absurd to think of the popular outrage at these things as no more than a 'matter of taste', rather than a re-affirmation of injured moral feeling.

These thoughts must lead us to perceive one further respect in which style is necessary. For the public order which we have described is not *given*: it is an achievement, an achievement which depends on being recognized. There is no public order until men can see it. But this recognition, because it must take place daily and hourly, during the course of a busy and distracted commerce, will necessitate something like the repeatable vocabulary, recognizable forms, interesting detail, that we described in the preceding chapter. The moral task which we have elicited from our 'aesthetics of everyday life' cannot be fulfilled by any lapse into originality, into the pursuit of the 'enveloping experience' that is so often proposed as the only serious ideal of art. Self-expression is no more than the attempt of individualism to perpetuate itself in the aesthetic sphere. Of course, no one doubts that the aesthetic understanding requires a special kind of freedom; but freedom has the sense given to it in the apt words of Spinoza: the 'consciousness of necessity'.[19] The architect must be constrained by a rule of obedience. He must translate his intuition into terms that are publicly intelligible, unite his building with an order that is recognizable not only to the expert but also to the ordinary uneducated man.

It may be wondered how far my remarks reiterate or confirm the Hegelian position that I described at the close of chapter 6. Certainly, Wölfflin recognized in the aesthetic aspect of architecture just the kind of public representation of human life that I have attempted to describe. However, he connected the *Lebensgefühlen* which architectural forms express with an intuitive apprehension of the form and movement of the human body. Now it is obvious that architectural forms wear human expressions; their divisions, like those of the classical column, often correspond to our anatomy; they appear to 'step', 'dance', 'stand' in human postures, to represent themselves as bodies. Nor did it require the refinements of Hegelianism to make this observation possible. The idea is there in Vitruvius and Alberti, and is reiterated, for example, by the eighteenth-century theorist Le Clerc, who wrote in his *Traité d'Architecture*:

> Vitruvius . . . maintains that the Doric column, being composed upon the model of a naked, strong, muscular man, resembling a Hercules, should have no base – pretending that the base of a column is the same as a shoe to a man. But I must own, that I cannot consider a column without a base in comparing it to a man, but I am, at the same time, struck with the idea of a person without feet rather than without shoes. . . .[20]

a passage quoted with considerable approval by Sir William Chambers. But one must distinguish such (slightly comic) observations from the thoughts that I have adumbrated. To say that architecture is seen in terms of a perception of the human body is to say something highly ambiguous, until it is made clear whether one is referring to the body as organism, or to the body as expression of self. Wölfflin, in identifying his *Lebensgefühlen* with specific experiences of the body, made it clear that he included in those experiences every cultural and rational value that the body is able to convey. For him the human body was as far from being seen under the aspect of mere 'organism' as any work of architecture. Adrian Stokes, by contrast, tries to use the doctrine to refer architecture (as he refers the self) to experiences that are decidedly organic – the pre-rational experiences of the infant at the breast. One would like to say – yes, there are such experiences, but why should their importance be anything more than causal? Why should they provide a paradigm? It is only one body that we experience in Stokes's way; is every body that we encounter in later life therefore seen under the aspect of suckling? (If you believe that, then you'll believe anything.) Wölfflin's view, by contrast, emphasizes the human body not as organism, but (to use an Hegelian phrase) as expression of spirit. (Which is not to imply that body and spirit are two separate *things*.) The human body, seen as person, wears on its surface, in its movements, gestures, expressions, habits and clothing, the very same insignia of rational activity with which we console ourselves in architecture.

However, to construe the bodily analogy in that way is also to show how very little it advances our understanding. It is only because we can see that the activity of building belongs to the process of self-realization in a public world, that we see what is meant by the assertion that there is a significant correspondence between architecture and the human frame. I argued that the correspondence of part with part exhibited by successful architecture is also a correspondence between inner and outer. It arises because we can see inert materials as endowed with impulses which have their origin in us; in fulfilling those impulses in architecture we 'realize' a conception of ourselves, not as isolated subjectivities, but as self-conscious beings with an enduring identity in a public world. That process of self-realization through building can be described independently. And it is only because it can be described independently that the deep relation between architecture and the stances of the human body (the human body construed as self-expression) can be understood. It is, therefore, not the relation with the body that *explains* what we see – not, that is, unless we reduce the whole web of rational experience to the subconscious paradigms of the Freudian school.

The reader will perhaps expect me to extract from my arguments some precepts for the builder. For I have tried to situate the activity of architecture so centrally in the moral order as to uphold the claim to objectivity with which aesthetic judgement is imbued. And in doing so I have made a claim for style in building. However, to insist on the need for style is to provide no rule or recipe for its exercise. We have nothing more than an *intimation* of what good architecture consists in. We have arrived at a sense of a deep, *a priori*, connection between moral and aesthetic understanding; but we have no rule whereby to translate that sense into a critical canon. Nor is this surprising. For, if we reflect on the Aristotelian considerations which earlier occupied us, we must surely come to recognize that the reasons for the value of taste will not be criteria for its exercise: they will issue in no rules of critical discrimination. As I tried to show in chapter 6, the attempt to translate a Freudian theory of the value of architecture into a critical method was doomed to failure: and similar considerations could be brought to show that there could be no 'Hegelian' criticism established by the Heglian theory of value. It is a mark of moralism in aesthetics that it seeks to translate the moral nature of aesthetic taste into a *formula*; into a simple rule of right and wrong. (It is moralism, for example, that persuaded Pugin that he was *obliged* to build in the 'pointed' style, and which persuaded the advocates of the modern movement of the moral impeccability, indeed the moral necessity, of their enterprise.[21]) But this connection of moral with aesthetic *criteria* is a fantasy. The attempt to force the connection, to translate the moral sense into aesthetic standards, without first recognizing the measure of autonomy which aesthetic understanding must always preserve, that attempt is mere ideology, of no persuasive force. For while aesthetic values contain an intimation of the moral sense (the sense of ourselves as social beings, tied to an order greater than ourselves) moral values do not in their turn contain any intimation of their aesthetic embodiment. (And that is why there are good people with appalling taste.) The embodiment of moral truth in architectural form is an achievement, to be won afresh by the builder in the varied circumstances of day to day, working always with one eye on necessity, and with one eye on the visual tradition from which his aesthetic sense derives.

Nevertheless, we should not be sceptical. For, if we can provide an objective theory of the value of aesthetic taste, we will have *some* basis for translating our accumulated critical judgements into an architectural *ideal*. We shall know what kind of thing we are looking for in architecture, and what kind of style might serve to thwart or further it. For example, we can at least say that certain features of good architecture, while they may not be *necessary* in every successful style, bear a relation to architectural success which is far from accidental. Perhaps it is appropriate to end on a note of speculation, concerning the perennial value of two distinctive features of the buildings of the past.

First, the use of mouldings. The habit of moulding, whereby stark horizontals and sharp angles are etched out with parallels, undercut with shadows, pointed and emphasized in a seemingly infinite variety of ways, is no accidental feature of the successful styles that we have known. Moulding has disappeared from much modern architecture (surviving residually in the architecture of Mies, as in his use of close lying parallels at the Farnsworth House). And yet it is an obvious and intelligible way of giving richness to a space or line: through moulding, lines can be sharpened or softened, emphasized or subdued, brought to rest or set in motion – in short they can be articulated in the manner which lends itself to the accumulation of meaning. An architect who dispenses with mouldings must find an effective substitute; otherwise, he stands in danger of giving to every line in his building an appearance that is stark and unending, as cold and abstract as a mathematical proof.

Second, the division between inside and outside, and the consequent vesting of architectural significance in a built façade. The façade is the face of the building: it is what 'stands' before us; it wears the 'expression' of the whole. In the upward movement of lines on a façade we feel the moral force of human posture. And yet, once again, it seems that this law of architectural composition has been brushed aside, held in abeyance, or confusedly ignored. The change has in part resulted from the use of reinforced concrete, the aesthetic consequence of which was correctly anticipated by Le Corbusier, in *Vers une Architecture*:

> Reinforced concrete has brought a revolution in the asthetics of construction . . . suppressing the roof and replacing it by terraces . . . these setbacks and recessions will . . . lead to a play of half lights and heavy shades, with the accent running not from top to bottom, but horizontally, from left to right.[22]

Yet why should we accept that proliferation of horizontal movement, which seems so inimical to the outward projection of self into form? It is surely not an accident that we like to see our buildings *stand* before us (see Plate 90), not if we derive our conception of unity and humanity in building from our own sense of self. Nor is it an accident that we like to see a street as formed from a series of façades, or that the brutalist's 'street in the air'[23] seems such an inadequate visual substitute for the back-to-back slums which preceded it.

One ingenious modern architect, recognizing the values implicit in the classical façade, the values of publicity, order and the felt representation of human life, has tried to answer the objection. He has tried to demonstrate that the façade may be, as it were, dissolved, and reconstituted as a series of planes, cantilevered out into platforms; seen from below, these present in their soffits the same upward accumulation of detail as the classical façade, and yet, seen frontally, they present no façade, being permeated at every level by the horizontal movement of human life.

One might remain sceptical of the attempt. A façade gives a building some independent stance, a meaning that is *not* merely borrowed from the activity which it contains. The visible commotion of its inmates no more gives humanity to a building than the wriggle of worms gives vitality to a corpse. The soul of a thing is of its essence; it cannot be simulated, borrowed or stolen from some foreign source. A building without a façade is not just a building without a face – it is a building without expression, and hence a building without life. So, at least, it might be argued.

But let us admit that the question is of the greatest difficulty: at least we see that it has lost some of its air of 'subjectivity'; the question of the façade, however difficult to settle in a manner agreeable both to modern engineering and to the aesthetic sense, is a question that is accessible to rational thought. Such vital aesthetic questions, while they cannot be settled by legislation, may avail themselves of thoughts and

PLATE 90 S. Maria in Campitelli, Rome, façade

perceptions which all rational beings might be brought to share. The architect to whom I have referred – Sir Denys Lasdun – has himself conceded that his treatment of the horizontal plane is an attempt to *reconstitute* something, the value of which he cannot question. As he writes:

> all these ideas return to the perennial lessons of Greece. There is an attempt . . . to recapture in some small way that exquiste reciprocal relationship which [the Greeks] achieved between geometrical form, siting and spirit of place – a sense of belonging to time, place and people and being at home in the world.[24]

Like Lasdun, we have begun to see that the achievement represented by the classical tradition, the translation of the aesthetic demand into an agreed and flexible language of signs, a language which facilitates at every juncture the outward projection and realization of the self, is not just a passing object of respect, a temporary speciality in the arcanum of taste, but on the contrary, the perfect representative of all that is good in building, all that building contains by way of decency, serenity and restraint. But it is perhaps best left to the reader to deduce, from our reflections, some suitable apologetic for his favourite style. Let him only reject the superstition that any style, or any lack of it, will equally do.

PART III

SUMMARY

IN THIS work I have covered a great many topics in both philosophy and architectural theory, and, constrained at every point by the exigencies of contrasting disciplines, I have often contorted or loosened the argument. I therefore append this brief summary, for those who have been lost, as much as for those who have not been convinced, by my reasoning.

Chapter 1 explored the most fashionable, but perhaps least important, concept in aesthetics, the concept of art, as this has been formed under the pressure of romantic and post-romantic thinking. I tried to show how inadequate is this concept – and such distinctions as that between art and craft which have been thought to clarify it – to the discussion of architecture. Like all decorative arts, architecture derives its nature not from some activity of representation or dramatic gesture, but from an everyday preoccupation with getting things right, a preoccupation that has little to do with the artistic intentions of romantic theory. My thesis has been that the aesthetic sense is an indispensable part of this preoccupation, and that the resulting 'aesthetics of everyday life' is as susceptible of objective employment as any other branch of practical reason.

The discussion that followed divided into two parts; each began in a low key and proceeded towards a higher. The first part presented a theory of the experience of architecture, while the second part applied that theory to architectural practice and criticism. Finally, the conclusion drew together the threads of the argument and answered the question posed by the introduction, the question of the value of aesthetic judgement in the activity of building.

Chapter 2 began by exploring the attempt to detach aesthetics from architecture, to see aesthetic preoccupations as subordinate to some more important aim. On this view, architecture is seen as a species of 'problem-solving', and beauty as at best a consequence, and certainly not an aim, of the ideal solution which the architect requires. I argued that such an approach, which often claims to be uniquely 'reasonable', shows nothing so much as a confusion about the nature of practical reason: the reader was therefore introduced to the philosophy of rational action which was elaborated in later chapters. This showed that there is something left out of account by this 'rationalistic' approach to architecture, something which, far from being secondary, is the most important ingredient in the architect's endeavour. I tentatively suggested (and later tried to prove) that what is left out is aesthetic experience, and the values which that experience implies.

But what is this 'aesthetic' experience? How is it exercised, what is its object, and by what is it guided? *Chapter 3* proceeded to consider certain influential doctrines concerning the nature of building doctrines which attempt to describe the experience of architecture in terms of some conception of the essence of architectural forms. Each doctrine depends upon the elaboration of some ruling concept – function, space, historical meaning, proportion – and I argued that each concept is inadequate to its stated aim. The chapter was designed to undermine some of the intellectual rhetoric of architectural theory, and also to prepare the way for a positive conception. It emerged incidentally that the theories which have, from its beginning, surrounded and given support to the 'modern movement' in architecture, are intellectually vacuous.

Chapter 4 presented a positive account of the experience of architecture, and introduced one of the most important concepts in aesthetics, the concept of imagination. I began by distinguishing the experience of architecture from merely sensuous experience, showing that, in the former case, experience is informed by and expressive of a thought or concept. But there are two ways in which experience and concept can combine: the way of literal perception, and the way of imagination. I showed that, in the experience of architecture, it is the imagination that prevails. This means not merely that architectural experience is inherently interpreted, but that it can be modified through argument, remains free of literal-minded preconceptions, and acquires a status wholly unlike that of common perception, namely, the status of a symbol. I went on to apply the theory, by showing that we can now describe the unity of our experience of architecture, and the felt unity of its object. It also became possible to distinguish building from ornament, and to show that the romantic's contrast between the sublime world of the imagination and the pettifogging world of taste is totally misguided. It is because the experience of architecture is imaginative that architecture can be judged right or wrong. And it is because of aesthetic discrimination that imaginative experience acquires its interest and meaning.

Chapter 5 proceeded to analyse the notion of taste or aesthetic judgement. I argued that, in imaginative experience, reasoned reflection, critical choice and immediate experience are inseparable. I tried to show that in the exercise of taste experience is transformed into a sign of deeper values, by being brought into relation with procedures of critical reflection and comparison, procedures which may be wholly inexplicit, but which inform the perception of the normal sensitive eye. I showed how experience, reason and preference each lay their separate constraints on aesthetic judgement. In spite of that, however, aesthetic judgement maintains an ideal of objectivity, and moreover a continuity with the moral life. It became clear that aesthetic experience is not only a peculiarity of rational beings, but also an essential part of their understanding, both of themselves and of the world which surrounds them. It is inevitable, therefore, that it should issue in criticism of its object, and that it should attempt to find in the object a premonition of some real and objective moral order.

The argument had reached a turning point. I had tried to describe the experience of architecture as comprehensively as possible, and to show that it cannot be separated from the exercise of aesthetic taste. I had also given a theory of the nature of taste, a theory which shows that all architectural experience contains the intimation of an objective validity, of a true critical standard, of a right and a wrong way to build. The discussion in Part II took up that suggestion. I began, in an uncomplicated way, by exploring certain critical theories, theories which claim to provide some general method for deciphering and understanding architectural forms, and therefore some general procedure for evaluating buildings.

Chapter 6 considered Freudian and Marxist analysis, together with certain of their intellectual antecedents. Both these theories have claimed to provide methods for understanding not only artistic but every other human activity. Moreover, both theories have achieved considerable critical importance and raise questions which must be answered by any satisfactory theory of aesthetic taste, questions about the relation between criticism and psychological analysis, between aesthetic and moral or political judgement. I suggested that in fact both

Freudian and Marxist analysis are largely irrelevant to the understanding of architecture, being either generalized beyond the point where aesthetic significance expires, or else devoted to a systematic falsification of architectural experience, in order to present an illusion of critical method. Both of them, however, contain a residue of truth, which I attempted to describe.

Chapter 7 explored another important suggestion, the suggestion that architecture is a language, or something like a language, and to be understood accordingly. I discussed the influential 'semantic' and 'semiological' theories of art, theories which consider all art and architecture as forms of quasi-linguistic symbolism. These theories also turned out to be vacuous, having neither theoretical basis, nor critical application. It began to emerge that the 'meaning' enshrined in aesthetic understanding is in some way *sui generis*, and also that it is perhaps more obvious, and more on the surface, than the advocates of these critical 'methods' are prepared to countenance. However, something remained to the analogy with language. The concept of an architectural 'syntax' was rejected, along with that of architectural 'semantics'. Nevertheless, a sense of the ordered achievement of meaning, rather than its random accumulation, remainded as a principal characteristic of architecture, as of every aesthetic enterprise, and it is that characteristic which I went on to describe.

Chapter 8 began to take up again the intellectual problems posed in Part I. I explored the kinds of 'meaning' that are proper objects of aesthetic understanding, and discussed two important concepts in aesthetics, the concepts of representation and of expression. I tried to show that the first of these does not apply to architecture, while the second applies only in a special sense, a sense which creates an important distinction between fine and decorative art. It emerged that there is no simple way of analysing the relation between a building and its 'meaning', and that the process of attachment between the two should first be described genetically rather than analytically. I therefore turned my attention to exploring the genesis of aesthetic judgement in the practice of the builder, and the manner in which form and meaning become conjoined.

The point was pursued in *chapter 9*, where it was argued that the aesthetic understanding is inseparable from a sense of detail, and that all the major concepts employed in it – the concepts of the appropriate, the proportionable, the expressive, the beautiful – take their meaning from the exercise of that sense. Implicit in the argument was an account of what is meant by such terms as 'right' and 'wrong' in aesthetic argument, and a suggestion as to where the objectivity of critical judgement lies. It became clear that style is an indispensable adjunct to architectural knowledge, and that the cultivation of a sense of appropriate detail is immensely more significant than any pursuit of pure 'proportion' or 'form'. It also became clear that only certain approaches to form and detail answer to the demands of the aesthetic sense, and these approaches all lead away from prevailing fashions to some more settled 'classical' style.

The defence of classicism (classicism not in its historical meaning, but in a more comprehensive sense) was taken up again in *chapter 10*, where the fundamental question of the relation between the aesthetic and the moral was explored. I drew together the threads of previous argument, and returned to the questions raised in the first two chapters, showing that it is indeed the aesthetic sense which is left out of consideration in the rationalistic approaches there considered, and that it is the aesthetic sense which can transform the architect's task from the blind pursuit of an uncomprehended function into a true exercise of practical common sense. The attempt to subordinate aesthetic standards, either to an overriding function, or to the 'moral rightness' of a style, shows a confusion that is both intellectual and moral. The confusion was shown to derive from certain widespread misapprehensions concerning the nature of human action. These in their turn reflect a false conception of the self, a conception which has penetrated the theory and the practice of architecture since the start of the modern movement. A true understanding of the self led us to uphold, not only the primacy of aesthetic values, but also the objectivity which they implicitly claim. It became possible to arrive at a conception of critical reasoning, reasoning which is at once aesthetic and moral but which remains, for all that, free from the taint of moralism. We were drawn tentatively to conclude that some ways of building are right, and others (including many that are currently practised) wrong.

NOTES

CHAPTER 1 INTRODUCTION: THE PROBLEM OF ARCHITECTURE

(1) Kant's division is expounded in the three great critiques: *The Critique of Pure Reason* (2nd edn 1787), in which he explores the nature and limits of the human understanding, and the fundamental principles of empirical enquiry; *The Critique of Practical Reason* (1788), which expounds a system of morality; and *The Critique of Judgement* (1790). The last, devoted to aesthetics, is the least thorough of the three *Critiques*. Nevertheless, it laid a foundation for all major idealist theories, and its doctrines reappear in Herder, Schiller, Schopenhauer and Hegel, modified and expanded into developed philosophies of art. The second part of the *Critique of Judgement*, which is concerned with teleological thought (the general capacity to see and understand the *ends* of things, as I may see flight in the wings of a bird) contains passages which indicate that Kant too would have wished to reaffirm the connection between aesthetic judgement and practical reason.

(2) Such an explanation is offered by Adrian Stokes, whose theories are discussed at length in chapter 6. See especially his *Smooth and Rough* (London 1951), reprinted in volume 2 of *The Critical Writings of Adrian Stokes*, ed. L. Gowing (London 1978).

For an example of psychological explanation in architectural aesthetics which tries to rely on the scientific claims of 'empirical' psychology, see M. Borissavlievitch, *Les Théories de l'architecture*, and *Ésthétique de l'architecture* (both Paris 1926). These contain useful resumés of late nineteenth-century psychological theories, in particular of the introspectionist psychologists, Lipps, Volkelt and Wundt, but neither makes any serious contribution, either to the science or to the philosophy of design, beginning as they do from the false assumption that there is a certain identifiable aesthetic 'sensation' and that it is the sole task of scientific aesthetics to analyse its nature and cause. For other work, not specifically applied to architecture, see T. Munro, *Scientific Methods in Aesthetics* (London 1928); J. Bullough, 'Psychical Distance', *British Journal of Psychology* (1928), in which an important philosophical doctrine is oddly presented as a psychological *observation*; R. M. Ogden, *The Psychology of Art* (London 1937); and K. Koffka, *Problems in the Psychology of Art* (New York 1940), an application to aesthetic judgement of the idea of a 'good gestalt'. None of these contain any sustained contribution either to science or to philosophy. Indeed, I think it is fair to say that the subject of empirical aesthetics has yet to find that initial description of its subject matter without which it cannot proceed. Interesting 'results' – such as the supposed discovery of 'empathy' or '*Einfühlung*', by Volkelt and Lipps – seem to be philosophical doctrines masquerading as empirical observations, and the true test of their adequacy is not empirical but conceptual.

(3) Scepticism about the distinction between science and philosophy arises from the tradition of American pragmatism, launched by C. S. Peirce in the nineteenth century, and given its most effective recent exposition by W. V. Quine in *From a Logical Point of View* (Cambridge, Mass. 1953), and *Word and Object* (Cambridge, Mass. 1960). Quine argues that the distinction between conceptual and scientific truth is without a satisfactory basis, and indeed that to speak of 'concepts' is both sloppy and dispensable. While there have been serious attempts to reply to Quine's arguments (notably by H. P. Grice and P. F. Strawson, 'In Defence of a Dogma', *Phil. Rev.* 1956; and M. Dummett, *Frege, Philosophy of Language,* London 1973, ch. 17) the arguments themselves have a dogged persistence which refuses to be appeased. It is no longer possible to assume with confidence that the proper sphere of philosophy can be uncontentiously defined. The Quinean attack on the 'concepts' of the analytical philosopher would apply equally to the 'noematic content' which is the favoured candidate of the phenomenologists for the true object of philosophical understanding.

(4) The arguments for the theory that a mental state and its object are essentially connected have been recently rehearsed by A. J. Kenny, *Action, Emotion and Will* (London 1963). The doctrine is an ancient one, given fine elaboration by St Thomas Aquinas, in *Summa Theologiae,* 1a, 2e, which remains the most systematic and convincing philosophical treatise on the nature of emotion. See also the (now classical) exposition by F. Brentano in *Psychology from an Empirical Standpoint* (1874, trans. L. McAlister *et al.*, London 1973), a book which provided some of the inspiration for modern phenomenology. The idea that a mental state has an object is sometimes referred to as the idea of the 'intentionality' of the mental, and the object is often referred to as the 'intentional object', in order to make clear that its nature depends not on the world but upon how the world is seen. (The subject may be mistaken; his jealousy may be concerned with something imaginary or unreal.) The word 'intentionality' – from the Latin, *intendere*, to aim – records the fact that many (some would say all) mental states *aim outwards* from subject to object, and are not

merely the passive 'impressions' that they have sometimes been taken to be.

(5) My method involves abstracting from the actual or 'material' objects of aesthetic experience, and attempting to discover only what is formally required in aesthetic experience. This species of abstraction has been referred to by Husserl (the founder of modern phenomenology) as the 'bracketing' (*epoche*) of the object (see E. Husserl, *Ideas, General Introduction to Phenomenology*, 1913, trans. W. R. Boyce Gibson, London 1931). But my method of argument in this book will not be phenomenological. As I try to argue in my *Art and Imagination* (London 1974) ch. 1, I do not think that there can be such a thing as phenomenology, even though there are what might be called 'phemomenological puzzles', one of which I discuss here in chapter 4.

(6) The great exception to this rule is Hegel, in his *Lectures on Aesthetics* (1835, trans. T. M. Knox, London 1975). Among modern writers who have tried to give a philosophical aesthetics which is also applied, one might mention S. Cavell (*Must We Mean What We Say*? 2nd edn, London 1976).

(7) See, e.g. Kant's account of 'dependent' beauty, *Critique of Judgement* (trans. J. C. Meredith, Oxford 1952) pt. 1 s. 16; and Schopenhauer's appendix on architecture in the second volume of *The World as Will and Representation* (trans. E. F. J. Payne, Colorado 1958).

(8) Hegel, op. cit.

(9) R. G. Collingwood, *The Principles of Art* (Oxford 1938). Collingwood's theory has been applied to architecture by Bruce Allsop, with the intention (largely unrealized, I think) of distinguishing that part of architecture which is art from that part which is merely craft (*Art and the Nature of Architecture*, London 1952). Collingwood's theory derives from the father of expressionism, Benedetto Croce, whose *Aesthetic* (1902, 4th edn, trans. D. Ainslee, London 1922), has been the most influential work of philosophical aesthetics written in modern times. Croce's theory of art as pure 'intuition' has been applied to architecture (with predictably odd results) by S. Vitale, *L'Estetica dell'Architettura* (Bari 1928).

(10) I refer here to Kant's view, in the *Critique of Judgement*, that the *pure* experience of beauty is unmediated by any concept.

(11) See especially L. H. Sullivan, *Kindergarten Chats* (New York 1901); and H. Morrison, *L. Sullivan, Prophet of Modern Architecture* (New York 1952). As a matter of fact Sullivan's interiors are as far from his functionalist ideal as are any of the contemporary Art Nouveau works which provided his principal (though unacknowledged) inspiration. The functionalist cause was pleaded by Viollet-le-Duc in his *Entretiens sur l'architecture* (Paris 1863, 1872, trans. B. Bucknell, *Discourses on Architecture*, Boston 1889), especially volume 2. This is one of the source books for the myths which have proved necessary in order to persuade people that there is a truly 'modern' architecture.

(12) See A. W. Pugin, *The True Principles of Pointed or Christian Architecture* (London 1841), and Viollet-le-Duc. op. cit.

(13) For a brilliant description of the piazza and of the effect of subsequent clearance, see R. Wittkower, *Art and Architecture in Italy 1600–1750* (London 1958) p. 128.

(14) But see the reservations contained in Sir John Summerson's description of this church (*Georgian London*, London 1963, pp. 216–19).

(15) Schopenhauer, op. cit.

(16) The effect of this church, previously difficult to appreciate, has been rendered particularly striking by the clearance of the site of the Halles.

(17) These bridges have been praised in the most enthusiastic and intemperate terms by S. Giedion, in an article which first appeared in *Circle* (N. Gabo, B. Nicholson and L. Martin (eds), London 1937).

(18) Among such critics one must count, as principal ideologist and intellectual master, Sir Nikolaus Pevsner, in his *Pioneers of the Modern Movement* (London 1936), as well as S. Giedion, *Space Time and Architecture* (5th edn Cambridge, Mass. 1967). For the view that change in style is in fact always the enforcement of a change in technique, see A. Choisy, *Histoire de l'architecture* (Paris 1899).

(19) See, especially, the collection of essays known as *Style and Idea* (trans. D. Newlin, New York 1950, reissued, in expanded form, London 1975).

(20) T. S. Eliot, 'Tradition and the Individual Talent', reprinted in *Selected Essays* (London 1932). Cf. also, *Faust*, 1.1:

> *Was du ererbt von deinem Vätern hast,*
> *Erwirb es, um es zu besitzen.*

(21) See J. Ruskin, *Seven Lamps of Architecture* (London 1849), Introduction and chapter 1. The doctrine of architecture as *the* 'political art' has received repeated expression in the present century, and has led to a peculiar brand of architectural utopianism, seen at its clearest in the works of Lewis Mumford (e.g. *The Culture of Cities*, London 1938), Le Corbusier (e.g. *Vers Une Architecture*, Paris 1923) and Bruno Taut, *Die Neue Baukunst*, (Berlin 1929, trans. as *Modern Architecture*, London 1929). See also Charles Jencks, *Modern Movements in Architecture* (London 1973), in which a great deal of addled political theory is brought to bear, both by the author and by the architects from whom he quotes, upon the problems of architectural aesthetics.

(22) See, e.g. C.-N. Ledoux, *L'Architecture considérée sous le rapport de l'art, des moeurs et de la legislation* (1804), and the discussion in E. Kaufmann, *Architecture in the Age of Reason* (Cambridge, Mass. 1955).

(23) See Sir John Summerson, *Heavenly Mansions* (London 1949) p. 212. Some might, of course, wish to argue that the merits of the vernacular are so great that architects should be dispensed with wherever possible. For some persuasive visual reasons for such a view, see B. Rudofsky, *Architecture without Architects* (London 1964).

(24) Sir Henry Wotton, *Elements of Architecture* (London 1624), translating Vitruvius, Bk.I.c.3.

CHAPTER 2 ARCHITECTURE AND DESIGN

(1) See L. B. Alberti, *De Re Aedificatoria* (Florence 1485, Book X, trans. Bartolo and Leoni, London 1726, as *Ten Books on Architecture*, reprinted, ed. J. Rykwert, London, 1965). For an exposition of Alberti's thought on architecture, see R. Scruton, 'The Art of the Appropriate', *Times Literary Supplement* (16 Dec. 1977).

(2) *Seven Lamps of Architecture* (London 1849) ch. 1. Ruskin's actual discussion of individual buildings indicates that he might have regarded his own didactic pronouncements as exaggerated.

(3) Alberti, op. cit., Book I, ch. 1.

(4) For an analysis of this concept, see chapter 9, and for a discussion of the terminology used by Alberti to give expression to it, see Scruton, op. cit.

(5) The term 'aesthetic' is a philosophical coinage whose present use we owe to the eighteenth-century German philosopher A. G. Baumgarten (see his *Aesthetica*, 1750). The term has remained a technicality of philosophy, dependent for its sense upon the philosophical theory with which it is associated. This artificial nature of the concept has, I think, important consequences for the method of philosophical aesthetics.

(6) For the general philosophy of the 'design methods' school, see Christopher Jones, *Design Methods* (London 1970). The main inspiration of the school has been the work of the mathematician and architectural theorist, Christopher Alexander, who, in his influential book, *Notes on the Synthesis of Form* (Cambridge, Mass., 1964), attempted to provide the foundation for a mathematical theory of design. His ideas were also formulated in an article called 'The Determination of the Components for an Indian Village', in J. C. Jones and D. G. Thornley (eds), *Conference on Design Methods* (London 1963) (a book which contains other important theoretical articles by the editors and by Joseph Esherick), and in 'Houses Generated by Patterns' (Project for a Peruvian Village), published in Berkeley, California in 1971.

(7) Joseph Esherick, in P. Heyer (ed.), *Architects on Architecture, New Directions in America* (New York 1966) p. 113. The same view was expressed by Bruno Taut in 1929, *Modern Architecture*, p. 29.

(8) See, for example, El Lisstizky, *Russia, an Architecture for World Revolution* (trans. E. Dluhosch, London 1970) and the writings of the engineer-architects L. Komarova and N. Krail'nikov in *Sovremennaya Arkhitektura* (1928), quoted in L. March (ed.), *The Architecture of Form* (Cambridge 1976) preface.

(9) See for example the introduction to L. March, *The Architecture of Form*, in which the basis of this identification is given in terms of a common search for the 'rational solution' to 'design problems'. In fact constructivism was many things, and even in its early phase it is virtually impossible to pin it down to a doctrine. It seems to have started life as a kind of sloganizing anti-aestheticism, typified by the shrieks of A. Rodchenko and U. Stepanova, circulated in 1920, among which the following are by no means uncharacteristic: 'Kill Human thinking's last remaining attachment to art!', and 'Down with art which only camouflages humanity's incompetence!'. These were followed, in 1922, by the *International Constructivist Manifesto*, in which the tone was somewhat less shrill, although scarcely more coherent. A sympathetic reader of constructivist theory, remembering that architectural theory is usually the gesture of a practical man unused to words, attempting to rationalize with hindsight something which he understood intuitively only while seeing it done, might prefer to interpret these slogans as the preparation for a new aesthetic, rather than a radical break with all aesthetic values. But the history of the

movement is immensely complicated. It has been discussed at length by Reyner Banham in his *Theory and Design in the First Machine Age* (London 1960) ch. 14. Banham attempts to separate the conflicting currents of machine worship and stylistic adventure which run through the constructivist manifestos, and at the same time to show their complex reflection to the Dutch De Stijl movement.

(10) Cf. E. Kaufman, *Architecture in the Age of Reason* (Cambridge, Mass. 1955).

(11) Of course, the term 'constructivist' is a word that I have appropriated to name a specific ideology. Cultural historians will no doubt differ considerably in their views as to the nature (or even the existence) of a specifically 'constructivist' *movement*. However, it is of some interest to note that the ideology that I describe has flourished wherever the Leninist ethos has been influential. Hannes Meyer, who captured the Bauhaus in 1928 and held it until 1930, expressed the ethos as follows:

> The Leninist architect is not an aesthetic lackey, and unlike his colleague in the West, not a lawyer and custodian of the interest of the Capitalist ruling class there. . . . For him architecture is not an aesthetic stimulus but a keen-edged weapon in the class struggle. (Manifesto in the Swiss magazine *ABC* (1928), called 'ABC Demands the Dictatorship of the Machine')

It is worth remembering that the ethos of large-scale comprehensive development came to England with the firm of Tecton, founded by the constructivist ex-patriate Lubetkin (along with the engineer Ove Arup). Nobody could accuse either Sir Ove Arup or Sir Denys Lasdun (another erstwhile partner in that firm) of the anti-aesthetic ideology of their master. Nevetheless it is interesting that wherever the constructivists have flourished – in Germany, England and America – there has flourished with them a conception of architecture as irremediably wedded to stark and isolated forms, to 'comprehensive redevelopment', and to the anti-aesthetic ideology which sometimes pretends to be merely anti-Beaux-Arts, sometimes frankly confesses itself as Brutal. The history of the movement in England has been documented (somewhat uncritically) by Anthony Jackson, in *The Politics of Architecture; A history of modern architecture in Britain* (London 1970).

In fact, the whole enterprise was so fragmentary, that I do not think that it ever amounted to a single movement, or ever had a single dominant idea.

(12) C. Jones, op. cit. p. 10.

(13) Alexander, op. cit.

(14) As is attempted – though without success – in *The Architecture of Form* (ed. L. March), in which various standard techniques of computer representation are applied in a desultory way to architectural problems.

(15) The work of the 'design methods' school and their critics has as yet brought us no nearer to that ideal, as can be seen from Alexander's clumsy and impracticable village projects (see note 6).

(16) See Le Corbusier, *Vers Une Architecture* (Paris 1923), and the pertinent criticisms of the whole process of thought made by Peter Blake, in 'The Folly of Modern Architecture', *Atlantic Monthly* (September 1974). It is fair

to say that the idiosyncracy of Le Corbusier's own conception of a human need (a conception which led him to deny windows to those convalescing in his Venice hospital – see *Le Corbusier 1910–1965*, Edition Ginberger, Zurich, 1967, p. 176), is now fairly widely recognized. But the concept survives as a major part of the intellectual rhetoric through which large-scale development is advocated. See, for example, Sir Leslie Martin, 'Architects' approach to Architecture', *RIBAJ* (1967), and Alexander's wierd definitions of architectural features in the Indian Village Project (note 6), the street being defined as 'the coming together of the need for circulation space, the need for access to houses, the need for light and air between buildings, etc.' (p. 88).

(17) The point was made by Aristotle (*Metaphysics* Δ 5), has been put forward (in a slightly distorted form) by P. Foot, for example, in 'Moral Beliefs' PAS (1959), and in other aspects of her moral philosophy. I am grateful to David Wiggins and Sirah Derman, both of whom have worked to clarify the complex relation of a need.

(18) The identity of rationality and personhood is an ancient thesis of philosophy, upheld most convincingly by Kant in his moral theory, and by Hegel in *The Phenomenology of Spirit* (1807).

(19) This tendency, which has its seeds in Bentham's 'hedonic calculus', has found renewed expression in the science of 'preference theory', and in the attempt to quantify all human satisfaction in terms of the satisfaction of individual needs and desires. This has given rise to a study quaintly called 'human factors engineering' in America. See, e.g. E. J. McCormick, *Human Factors Engineering* (New York, 1957, 2nd edn, 1964). The whole enterprise rests upon a philosophical theory of human nature, and yet seems uninformed by any sense of the massive objections to that conception which have accumulated since Aristotle. Some of these objections are sketched in chapter 10.

(20) See for example the theoretical work of the Italian architect, Pier Luigi Nervi (*Costruire Correttamente*, Hoepli 1955). Nervi, who has built some of the finest of modern buildings, illustrates how wide the gap may be between an architect's practice and his theory.

(21) See N. Negroponte, *The Architectural Machine* (Cambridge, Mass. 1970), and the euphoric writings of Buckminster Fuller, more than adequately represented in James Meller (ed.): *The Buckminster Fuller Reader* (London 1970). For the influence of Fuller see Reyner Banham's advocacy of the 'unhouse', *Art in America* (April 1965), and the amusing irreverences of *Archigram*, whose writers have managed to reduce the human being to a 'node', 'plugged in' to a 'giant needery' (David Greene, in *Archigram* 1968).

(22) The comparison between clothes and architecture is a deep and fascinating subject, some first steps in the exploration of which have been taken by James Laver, *Style in Costume* (Oxford 1949).

(23) Theodor Adorno, *Minima Moralia* (London 1974).

CHAPTER 3 HAS ARCHITECTURE AN ESSENCE?

(1) This is certainly true, for example, of the functionalism of Viollet-le-Duc,

Sullivan and Lethaby (see especially, Lethaby's *Architecture*, London 1911).

(2) Sir Denys Lasdun (*RIBAJ*, September 1977, p. 367). A philosophical defence of the doctrine occurs in the theory of 'virtual space' presented by S. K. Langer in *Feeling and Form* (London 1953).

(3) Bruno Zevi, *Architecture as Space* (originally *Sapere Vedere L'Architettura*, trans. M. Gendel, ed. J. A. Barry, New York, 1957) p. 30.

(4) This distinction, and its architectural application, have been finely, and perhaps slightly preciously, elaborated by Adrian Stokes, in *Stones of Rimini* (London 1964) pp. 108ff.

(5) P. Frankl, *Principles of Architectural History, The Four Phases of Architectural Style, 1420–1900* (trans. and ed. J. F. O'Gorman, Cambridge, Mass. 1968), p. 43.

(6) ibid., p. 27.

(7) It is perhaps important to remember Giedion's enormous influence as secretary to the Centre International de l'Architecture Moderne (CIAM), between the wars.

(8) S. Giedion, *Space Time and Architecture*, (5th edn, Cambridge, Mass. 1967) p. lv.

(9) By Sir Ernst Gombrich, for example, in his compelling essay *In Search of Cultural History* (Oxford, 1969). The argument has been carried over into architectural theory by David Watkin, in *Morality and Architecture* (Oxford 1977), where many established myths are demolished.

(10) H. Wölfflin, *Renaissance and Baroque* (trans. K. Simon, London 1964) p. 78. For a theoretical underpinning to this brilliant work, see the same author's *Principles of Art History* (trans. M. D. Hottinger, New York 1932).

(11) For example, it has served as the basis of Pevsner's rejection (in *Pioneers of the Modern Movement from William Morris to Walter Gropius* (London 1936, later revised edns entitled *Pioneers of Modern Design*) and in *An Outline of European Architecture*, London 1943, 7th edn 1963) of 'historicism' (meaning the pursuit of a pre-existing style), and of the influential criticism of Giedion and Sedlmayr.

(12) Giedion, op. cit., and C. Norberg-Schulz, *Meaning in Western Architecture* (London 1975 (Italian edn 1974)). Norberg-Schulz's book is perhaps the most comprehensive recent manifestation of criticism in the *kunstgeschichtlichem* tradition.

(13) Norberg-Schulz, op. cit., *passim*.

(14) By Sir Karl Popper, *The Poverty of Historicism* (London, 1957). This use is not to be confused with that of Pevsner, mentioned in note 11, and succinctly explained in N. Pevsner, J. Fleming and H. Honour, *A Dictionary of Architecture* (expanded edn, London 1975).

(15) Giedion, op. cit., p. 108.

(16) ibid., p. 529.

(17) Watkin, op. cit.

(18) For an example of this particular critical method, see Norberg-Schulz, op. cit.

(19) Cf. J. B. Ache, *Eléments d'une histoire de l'art de bâtir* (Paris 1970) p. 322.

(20) See Alois Riegl, *Stilfragen* (Berlin 1873); Wilhelm Worringer, *Abstraction and Empathy* (trans. M. Bullock, London 1953); and especially Erwin

Panofsky's brilliant essay, 'The History of the Theory of Human Proportions as a Reflection of the History of Styles', reprinted in E. Panofsky, *Meaning in the Visual Arts* (New York 1955).

(21) J. Ruskin, *Stones of Venice* (London 1851, 1853) ch. 5, and E. Panofsky, *Gothic Architecture and Scholasticism* (Latrobe, 1951).

(22) The idea of an 'intentional fallacy' in aesthetics originated in a paper of that name by W. K. Wimsatt and M. C. Beardsley (*Sewanee Review*, 1946, reprinted in W. K. Wimsatt Jr, *The Verbal Icon*, Lexington Kentucky, 1954), who argued that, since what matters in aesthetic understanding is the object itself and not the extraneous circumstances of its production, to seek for the artist's intention is not to engage in genuine criticism of his work, and therefore not to advance aesthetic appreciation. The recognition of this argument as a reiteration of the Cartesian view of consciousness (the view which sees the connection between inner and outer, mind and expression, intention and act, as always contingent) is implicit in R. Wollheim, *Art and its Objects* (New York, 1968) s. 33.

(23) Sir Henry Wotton, *Elements of Architecture* (London 1624).

(24) G. Vasari, *Lives of the Artists* (London 1970) preface to Part III. It must be said, however, that while Vasari here imitated Vitruvius, he was speaking as much of painting as of architecture.

(25) The major source of this view is of course Rudolf Wittkower's seminal work *Architectural Principles in the Age of Humanism* (3rd edn, London 1962). The theory was delivered in many forms by the Renaissance theorists and their followers: sources are detailed by Wittkower in the third appendix to his work. The influence of Wittkower's study has been so great that it has not only led architectural critics to extend its application to the discussion of modern architecture (cf. Colin Rowe, 'The Mathematics of the Ideal Villa' in *The Mathematics of the Ideal Villa and Other Essays*, Cambridge, Mass., 1972), but has also in fact influenced the practice of modern architecture itself, so that a selfconscious Wittkoverian style can often be recognized (see Henry Millon's study of this influence in *Journal of the Society of Architectural Historians*, no. 2, 1972, pp. 83–91). As I go on to argue, this attempt to translate an ideal of 'proportion' from the style which made it intelligible is inherently confused. See also Panofsky, The History of the Theory of Human Proportions'.

(26) The theory is typified by Alberti (*De Re Aèdificatoria*, Florence 1485, trans. Bartolo and Iconi, London 1726, as *Ten Books on Architecture* Book X, chs 5 and 6; see also the famous letter to Matteo da Pasti, Alberti's assistant at Rimini). The Platonist tradition, which derived its principal inspiration from the doctrines of the *Timaeus*, was given its model expression for the mediaeval mind in Macrobius's Commentary on the *Somnium Scipionis* of Cicero, and in Boethius's beautiful and compelling work, *On the Consolation of Philosophy* (see in general, R. Klibansky, *The Continuity of the Platonic Tradition*, London 1939). Both St Augustine and Boethius wrote treatises on music in which the Pythagorean laws of harmony are emphasized as reflections of a harmony that transcends the realm of music, infusing the entire natural order with the properties of number. The detailed working of Pythagorean mathematics into the rules of architectural harmony was not, I think, ever carried out in the ancient works that have come down to

us, but it is clear from Vitruvius' remarks concerning mathematics, proportion and the human body (III.c.1), and from the actual proportions used in Egypt, Greece and Rome, that the Pythagorian theory, or something like it, was the commonly accepted one. Moreover, St Augustine clearly says in his *De Musica* that the laws which determine musical harmony must determine visual harmony too.

(27) The principal figurehead of that school at the time of building was the great 'humanist' Alain de L'Isle, whose philosophy of natural harmony, expounded in the *De Planctu Naturae*, has architectural implications acceptable to any early Renaissance thinker. The proof of the use of Pythagorean ideas in the proportions of the Gothic cathedrals is undertaken in O. von Simson's splendid work *The Gothic Cathedral* (New York 1956).

(28) von Simson, op. cit.

(29) Cf. Vitruvius, III.c.i: *Proportio est ratae partis membrourum in omni opere totiusque commodulatio, ex qua ratio efficitur symmetriarum.* (Vitruvius's concept of *proportio* is not quite identical with our 'proportion': indeed the latter term often corresponds more nearly to *eurythmia*, which Vitruvius is far less ready to reduce to a mathematical rule.) See also Le Corbusier, *The Modulor* (trans. P. de Francia and A. Bostock, London 1951); G. D. Birkhoff, *Aesthetic Measure* (Cambridge, Mass. 1953); and, for surprising Gothic examples, von Simson, op. cit., pp. 207–8.

(30) The use of this system by the Greeks is suggested in P. H. Scholfield, *The Theory of Proportion in Architecture* (Cambridge 1958). For the Golden Section as it occurs in Euclid's geometrical proofs see L. Heath, *The Thirteen Books of Euclid's Elements* (Cambridge 1926) vol. II, pp. 97 ff. For a general discussion of the Golden Section in art, see also R. Wittkower, 'The Changing Concept of Proportion', *Daedalus* (Winter 1960) pp. 201ff.

(31) The point here is of some independent interest, in the light of the often noticed similarities between Greek and Mexican mouldings, and of the occurrence in Mexican architecture of decorative motifs which imitate the famous 'Greek Fret' (see Owen Jones, *The Grammar of Ornament*, London 1868, p. 35).

(32) The analysis here derives from Wölfflin, op. cit., pp. 66–7.

(33) Le Corbusier, op. cit., 2nd edn, p. 44.

(34) Palladio, *Quattro Libri* (Venice 1570) Book IV, preface.

(35) Magnini, *Memorie Intorno Andrea Palladio* (1845) Appendix, p. 12; quoted in Wittkower, op. cit., p. 113 fn.2.

(36) Thus by the end of the classical tradition as the Beaux-Arts school had preserved it, laws of proportion had a character that was considered to be wholly *a posteriori*. For example, in *The Principles of Architectural Composition* (London 1924), H. Robertson wrote that his aim was to give a theory of proportion which resumes 'certain principles of which an analysis of good architecture has proved the existence' (p. 2). And the principles that he gives are so sparse and elementary as scarcely to deserve description.

(37) For example by Temanza, summarized in Wittkower, op. cit., p. 147.

(38) Hogarth, *The Analysis of Beauty* (London 1753) p. 76f.

(39) Guarini, *L'Architettura Civile* (Turin 1737, ed. B. Tavassila La Greca, Milan 1968) p. 6.

(40) See the introduction to Serlio's second book, and the general tenor of such writers as Sir William Chambers.
(41) In fact, if we look back to Vitruvius's explanation of *eurythmia*, variously translated, and, while seemingly distinct from *proportio*, filling a similar critical role, we find an explicit afffirmation of the interdependence between 'proportion' and 'detail' (*Eurythmia est venusta species commodusque in conpositionibus membrorum aspectus*, I.c.II).
(42) On the possible derivation of the cathedral façade from the Roman city gate, see von Simson, op. cit., pp. 109f.
(43) Sir John Summerson, *The Classical Language of Architecture* (London 1963) p. 38.
(44) A. W. Pugin, *The True Principles of Pointed or Christian Architecture* (London 1841) p. 18.
(45) Alec Clifton-Taylor, *The Pattern of English Building* (2nd edn, London 1972) pp. 43–50.
(46) It is, of course, a gross simplification to attribute these churches to Rainaldi, although the precise extent to which they are also the work of Bernini may be doubted. The churches exemplify perfectly the attempt to achieve proportion and harmony in a site that obeys no mathematical order, and to create a composition that destroys the least amount of the surrounding disarray. See R. Wittkower, 'Carlo Rainaldi and the Architecture of the High Baroque in Rome' (*The Art Bulletin*, XIX, 1937, reprinted in R. Wittkower, *Studies in the Italian Baroque*, London 1975).
(47) For this notion of a 'formal object' see A. J. Kenny, *Action, Emotion and Will* (London 1963) p. 189.

CHAPTER 4 EXPERIENCING ARCHITECTURE

(1) The theory of aesthetic experience given in this chapter is more fully elaborated in R. Scruton, *Art and Imagination* (London 1974), Parts II and III.
(2) That is, in the tradition which recognizes a specific technical usage of the term 'aesthetic', the tradition initiated by A. G. Baumgarten in his *Aesthetica* (1750).
(3) The distinction, central to much idealist philosophy, is not always presented very clearly (see G. E. Moore: 'External and Internal Relations', in *Philosophical Studies*, London 1922). In brief, the relation between *a* and *b* is external if (i) *a* and *b* could each exist independently of that relation; (ii) *a* and *b* could each be fully and separately identified. Otherwise the relation is internal. This leaves room for a great variety of relations which might deserve the name 'internal' – in what follows I to some extent draw on arguments presented by Bernard Williams in 'Pleasure and Belief' *Aristotelian Society Supplementary Volume* (1959).
(4) See O. von Simson, *The Gothic Cathedral* (New York 1956) ch. 3, and also Panofsky, *Meaning in the Visual Arts* (New York 1955) ch. 3.
(5) See again von Simson, op. cit., and for an extreme interpretation of this kind, H. Sedlmayr, *Die Enstehung der Kathedrale* (Zurich, 1950).
(6) Sir John Summerson, *Heavenly Mansions* (London 1949) ch. 1.
(7) On this point, see D. W. Hamlyn, *The Psychology of Perception* (London,

1957). The Kantian argument which follows is, in its developed form, enormously difficult. See the passage in the *Critique of Pure Reason* entitled 'The Transcendental Deduction of the Categories', and, for a modern (although I think invalid) version, P. F. Strawson's commentary on the same passage in *The Bounds of Sense* (London, 1966). For a possibly valid version, in no way intended as a commentary upon Kant, see L. Wittgenstein, *Philosophical Investigations* (London, 1953) pp. 200ff.

(8) In German, *Einbildungskraft*. This concept is treated neither clearly nor consistently by Kant, but one central strand in his thought concerning it has been expounded and defended recently by P. F. Strawson in 'Imagination and Perception', in L. Foster and J. W. Swanson (eds), *Experience and Theory* (Cambridge, Mass. 1970, reprinted in P. F. Strawson, *Freedom and Resentment*, London 1974); and by Mary Warnock in *Imagination*, (London 1976) Parts I and II.

(9) This dependence, between the knowledge of what is and the knowledge of what is possible, provided one of the starting points for Kant's philosophy – see the arguments in the 'Analogies', in the *Critique of Pure Reason*. The idea is that I can only know that this before me is a real substantial table if I also know what my experience *would* be like were I to advance towards it, retreat from it, lean against it and so on. Thus the idea of an object is already an idea of systematic *possibilities*.

(10) J. P. Sartre, *L'Imaginaire* (Paris 1940, trans. 'The Psychology of the Imagination', New York, 1948); Wittgenstein op. cit., Part II, s. xi. Wittgenstein does not in fact claim to be presenting a theory of imagination, but for the defence of his views as embodying such a theory see R. Scruton, *Art and Imagination* (London 1974) part II.

(11) S. T. Coleridge, *Biographia Literaria* (London 1817) vol. I, ch. XIII. Hegel, *Lectures on Aesthetics* (1835, trans. T. M. Knox, London 1975).

(12) See Scruton, op. cit., chs 7 and 8.

(13) D. Hume, *A Treatise on Human Nature* (London 1739) Bk.I, Part IV, s. 2.

(14) Among the principal works of phenomenology are those of Husserl (especially his *Ideas, General Introduction to Phenomenology*, 1913, trans. W. R. Boyce Gibson, London 1931), and Merleau-Ponty (whose work is best represented by the treatise *The Phenomenology of Perception*, trans. C. Smith, London 1962). Sartre's works on the imagination could be called 'phenomenological' investigations, as could his treatise *Being and Nothingness*, and as could also the major works of Martin Heidegger. For applications of phenomenology to aesthetics see R. Ingarden, *Das Literarische Kunstwerk* (2nd edn, Tubingen 1960), and M. Dufrenne, *La Phénoménologie de l'expérience ésthétique* (Paris 1953). The phenomenology of musical perception has been touched on by Husserl in his impenetrable work *The Phenomenology of Internal Time Consciousness* (ed. M. Heidegger, trans. J. S. Churchill, Indiana, 1964). To catalogue all the various philosophies and pseudo-philosophies that have claimed a 'phenomenological' basis would be impossible. But – without arguing the point – I would suggest that there is no particular 'method' which this label is used to denote.

(15) I defend this view in *Art and Imagination*, especially ch. 1. See also Wittgenstein, op. cit., *passiom*.

(16) The arguments for this position are complex; I return to them in chapter 10.

(17) For the use of this kind of argument in the study of animal mentality, see especially J. F. Bennett, *Rationality* (London 1964), and *Linguistic Behaviour* (Cambridge, 1976); also D. C. Dennett, *Content and Consciousness* (London 1969).

(18) In other words we can impute mistakes to animals; hence we can apply to their behaviour the concepts of the true and the false; hence we can explain what they do in terms of the 'information' available to them; hence (with a slight stretch) we can usefully attribute to them beliefs.

(19) Assuming, that is (what I shall not argue for), that a bird lacks the concept of self.

(20) Whether 'concept' is quite the right word here depends, I think, on whether our attribution of concepts is ancillary to our attribution of beliefs. It seems to me fairly plausible to suppose that the evaluation of an animal's behaviour in terms of the concepts of truth and falsity already presupposes certain 'conceptual' abilities on the animal's part.

(21) Cf. L. Wittgenstein, *Zettel* (trans. G. E. M. Anscombe and L. Von Wright, ed. G. E. M. Anscombe, Oxford, 1967), section 173: 'I think of a quite short phrase, consisting of only two bars. You say "What a lot that's got in it!" But it is only, so to speak, an optical illusion if you think that what is there goes on as we hear it . . .'.

(22) See Kant, 'Concerning the Ultimate Foundation of the Differentiation of Regions in Space' (1768), in *Selected Pre-Critical Writings* (trans. G. B. Kerferd, and D. E. Alford, Manchester 1968).

(23) The philosophical significance of this axiom, as an essential pre-condition of our concept of identity over time, is explored in P. F. Strawson, *Individuals* (London 1959) chs. 1 and 3. Recently, however, both Strawson and also Saul Kripke have argued that the axiom needs qualifying, and that it is not true in its classical form. The problem is a complex one, but whatever qualifications might need to be introduced, they will not, I think, affect my argument.

(24) See Scruton, op. cit., ch. 10

(25) Cf. the duck-rabbit figure discussed by Wittgenstein, *Philosophical Investigations*, part II, section xi.

(26) Noticeable in many Roman buildings, mentioned by Vitruvius, and explicitly recommended by Alberti, *De Re Aedificatoria* (Florence 1485, trans. Bartolo and Leoni, London 1726, as *Ten Books on Architecture*) Book VII, ch. V.

(27) The method here (that of classifying mental states in terms of what one might call their 'formal' properties) derives from Wittgenstein – see especially, *Zettel*. A fuller account of imaginative experience is given in Scruton, op. cit., part II.

(28) See, for example, R. Wittkower, 'Carlo Rainaldi and the Architecture of the High Baroque in Rome' (*The Art Bulletin*, XIX, 1937, reprinted in *Studies in the Italian Baroque*, London 1975).

(29) Alberti, op. cit., Book I, Ch. X: 'a row of columns being indeed nothing else but a wall open and discontinued in several places. And were we to define a column, it would not be improper to describe it as a strong

continued part of the wall, carried perpendicularly up from the foundation to the top . . .'.

(30) On this point, see Sir John Summerson's *Georgian London* (London 1963).

(31) See R. Wittkower's persuasive description of the dramatic geometry of this church in *Architectural Pinciples in the Age of Humanism* (London, 3rd edn, 1962) pp. 97ff.

(32) See, for example, the excellent discussion of the range of architectural experience in S. E. Rasmussen, *Experiencing Architecture* (Cambridge, Mass. 1959).

(33) See, for example, the subtle discussion by H. P. Grice in 'Some Remarks Concerning the Senses', in R. J. Butler (ed.), *Analytical Philosophy, First Series* (Oxford 1966).

(34) See, for example, Ruskin's comments in *Seven Lamps of Architecture* (London 1849) ch. 2.

(35) Alberti, op. cit., especially Book VI, ch. 2.

(36) For an explanation of Bernini's *'concetto'* see Wittkower's discussion of Bernini's work at St Peter's, *Art and Architecture in Italy, 1600–1750* (London 1968) pp. 115ff.

CHAPTER 5 JUDGING ARCHITECTURE

(1) J. Ruskin *Stones of Venice* (London 1861, 1863) ch. 1.

(2) Geoffrey Scott, *The Architecture of Humanism* (London 1914) p. 232.

(3) Ruskin, op. cit., Appendix II, S. Even Ruskin concedes that the effect of mass gives to this church a certain beauty when seen from afar. As a corrective to Ruskin, see Wittkower's analysis in *Studies in the Italian Baroque* (London 1975).

(4) The intentional object of a state of mind is the object as the subject sees, describes or 'posits' it (see chapter 1, note 4).

(5) See, for example, F. N. Sibley, 'Aesthetic and non-Aesthetic', *Phil. Rev.* (1965; and S. N. Hampshire, 'Logic and Appreciation', in W. Elton (ed.), *Aesthetics and Language* (Oxford 1954). The view is anticipated in D. Hume's essay 'Of the Standard of Taste', in *Essays Moral, Political and Literary* (London 1741).

(6) The idea of an action as a 'conclusion' of an argument derives from Aristotle (*Nichomachean Ethics*, 1147a, 27–8). Alternatively, practical reasons are reasons not for thinking but for doing something. The point has been well discussed by G. E. M. Anscombe in *Intention* (Oxford 1957) sections 33ff.

(7) On the notion of the autonomy of the aesthetic judgement (which is related to the view that aesthetic judgement arises from treating its object not as a means but as an end), see Kant and Collingwood. The question of what this 'autonomy' really amounts to is a deep and difficult one; I am not sure that I have any satisfactory answer to it.

(8) The idea that a connection may be necessary but not universal derives from L. Wittgenstein, *Philosophical Investigations* (London 1953) Part I.

(9) Cf. B. Williams, 'Pleasure and Belief', *Aristotelian Society Supplementary Volume* (1959).

(10) See in particular the beautiful speech given by Socrates at the end of the *Symposium*. Plato's thought – reconstituted by Augustine and Boethius,

and embellished with all the symbolic trappings of mediaeval courtly love – achieved its finest expression in Dante's *Divine Comedy*, a work in which the conflict between the carnal and the spiritual, the temporal and the eternal, is confronted and resolved.

(11) See, for example, *Summa Theologica*, 1a 2ae, 27, 1. Also Hegel's introduction to the *Lectures on Aesthetics* (1835, trans. T. M. Knox, London 1975).

(12) Cf. Hume, op. cit.

(13) Kant was the first philosopher to take this point really seriously, as defining the basis of aesthetic judgement. He spoke in this connection of the 'universality' of taste, of the fact that it always claims for itself a *right* which others ought to acknowledge or obey (*Critique of Judgement*, 1790, *passim*).

(14) Cf. L. Wittgenstein, *Lectures on Aesthetics, Freud, etc.* (ed. C. Barrett, Oxford, 1966).

(15) For the story of the erection of this building, see R. Wittkower, 'F. Borromini, his Character and Life', in *Studies in the Italian Baroque*.

(16) F. Borromini, *Opus Architectonicum* (written 1641–1656, published, ed. Giannini, Rome, 1725).

(17) See chapter 3, note 22, on the so-called 'intentional fallacy'.

(18) For further speculations of this kind see Geoffrey Scott's impressive polemic *The Architecture of Humanism*, chs. VIII and IX. For the extreme opposite view, that baroque architecture is essentially an expression of the spirit of the Counter-Reformation, and must so be seen, see Werner Weisbach's *Der Barock als Kunst der Gegenreformation* (Berlin 1921).

(19) A. W. Pugin, *The True Principles of Pointed or Christian Architecture* (London 1841) and Viollet-le-Duc, *Entretiens sur l'architecture* (Paris 1863, 1872, trans. B. Bucknall, *Discourses on Architecture*, 2 vols, Boston 1889, vol. 1).

(20) Especially in *Stones of Venice*, and followed therein by A. Stokes in *Stones of Rimini* (London 1964) pp. 108ff.

(21) See S. K. Langer, *Feeling and Form* (London 1953) ch. 1) It is the term 'virtual' that I borrow. The same idea has been expressed by N. L. Prak in *The Language of Architecture* (The Hague 1968) p. 30, as 'phenomenal structure'.

(22) See the discussion of these examples in Peter Murray, *The Architecture of the Italian Renaissance* (London 1963) p. 67ff.

(23) A. Schopenhauer, *The World as Will and Representation* (trans. E. F. J. Payne, Colorado 1958).

(24) Serlio, *Six Books on Architecture*, with supplement by V. Scamozzi (Venice 1619) p. 101.

(25) Alberti, *De Re Aedificatoria* (Florence 1485, trans. Bertolo and Leoni, London 1726 as *Ten Books on Architecture*) Book IX, ch. V: *'non opinio, verum animis innata quaedam ratio efficiet'*.

(26) A. Trystan Edwards, *Good and Bad Manners in Architecture* (London 1949) pp. 83ff.

(27) S. Freud, *Leonardo* (trans. A. Tyson, London 1963).

CHAPTER 6 FREUD, MARX AND MEANING

(1) See, for example, the essays by Addison in the *Spectator*, 1712, entitled 'The Pleasures of the Imagination', and also the many discussions

inspired by E. Burke's dissertation *Of the Sublime and the Beautiful* (London 1757) e.g. R. P. Knight (architect of Downton Castle), *An Analytical Enquiry into the Principles of Taste* (4th edn, London 1808) Part II, ch. III and V. Price, *Essays on the Picturesque* (London 1810). The history of the movement in architecture and its mode of thought are well set out in Peter Collins, *Changing Ideals in Modern Architecture* (London 1965) ch. 1. The influence of the theory of 'association' was great, first as providing the theoretical foundations for a rejection of classical architectural thought, second, as introducing a love of age and decay for their own sake. See Paul Zucker, *The Fascination of Decay* (New Jersey, 1968), for the many striking pieces of anti-architecture which the theory thereby inspired.

(2) For this objection, see B. Bosanquet, 'On the Nature of Aesthetic Emotion', in B. Bosanquet, *Science and Philosophy* (London 1927).

(3) D. Hume, *A Treatise on Human Nature* (London 1739, Book II, Part 1, s. iii – Selby-Bigge edn, p. 229).

(4) See Sinclair Gauldie, *Architecture* (New York and Toronto, 1969) p. 27, where the aesthetic nature of such constructions is effectively described.

(5) On the general distinction between object and cause, see A. J. Kenny, *Action, Emotion and Will* (London 1963).

(6) Consider in particular the phenomenon of 'double intentionality' which I attempt to describe in *Art and Imagination* (London 1974) ch. 15.

(7) This feature of the knowledge of the 'content' of one's mental state has been much discussed, for example by G. E. M. Anscombe in her treatment of 'mental causes', *Intention* (Oxford 1957) pp. 16f., and by Wittgenstein in his 'Conversations on Freud' (*Lectures on Aesthetics, Freud etc.*, ed. C. Barrett, Oxford 1966). See also Douglas Gasking, 'Avowals', in R. J. Butler (ed.), *Analytical Philosophy, Second Series* (Oxford, 1963).

(8) See, e.g. Freud's essay on Dostoevsky, reprinted in *Collected Papers* (ed. J. Strachey, London 1950) vol. V.

(9) Hannah Segal, 'A Psychoanalytic Approach to Aesthetics', *International Journal of Psychoanalysis* (1952), pp. 196–207; Robert Waelder, *Psychoanalytic Approach to Art* (London, 1961) which contains a bibliography of relevant material; Ernst Kris, *Psychoanalytic Explorations in Art* New York, 1952); and Anton Ehrenzweig, *The Psychoanalysis of Artistic Vision and Hearing* (London 1953), and *The Hidden Order of Art* (London 1967).

(10) See, for example, Melanie Klein, *The Psychoanalysis of Children* (London 1932).

(11) See especially the essays collected as volumes 2 and 3 of *The Critical Writings of Adrian Stokes* (ed. L. Gowing, London 1978). An excellent short summary of Stokes's thought from a Kleinian point of view is given by R. Wollheim, 'Adrian Stokes, Critic, Painter, Poet', in *The Times Literary Supplement* (17 Feb. 1978). Wollheim draws attention to a further distinctive feature of Kleinian psychiatry that makes it peculiarly relevant to aesthetics, which is that it is able to treat the artist's relation to his work, and the audience's relation to that work, in precisely the same terms, and therefore does not degenerate (as Freud's studies of Leonardo and Michelangelo degenerate) into mere armchair psychology of creation.

How far Stokes's view of the nature and value of architecture is in fact dependent upon its Kleinian dressing is not clear. The theory that the appreciation of beauty involves a 'sense of wholeness' arising from the reconciliation of two conflicting mental principles, one aggressive, one 'melting' or submissive, derives from Schiller (see *The Aesthetic Education of Man, in a Series of Letters,* revised edition 1801 (reprinted, with translation and commentary, ed. M. Wilkinson and C. A. Willoughby, Oxford 1967) especially letter 17). On one level Schiller's view that 'energy' and 'meltingness' derive from two separate aspects of the human mind, reconciled only in the 'play' of the understanding as it contemplates art, is identical with that of Stokes (and for both Stokes and Schiller there is a sense in which the resulting feeling is 'oceanic'). However, Schiller, who derived his theory directly from Kant, was referring to conscious principles of the rational understanding, and would have looked on the infantile experience, not as the essence of mental life, but as no more than a premonition of something that must be understood in its mature manifestations.

(12) The example is a favourite of Stokes (see *The Quattro Cento*, London 1932) ch. 5. The whole building has been excellently analysed by Pasquale Rotondi in *The Ducal Palace of Urbino* (London 1969).

(13) J. Ruskin, *Seven Lamps of Architecture* (London 1849) ch. III, s. 8.

(14) L. Wittgenstein, *Lectures and Conversations on Aesthetics, etc*. (ed. Barrett, Oxford 1966).

(15) The concept of 'self-ascription' here expressed, and its importance in determining the nature and content of the mind, are further explored in R. Scruton, 'Self-Knowledge and Intention' (*Proceedings of the Aristotelian Society*, 1977–8). A full theory of the self along these lines lies beyond the scope of the present work, but I adumbrate some small parts of it in chapter 10.

(16) A. Stokes, *Stones of Rimini* (London 1934, *passim*).

(17) It goes without saying that, in invoking the concept of 'ideology' here, I am referring to what has been called an 'essentially contested concept': a concept postulated in advance of any theory that might provide its full elaboration. Many who call themselves Marxists will disagree with my account of this concept, on the grounds that for them it belongs to a theory far more sophisticated than the one that I assume. Indeed Marxism now inclines to habits of sophistication and self-reference which make it impossible for an outsider to debate the main considerations of Marxist theory with any confidence that his opponents will admit to understanding him. Nor is it clear what Marxism means in the realm of aesthetics and critical theory – see, for example, A. Marcuse, *The Philosophy of Aesthetics* (New York 1972); G. Lucács, *Writer and Critic* (trans. and ed. A Kahn, London 1970); Raymond Williams, *Marxism and Literature* (Oxford 1977), all of which make ambitious statements of position which fail to translate from the jargon through which they are presented. For a more traditional position, see G. Plekhanov, *Art and Social Life* (trans. E. Fox *et al.*, London 1953).

The source for the concept of ideology is of course K. Marx and F. Engels: *The German Ideology* (London 1963), while that for the assignment of art to 'superstructure' is the preface to Marx's *Contribution to the Critique of Political Economy*, in *Marx on Economics* (ed. R. Freedman, London 1962).

It is this assignment which enables the Marxist to think that it is 'the responsibility of a Marxist aesthetic . . . to demonstrate how . . . objectivity emerges in the creative process . . . as truth independent of the artist's consciousness' (Lucács, 'Art and Objective Truth', op. cit.); but it is an assignment that has been questioned by recent Marxists, as has the whole simplistic relation between base and superstructure. Very few would now agree with Marx in thinking that

> the distinction should always be made between the material transformation of the economic conditions of production, which can be determined with the precision of natural science, and the legal, political, religious, aesthetic or philosophic – in short ideological – forms in which men become conscious of this conflict and fight it out. (Preface, *Critique of Political Economy*)

See, for criticism of this simple antithesis from a professedly 'Marxist' standpoint, Raymond Williams, op. cit., and Ernst Fischer, *Art against Ideology* (trans. A. Bostock, New York 1969) pp. 56ff. From all this it will be apparent that I have tried to take issue with a very simplified form of Marxist theory, in order to present the particular intellectual questions which interest me. Nevertheless, it seems to me that the questions are real ones, and that my arguments tend to show that there cannot be such a thing as a specifically 'Marxist' method in the criticism of architecture.

Despite the lack of any directly Marxist criticism of buildings, there is a considerable literature of Marxist comment on the role of building in the life of man and society, and this comment sometimes comes close to enunciating what could be taken as principles of architectural practice. Problems of urban planning have such an immediate impact on political life that it would of course be absurd for a political theory to ignore them. Hence Engel's interesting attempt to relate spoilation to the division of labour in capitalist industry (see the final chapters of *The Condition of the Working Class in England*, Stanford, California, 1968). The relation of the Marxist theory of history to the process of design is discussed, for example, by Manfredo Tafuri, *Progetto e Utopia* (trans. B. L. La Penta as *Architecture and Utopia: Design and Capitalist Development*, Cambridge, Mass., 1976). It is hard to derive any satisfactory architectural criticism from the result, however.

(18) See, for example, the bibliography in Raymond Williams, op. cit., and also the work of Walter Benjamin, *Illuminationen* (Frankfurt 1955), and Theodor Adorno, especially, *The Philosophy of Modern Music* (Frankfurt 1948, trans. A. G. Mitchell and W. V. Bloomster, New York, 1973).

(19) For refinements of this crude position see Fischer, op. cit., and Williams, op. cit.

(20) *The Cantos*, no. LXXXI: 'To have gathered from the air a live tradition or
from a fine old eye the unconquered flame
This is not vanity.'

(21) Schoenberg in *Style and Idea* (ed. L. Stein, London 1975); Thomas Mann in *Dr Faustus* (trans. H. T. L. Parker, London 1949).

(22) E.g. *De Moribus et Officio Episcoporum Tractatus*. See O. von Simson, *The Gothic Cathedral* (New York 1956) ch. 5.

(23) Viollet-le-Duc, *Entretiens sur l'architecture* (Paris 1863, 1872, trans. B. Bucknall, *Discourses on Architecture,* Boston 1889) vol. 1, pp. 230ff.
(24) See again, however, the disclaiming notes to chapter 2. It is worth pointing out that Lenin himself affected a kind of pragmatic tolerance in aesthetic matters which makes it difficult to attribute to him any particular view of their importance (see V. I. Lenin, *On Literature and Art,* Moscow 1967).
(25) See the discussion in K. Marx, 'On Alienated Labour', from the *1844 Manuscripts*, in *Marx's Concept of Man* (ed. Erich Fromm, trans. T. B. Bottomore, New York, 1961).
(26) See H. Wölfflin *Renaissance and Baroque* (trans. K. Simon, London 1964) pp. 77ff.
(27) R. G. Collingwood, *The Principles of Art* (Oxford 1938) pp. 39–40.

CHAPTER 7 THE LANGUAGE OF ARCHITECTURE

(1) The desire to see architecture – and indeed all forms of art – as kinds of language provides the most popular of all aesthetic theories. It is difficult to provide a simple diagnosis of this popularity, but it is evidenced in the following recent titles: C. Jencks, *Meaning in Architecture* (London 1969); N. L. Prak, *The Language of Architecture* (The Hague, 1968); S. Hesselgren, *The Language of Architecture* (Kristianstad, 1969); G. K. Koenig, *Analisi del Linguaggio Architettonico,* vol. 1 (Florence 1964); Sir John Summerson, *The Classical Language of Architecture* (London 1963); P. Portoghesi, *Borromini: Architettura come Linguaggio* (Milan 1967). It is also evident in the (for the most part desultory) attempts to apply information theory and semiology to the theory of architecture, the first by C. Jencks (*Modern Movements in Architecture,* London 1973) pp. 172–5, the second by Barthes, Eco and others (see notes 8 and 12). The general tendency has also made itself felt in analytical aesthetics – see, for example Nelson Goodman's *Languages of Art* (Indiana 1968), as well as in applied aesthetic theory (as in L. B. Meyer, *Emotion and Meaning in Music,* Chicago 1956, and Deryck Cooke, *The Language of Music,* Oxford 1959). I do not deal with 'information theory' in this chapter, it being now sufficiently evident that the theory is irrelevant to aesthetics, being a special branch of the science of prediction, and unconcerned with 'meaning'. (For a conclusive refutation of the relevance of information theory to aesthetics, see R. Wollheim, *Art and its Objects* (New York 1968) s. 56.) The fundamental idea is evidenced in the subtitle to Croce's great work – *Estetica come . . . linguistica generale* – and arises whenever the symbolic and communicative nature of art is presented as its most important aspect.
(2) For the philosophical elaboration of this distinction, see the seminal article by H. P. Grice, 'Meaning' (*Phil. Rev.,* 1957).
(3) The interdependence between intention and convention in language use is admirably illustrated by D. K. Lewis in his excellent work *Convention* (Oxford 1972). See also P. F. Strawson, 'Intention and Convention in Speech Acts', in P. F. Strawson, *Logico – Linguistic Papers* (London 1971).
(4) The theories in question are those of Charles Morris, *Foundations of a Theory of Signs* (Chicago 1938), and C. L. Stevenson, *Ethics and Language* (Yale, New Haven, 1945).
(5) One such theory is that of Koenig, op. cit.

(6) ibid, p. 15.

(7) L. B. Alberti, *De Re Aedificatoria* (Florence 1485, trans. Bartolo and Leoni, London 1726 as *Ten Books of Architecture*, reprinted ed. J. Rykwert, London 1965) Book VI, ch. 2

(8) By far the most compelling description of this 'grammatical' nature of the Orders is that given by Summerson in *The Classical Language of Architecture.*

(9) The concept of semiology (the 'general' science of signs) derives from F. de Saussure, *Cours de Linguistique Générale* (Lausanne, 1916). It was left to others to invent this general 'science', notably to Barthes (*Éléments de sémiologie,* Paris 1964; *S/Z*, Paris 1970, etc.) and to his associates in the review *Tel Quel*. For a critical discussion of semiology, and of Barthes in particular, see J. Casey and R. Scruton, 'Modern Charlatanism; III', *The Cambridge Review* (30 January, 1976). For an extended examination of the literary application, see Jonathan Culler, *Structuralist Poetics* (London 1975), and for an attempt to claim the territory of architecture in the name of semiotic analysis, see the German review *Konzept*, ed. A. Carlini and B. Scheider, Tubingen; especially *Konzept 1* ('Architektur als Zeichensystem', 1975) and *Konzept 3* (1976, entitled, in true semiological fashion, 'Die Stadt als Text', and containing a piece by Barthes, here called 'Semiotik und Urbanismus', and originally published in *Tel Quel* as 'L'Architecture d'aujourd'hui'). In the present chapter I argue from the basis of Fregean and Tarskian semantics, and therefore find it difficult to take seriously the pretensions of this pseudo-science. However, the search for a 'general' science of signs is not confined to continental semiology. Nelson Goodman, in *Languages of Art* develops such a theory from a basis of analytical nominalism.

(10) See especially the writings of Barthes, and *Mythologies* (Paris, 1957), in particular.

(11) The emphasis on structure is the point at which semiology seems to make contact with the anthropology of Lévi-Strauss (see, for example, *Anthropologie Structurale*, Paris 1958) and the linguistic theory of Chomsky (as in *Aspects of the Theory of Syntax,* Cambridge, Mass. 1965).

(12) Barthes, *Éléments de Sémiologie* (trans. A. Lavers and C. Smith as *Elements of Semiology*, London 1967, pp. 27, 62ff.).

(13) For U. Eco see *La Struttura Assente* (Milan 1968), in which the application to architecture is taken extremely seriously. The intellectual purpose of *Tel Quel* distances it from *Konzept,* the latter being in fact an architectural glossy designed for the coffee tables of the radical chic.

(14) See Barthes, *Mythologies*.

(15) This thought, brilliantly expounded by G. Frege ('On Sense and Reference', *The Philosophical Writings of Gottlob Frege*, ed. and trans. P. T. Geach and M. Black, Oxford, 1952), and developed formally by Alfred Tarski ('The Concept of Truth in Formalized Languages' in *Logic, Semantics, Metamathematics*, Oxford 1956), has been given renewed philosophical importance in recent years in the work of D. Davidson – see especially his 'Truth and Meaning', *Synthese* (1967).

(16) Frege, op. cit. See also M. Dummett, *Frege, Philosophy of Language* (London 1973).

(17) This was proved for formalized languages by Tarski, op. cit. Undeniable advances have been made in the understanding of natural languages by the attempt to extend Tarski's theory to cover them, either directly (see Davidson, op. cit., and the essays in *Truth and Meaning*, ed. G. Evans and J. McDowell, Oxford 1977), or indirectly, through the apparatus of model theory and the consequent 'relativization' of the concept of truth (see, for example, R. Montague, *Formal Philosophy*, ed. R. H. Thomason, London and Yale 1979).

(18) E.g. Eco, op. cit., and Barthes, *'L'Architecture d'aujourd'hui'*. For a truly pretentious example of architectural semiology, in which its extravagant claims and its ultimate vacuity are perfectly exemplified, see U. Eco, 'A Componential Analysis of the Architectural Sign/Column', in *Semiotica*, vol. 2, 1972.

(19) Eco, op. cit., pp. 207ff. The borrowing is from J. S. Mill's *System of Logic* (10th edn, London, 1879) vol. 1, Bk. I, ch. 2.

(20) A similar attempt to divorce denotation or reference from truth (i.e., to divorce the interpretation of 'signs' from the truth-conditions of 'sentences' (complexes) in which they might occur) is undertaken by S. K. Langer, in her analysis of music in *Philosophy in a New Key* (Cambridge, Mass. 1942). The same attempt is also implicit in Nelson Goodman's theory of the 'symbol systems' of art in *Languages of Art*. See R. Wollheim, 'On Nelson Goodman's *Languages of Art*', in R. Wollheim *On Art and the Mind* (London 1972), and also R. Scruton, 'Attaching Words to the World', *Times Literary Supplement* (2 August 1977).

(21) Eco, op. cit., p. 209.

(22) J. Ruskin, *Seven Lamps of Architecture* (London 1849, s. 8) ch. II.

(23) This 'holistic' view of meaning, adumbrated in 'Sense and Reference', cit., is given full elaboration and support in Dummett, op. cit.

(24) See Sir William Chambers, *Architecture* (ed. Gwilt, London 1825, 'Of Persians and Caryatids', pp. 191–2).

(25) See again chapter 6 note 1.

CHAPTER 8 EXPRESSION AND ABSTRACTION

(1) For arguments against the view that music is a representational art, see R. Scruton 'Representation in Music', *Philosophy* (1976).

(2) For a discussion of the problem, see N. Goodman, *Languages of Art* (Indiana 1968) and R. Wollheim's 'On Nelson Goodman's *Languages of Art*', in R. Wollheim, *On Art and the Mind* (London 1972).

(3) See R. Scruton 'Attaching Words to the World', *Times Literary Supplement* (12 August 1977).

(4) See G. Frege 'The Thought, a Logical Enquiry', trans. A. M. and M. Quinton, *Mind* (1956).

(5) See, for example, Goodman, op. cit. ch. 1, and R. Wollheim, *Art and its Objects* (New York 1968) s. 26. To take an example: a Dutch interior may contain a fragment which intentionally resembles a tree, but which is seen, not as a tree, but as a tree in a picture. For the fragment represents, not a tree, but a picture.

(6) The principal advocates of the distinction – Croce, and, following him, Collingwood – had in mind to abolish representation, or at least certain

kinds of representation, as merely accidental features of art, while retaining expression as the aesthetic essence.

(7) For the notion of 'Reference without description', see S. K. Langer, *Philosophy in a New Key* (Cambridge Mass. 1942); as the arguments in the last chapter suggest, it is little more than a *jeu de mots* to use the term 'reference' in this sense, legitimate only so long as one does not also see reference (as Frege saw it) as part of the theory of understanding.

(8) It is necessary here to separate the philosophical theory of 'expressionism' (the theory typified by Croce and Collingwood, which elevates some sense of the term 'expression' into the key concept in aesthetics), from the artistic movements which have gone by that name. These movements occurred in such close contiguity as to be regarded as in some sense parts of a single movement. In music, expressionism was typified by early Schoenberg, by Berg, and by the 'serious' (i.e. uninteresting) works of Kurt Weill; while, in painting, Kandinsky and Kokoschka made similar pronouncements and indulged in similar stylistic gestures. In architecture, various late offshoots of Art Nouveau and the Jugendstil (Rudolf Steiner, Hans Poelzig, the Werkbund, etc.) applied for membership of the expressionist club. In every case expressionism signified intensity, individuality, self-reference, the stretching, heightening and contorting of line and form into every possible suggestion of a 'meaning'. For the first stirrings of architectural expressionism, see Otto Kohtz, *Gedanken über Architektur* (Berlin, 1909). See, in general, W. Pehnt, *Expressionist Architecture* (London 1973).

(9) See Hans Sedlmayr, *Johann Bernhard Fischer von Erlach* (new edn, Vienna 1956) pp. 123ff.

(10) N. Pevsner, *An Outline of European Architecture,* (London 1943, 7th edn, 1963) p. 255.

(11) See Ludwig Wittgenstein, *The Blue and Brown Books* (Oxford, 1958) pp. 177–85, and R. Wollheim, *Art and its Objects,* s. 41.

(12) Vitruvius, IV.c.1.

(13) The difference here is something like the difference between metaphor and simile. The comparison effected by a metaphor is distinguished by the fact that it may be impossible to 'spell out' what it contains. See R. Scruton, *Art and Imagination* (London, 1974) Part I.

(14) S. Hesselgren, *The Language of Architecture* (Kristianstad 1969) vol. 2, fig. 36.

(15) H. Wölfflin, *Renaissance and Baroque* (trans. K. Simon, London 1964) chs 1 and 2.

(16) L. Wittgenstein, *Lectures and Conversations on Aesthetics, etc.* (ed. Barrett, Oxford 1966). My method at this point is also Wittgensteinian, in that it makes the analysis of a concept dependent upon an understanding of its genesis. (But the thought goes back to Hegel.)

(17) See, for example, *Art and Illusion* (London 1960), and *Meditations on a Hobby Horse* (London 1963).

(18) The image here, and the thought, are Hegel's. See the Introduction to the *Lectures on Aesthetics* (trans. T. M. Knox, London 1975).

(19) On the idea of knowledge by acquaintance, see Lord Russell, 'Knowledge by Acquaintance', in *Mysticism and Logic* (London 1917). On the extension

of this notion to the experience of art, see Scruton, *Art and Imagination*, pp. 105–6.

CHAPTER 9 THE SENSE OF DETAIL

(1) Despite the many views to the contrary – e.g. that of E. Bullough, *Aesthetics* (ed. E. M. Wilkinson, Stanford 1957) (for the philosophy of 'psychical distance'), and H. S. Langfeld *The Aesthetic Attitude* (New York 1920). But see G. Dickie, 'The Myth of the Aesthetic Attitude', in *American Philosophical Quarterly* (1964). In fact the question whether there is or is not an aesthetic attitude depends very much on what is meant by 'attitude'. Most sides to the discussion fail to make clear quite what they mean by the term.

(2) Cf. G. Frege, 'On Sense and Reference' *The Philosophical Writings of Gottlob Frege* (ed. and trans. P. T. Geach and M. Black, Oxford 1952), and M. Dummett, *Frege, Philosophy of Language* (London 1973).

(3) L. B. Albert, *De Re Aedificatoria* (Florence 1485, trans. Bartolo and Leoni, London 1726 as *Ten Books of Architecture*, reprinted, ed. J. Rykwert, London 1965) Book VI, ch. 2.

(4) See Guarini, *L'Architettura Civile* (Turin 1737, ed. B. Tavassila La Greca, Milan 1968).

(5) There are many Roman and Middle-Eastern examples of this ornament, and it was immediately adopted by the Renaissance masters as an essential part of their vocabulary, although later condemned by Sir William Chambers (*Architecture*, ed. Gwilt, London 1825, pp. 289f.), on the grounds that a niche should be a bare repository, with no character of its own.

(6) Giedion, *Space, Time and Architecture* (5th edn, London 1967) pp. 157–9. It is perhaps interesting to note Aalto's own description of the concrete baroque: 'Grown up children playing with curves and tensions which they do not control. It smells of Hollywood' (Alvar Aalto, in *Zodiac 3*, p. 78).

(7) In *Stones of Rimini* (London 1934), Stokes describes the distinction more traditionally. The Kleinian emphasis enters later, for example, in *Smooth and Rough* (London 1951), and the other essays collected in vols 2 and 3 of the *Collected Critical Writings of Adrian Stokes* (ed. L. Gowing, London 1978).

(8) In *Seven Lamps of Architecture* (London 1849) ch. 1. For the influence of Ruskin here see F. A. Paley's *Manual of Gothic Mouldings* (5th edn, ed. W. M. Fawcett, London 1891), a book which was widely read throughout the late nineteenth century, and whose influence on the buildings of the time is everywhere apparent.

(9) Willhelm Worringer, *Form in Gothic* (London 1927) ch. XIII.

(10) See, for example, I. Stravinsky, *La Poétique de la Musique* (trans. A. Knodel and I. Dahlas *Poetics of Music in the Form of Six Lessons*, London 1970).

(11) See Alberti, op. cit., Book IX, ch. 8.

(12) The richness of the vocabulary used by Alberti in articulating his concept of the appropriate is, I think, worthy of note, see Hans-Karl Lücke, *Index Verborum to Alberti's 'De Re Aedificatoria'* (Munich, 1970 onwards).

(13) Walter Gropius, letter to Goebbels, quoted in Barbara Miller Lane, *Architecture and Politics in Germany, 1918–1945* (Cambridge, Mass. 1968) p. 181.

(14) Hence the once popular theory that (in architecture at least) beauty consists in 'unity in variety' (see A. Göller, *Zur Aesthetik der Architektur*, Berlin 1887).

(15) Cf. D. K. Lewis, *Convention* (Oxford 1972).

(16) See Teshin Okakura, *The Book of Tea* (Tokyo 1906; English trans., Rutland Vermont and Tokyo 1956), in which the philosophy of the tea ceremony is finely expounded. It would of course be foolish to underestimate the enormous amount of thought and energy that has been expended in the development and instruction of manners in every civilization. Erasmus is not the only great Western thinker to have devoted a treatise to the topic. (*De Civitate Morum Puerilium*, 1526, a book which saw 130 editions.) See, in general, Norbert Elias *The Civilizing Process: The history of manners* (German 1936; vol. 1 trans. E. Jephcott, New York 1977). Perhaps it suffices to remind the reader of our own 'tea ceremony', not merely as satirized by Miss Mitford, but also as observed by the most self-consciously 'tragic' of all modern Japanese:

> When Englishmen drink tea, the pourer always asks each person whether he prefers 'milk first' or 'tea first'. One might suppose that it comes to the same thing whether it is the milk or the tea that is poured into the cup first, but in this seemingly rather trivial matter the English ideology of life is staunchly in evidence. Certain Englishmen are convinced that milk should be poured into the teacup first, then the tea, and if one were to reverse the order, doubtless they would see the act as the first step to violation of the principles they hold most dear. (Yukio Mishima, *On Hagakure,* trans. K. Sparling, London 1977, p. 55)

(17) Cicero, *De Officiis,* XXVII and XLI. The same concept was regularly used by Vitruvius as a term of architectural praise.

(18) The point is partly rendered explicit by Daniele Barbaro, in his edition of Vitruvius, where he says of the six Vitruvian categories – *ordinatio, dispositio, eurythmia, symmetria, decor, distributio* – that 'these terms are general and common and as such have their definition in the general and common science which is first and is called metaphysics. But when an artist wants to apply one of those elements to his own profession, then he restricts that universality to the particular and special needs of his own art' (*I dieci libri dell'Architettura di M. Vitruvio,* Venice 1556, quoted and discussed in R. Wittkower, *Architectural Principles in the Age of Humanism,* London, 3rd edn 1962, p. 68).

(19) How it is possible for a term to acquire such a 'freedom' of application and still retain its 'common' sense is a difficult question, and one which I have tried (with only limited success) to answer in *Art and Imagination* (London 1974) Part I).

(20) Kant, *Critique of Judgement*, especially Part I, section 17.

CHAPTER 10 CONCLUSION: ARCHITECTURE AND MORALITY

(1) The ancient distinction between theoretical and practical reason (subtly

expounded by Aristotle in *Nichomachean Ethics*) is here being extended to the notion of a reason for feeling, rather than for doing something. I take it as obvious, from Aristotle's discussion of the emotions, that he would have recognized the legitimacy of the extension.

(2) Kant, *Critique of Practical Reason*, and *Critique of Judgement*.

(3) This point is well argued by F. N. Sibley in 'Aesthetic and Non-Aesthetic' (*Phil. Rev.* 1965).

(4) A view upheld by Kant and recently argued in two influential books by R. M. Hare (*Language of Morals*, Oxford 1952, and *Freedom and Reason*, Oxford 1963).

(5) My thought in this paragraph has been greatly influenced by discussion with John Casey on the concept of virtue.

(6) On 'Knowing What to Feel', see R. Scruton, 'The Significance of Common Culture' in *Philosophy* (1979).

(7) Kant, *Critique of Judgement*, Introduction, section 5.

(8) See Paolo Portoghesi, *Roma Barocca* (Rome and Bari 1966) vol. 1, ch. 3.

(9) Sf. Ruskin: 'and when all was done, instead of the very doubtful advantage of the power of going fast from place to place, we should have had the certain advantage of increased pleasure in stopping at home' (*Seven Lamps of Architecture*, London 1849, ch. 7). And note Matthew Arnold's arguments in *Culture and Anarchy* (London 1869), in which the 'energetic absorption in external aims' is severely and convincingly castigated.

(10) See Hegel's *Philosophy of Right* and *Phenomenology of Spirit*, and also F. H. Bradley *Ethical Studies* (London 1876, 2nd edn, 1927).

(11) See R. Scruton, 'Self-knowledge and Intention' (*Proceedings of the Aristotelian Society*, 1977–8), and also D. C. Dennett, *Content and Consciousness* (London 1969).

(12) See, for example, the impressive argument of the *Phenomenology of Spirit*, and Bradley's eloquent borrowing from it in *Ethical Studies*, op. cit.

(13) See, for example, the papers by D. K. Lewis and D. C. Dennett, in A. O. Rorty (ed.), *The Identities of Persons* (Oxford, 1977).

(14) As an example of such a philosophy see J. S. Mill, *On Liberty* (London, 1859).

(15) ibid.

(16) John Locke, *An Essay on Human Understanding* (London 1698) II, 27.

(17) In a persuasive book Thomas Nagel has argued for a connection between the sense of self-identity and the ability to reason about one's satisfaction in a way that transcends reflection upon one's present desire. Nagel's arguments, phrased very differently, point in a similar direction to mine. See *The Possibility of Altruism* (Oxford, 1970).

(18) Sonnet, CXXIX:

All this the world well knows; yet none knows well
To shun the heaven that leads men to this hell.

(19) Spinoza, *Ethics*, Book II. See also the pertinent remarks by Ruskin concerning his 'Lamp of Obedience'.

(20) Le Clerc, *Traité d'Architecture* (Paris 1782 Art. v., p. 12). As a corrective to all this nonsense (I mean the nonsense involved in making a *premature* identification between the experience of architecture and that of the human body) it is worth remembering the equal number of architects who

have preferred to take trees rather than men as their main inspiration: for example, Palladio, *Quattro Libri* (Venice 1570) Bk. I. ch. xx and, of course, M. A. Laugier, in the *Essai sur L'architecture* (Paris 1753).

(21) On the moralism of the modern movement see the persuasive documentation and criticism in D. Watkin, *Morality and Architecture* (Oxford 1977), reiterating Geoffrey Scott's attack on the 'ethical fallacy', *The Architecture of Humanism* (London 1914) ch. V.

(22) *Vers Une Architecture*, p. 61.

(23) For a confused and rhetorical justification of this practice, see Alison and Peter Smithson, *Without Rhetoric – an Architectural Aesthetic 1955–1972* (London 1973).

(24) Sir Denys Lasdun, *RIBAJ* (September 1977).

BIBLIOGRAPHY

(1) THERE are few works of architectural theory which make any contribution to aesthetics, although there are many that claim to do so. It seems to me that the most reliable, and most interesting from the philosophical point of view, are:

L. B. ALBERTI, *De Re Aedificatoria,* Florence 1485, trans Bartolo and Leoni, London 1726, as *Ten Books of Architecture,* reprinted (ed. J. Rykwert), London 1965.

JOHN RUSKIN, *Seven Lamps of Architecture*, London 1849.

JOHN RUSKIN, *Stones of Venice,* London 1851 and 1853.

S. E. RASMUSSEN, *Experiencing Architecture*, Cambridge, Mass. 1959.

SINCLAIR GAULDIE, *Architecture,* London 1969.

GEOFFREY SCOTT, *The Architecture of Humanism,* London 1914, which remains the only modern attempt to defend classicism from a self-consciously philosophical standpoint.

SIR JOHN SUMMERSON, *Heavenly Mansions,* London 1949.

(2) For works of architectural theory and criticism which provide matter for philosophical enquiry and which cast light on the discussions in this book, the following are particularly important:

SIR JOHN SUMMERSON, *The Classical Language of Architecture*, London 1963. An excellent and clear account of classicism, with a useful bibliography of major sources.

SIR WILLIAM CHAMBERS, *Treatise on Civil Architecture*, London 1759. The most refined and reflective exposition of the Orders as these were understood at the time of their widest acceptance.

ADRIAN STOKES, *Stones of Rimini*, London 1934.

R. WITTKOWER, *Architectural Principles in the Age of Humanism*, London 1949,

3rd edn, 1962. An indispensible companion to the study of Renaissance theory.

H. WÖLFFLIN, *Renaissance and Baroque,* trans. K. Simon, London 1964. Still perhaps the most brilliant piece of architectural criticism in existence, and also the most succinct.

D. J. WATKIN, *Morality and Architecture,* Oxford 1977. A diagnosis of certain fallacies in architectural theory associated with the modern movement.

O. VON SIMSON, *The Gothic Cathedral,* New York 1956.

W. WORRINGER, *Form in Gothic,* London 1923.

For further works of theory and criticism the reader is referred to the notes.

(3) For works of philosophical aesthetics, relevant either to the present enquiry or generally, the following seem to me to be significant:

I. KANT, *Critique of Judgement.*

G. W. F, HEGEL, *Lectures of Aesthetics,* 1835, trans. T. M. Knox, London 1975.

F. SCHILLER, *On the Aesthetic Education of Man in a Series of Letters,* Oxford 1967.

B. CROCE, *Estetica,* Bari 1902.

R. G. COLLINGWOOD, *Principles of Art,* Oxford 1938.

M. DUFRENNE, *Phénoménologie de L'Expérience Ésthétique,* Paris 1953. A long-winded and derivative work, but clear and not technical.

R. WOLLHEIM, *Art and its Objects,* New York 1968. An introduction, with a useful bibliography, and many individual arguments of interest.

N. GOODMAN, *Languages of Art,* Indiana 1968. A difficult work, written in the spirit of analytical nominalism.

L. WITTGENSTEIN, *Lectures and Conversations on Aesthetics etc.,* ed. Barrett, Oxford 1966. This work requires a certain background understanding of Wittgenstein's philosophical position, which may be obtained from *The Philosophical Investigations,* Oxford 1952, and A. J. Kenny, *Wittgenstein,* London 1976.

It has often been pointed out that works of aesthetics in the analytical tradition tend to be philosophically slight and critically impoverished. The same is true of works on aesthetics in every other philosophical tradition. The reader in search of a comprehensive bibliography of this continuing intellectual disaster should consult: M. C. Beardsley, *Aesthetics, from Classical Greece to the Present,* New York and London 1966, and H. Osborne (ed.), *Aesthetics,* Oxford 1966.

INDEX OF NAMES

Aalto, Alvar, 219, 287
Ache, J-B., 272
Addison, Joseph, 280
Adorno, Theodor, 36, 271, 282
Ainslee, D., 267
Alain de L'Isle (Alanus de Insula), 274
Alberti, Leone Battista, 4, 23–5, 32, 36, 40, 47, 50, 58, 69, 93, 101, 102, 125, 132, 161, 174, 209, 210–11, 219, 223, 226, 229–30, 234, 251, 268, 269, 273, 277–8, 279, 284, 287, 291
Alexander, Christopher, 28f, 269, 271
Alford, D. E., 277
Allsop, Bruce, 267
Anscombe, G. E. M., 277, 280
Aquinas, St Thomas, 114, 266, 279
Archer, M., x
Areválo, Luis de, 208
Aristotle, 30, 239, 252, 271, 289
Arnold, Matthew, 289
Arup, Sir Ove, 270
Augustine, St, 59, 273–4, 279

Bach, J. S., 72, 179, 223
Balzac, Honoré de, 15
Banham, Reyner, 270, 271
Barbaro, Daniele, 288
Barrett, Father Cyril, 280
Barry, J. A., 272
Barthes, Roland, 162f, 283, 284
Bartolo, B., 268
Baudelaire, Charles, 165
Baumgarten, A. G., 269, 275
Beardsley, M. C., 273, 292
Beethoven, Ludwig van, 15, 86
Benjamin, Walter, 282
Bennett, J. F., 277
Berg, Alban, 286
Bernard of Clairvaux, St, 154
Bernini, Gianlorenzo, 69, 101, 102, 192–5, 275, 278
Birkhoff, G. D., 274
Black, M., 284
Blake, Peter, 270
Bloc, André, 8–9
Bloomster, W. V., 282
Boethius, 59, 273, 279
Boileau, L. C., 56–7
Borrisavlievitch, M., 265
Borromini, Francesco, 10, 47–8, 120–2, 200, 209, 216–17, 221, 279
Bosanquet, B., 280
Bostock, A., 274, 282
Bottomore, J. B., 283
Boullée, Étienne Louis, 26, 183
Boyce Gibson, W. W., 267, 276
Bradley, F. H., 244, 289
Brahms, Johannes, 15
Bramante, Donato (Donato di Pascuccio d'Antonio), 43, 172

Brentano, Franz, 266
Brown, Bernard, x
Brown, Maria Teresa, x
Brunelleschi, Filippo, 13, 64, 91, 223–4
Bucknell, B., 267, 279
Bullock, M., 272
Bullough, E., 266, 287
Burckhardt, Jacob, 53
Burke, Edmund, 280
Burns, Howard, x
Butler, R. J., 278, 280

Carlini, A., 284
Casey, John, x, 284, 289
Castilho, J. de, 8
Cavell, Stanley, 267
Chambers, Sir William, 171, 251, 275, 285, 287, 291
Choisy, A., 268
Chomsky, Noam, 284
Churchill, J. S., 276
Cicero, 60, 229, 288
Clifton-Taylor, Alec, 275
Cockerell, C. R., 176
Coleridge, S. T., 76, 276
Collingwood, R. G., 6–7, 75, 157, 267, 278, 283, 286
Collins, Peter, 280
Congreve, William, 196
Cooke, Deryck, 283
Croce, Benedetto, 267, 283, 286
Culler, Jonathan, 284

Dahlar, I., 287
Dante Alighieri, 73, 278
Davidson, Donald, 285
Dennett, D. C., 277, 289
Descartes, René, 58, 78, 244
Dluhosch, E., 269
Dostoevsky, Fyodor, 280
Dufrenne, Mikel, 276
Dummett, Michael, 266, 285, 287

Eco, Umberto, 163, 135–7, 283, 284
Edwards, A. Trystan, 132, 279
Ehrenzweig, Anton, 280
Einstein, Albert, 52
Elias, Norbert, 288
Eliot, George, 179
Eliot, T. S., 14, 82, 268
Elton, W., 278
Engels, Frederick, 281
Erasmus, 288
Esherick, Joseph, 25, 269
Euclid, 274
Evans, G., 285

Fischer, Ernst, 282
Fischer, von Erlach, J.B., 190
Fleming, J., 272
Fontana, Domenico, 243
Foot, Philippa, 271
Foster, L., 276
Fox, E., 281
Francia, P. de, 274
Frankl, Paul, 3, 43, 49–50, 53, 272
Freedman, R., 282
Frege, Gottlob, 164, 166, 176, 284, 285, 286, 287
Freud, Sigmund, 143, 154, 158, 162, 239, 252, 279, 280, 281
Fromm, Erich, 283
Fry, Maxwell, 227
Fuller, R. Buckminster, 271

Gabo, Naum, 268
Gasking, Douglas, 280
Gaudì, A., 7–9, 217
Gauldie, Sinclair, 138, 280, 291
Gautier, Théophile, 7
Geach, P. T., 284
Gendel, M., 272
Gibbs, James, 224
Giedion, Siegfried, 44, 51–7, 219, 267, 272, 287
Giorgio, Francesco di, 65
Giotto di Bondone, 104
Goebbels, Paul Joseph, 226, 288
Goethe, J. W. von, 268
Gombrich, Sir Ernst, 202, 272, 286, 292
Goodman, Nelson, 179–80, 283, 284, 285
Gowing, Sir Lawrence, 265, 280, 287
Greene, David, 271
Grice, H. P., 266, 278, 283
Gropius, Walter, 119, 173, 226, 288
Guarini, Guarino, 65, 214, 275, 287
Gwilt, Joseph, 287

Hamlyn, D. W., 276
Hampshire, S. N., 278
Hare, R. M., 289
Hawksmoor, Nicholas, 116, 175, 232
Heath, L., 274
Hegel, G. W. F., 5, 17, 52–3, 55, 58, 76, 151, 156–7, 187, 221, 239, 244, 245, 246, 247, 250, 251, 252, 265, 267, 271, 276, 278, 286, 289, 292
Heidegger, M., 276
Herder, J. G., 265
Hesselgren, S., 283, 286
Heyer, P., 269
Hogarth, W., 65, 219, 274
Homer, 52
Honour, H., 272

Horace, 229
Hottinger, M. D., 272
Hume, David, 75–7, 138, 139, 196, 276, 278, 279, 280
Husserl, E., 78, 267, 276
Huysmans, J. K., 115

Ingarden, R., 276

Jackson, A., 270
Jephsott, E., 288
Jencks, Charles, 268, 283
Jentsch, Anton, 128
Jones, Anthony, x
Jones, J. Christopher, 269, 270
Jones, Owen, 274
Jordan, R. Furneaux, 55
Jung, Carl, 144

Kandinsky, Wassily, 286
Kant, Immanuel, 1, 5, 10, 75–6, 77, 81, 234, 238, 244, 247, 265, 267, 271, 276, 277, 278, 279, 281, 288, 289, 292
Kaufmann, E., 268, 270
Kenny, A. J., 266, 275, 280, 292
Kerferd, G. B., 277
Klein, Melanie, 2, 144–7, 156–7, 219, 280
Klibansky, R., 273
Knight, R. P., 280
Knodel, A., 287
Knox, T. M. (Sir Malcolm), 267, 276, 279, 286
Koenig, G. K., 283, 284
Koffka, K., 266
Kohtz, Otto, 286
Kokoschka, Oskar, 286
Komarova, L., 269
Krail'nikov, N., 269
Kripke, Saul, 277
Kris, Ernst, 280

Lane, B. M., 288
Langer, S. K., 125, 272, 279, 285, 286
Langfeld, H. S., 287
La Penta, B. L., 282
Lasdun, Sir Denys, x, 43, 255–6, 270, 272, 290
Laugier, L'Abbé M. A., 290
Laurana, L., 149
Laver, James, 271
Leavis, F. R., 18
Le Clerc, S., 251, 289
Le Corbusier (C.–E. Jeanneret), 4, 30, 31, 59, 60, 61, 127, 132, 138, 161, 173, 234, 254, 268, 270, 271, 274
Ledoux, C.–N., 16, 26–7, 32, 268
Lenin, V. I., 283
Leonardo da Vinci, 281
Leoni, G., 268
Lethaby, W. R., 55, 272
Levi-Strauss, C., 284
Lewis, D. K., 284, 288, 289
Lipps, Th., 265–6
Lissitzky, El, 269
Locke, John, 247, 289
Longhena, B., 108
Lubetkin, B., 270
Lucács, G., 281
Lücke, H.–K., 288
Lutyens, Sir Edwin, 56

McCormick, E. J., 271
McDowell, J., 285
Macrobius, 59, 273
Magnini, 274
Maillart, R., 12, 56
Manet, E., 179
Mann, Thomas, 153, 283
Mansart, J. Hardouin, 54
March, L., 269, 270
Marcuse, A., 281
Martin, Sir Leslie, 268, 271
Marx, Karl, 158, 244, 282, 283
Masaccio, 180
Meager, R., x
Meller, James, 271
Mendelsohn, Erich, 105, 217
Meredith, George, 115
Meredith, J. C., 267
Merleau-Ponty, M., 78, 276
Meyer, Hannes, 270
Meyer, L. B., 283
Michelangelo Buonarroti, 43, 161, 163, 171, 172, 176, 183, 187, 232, 281
Michelozzo di Bartolommeo, 50, 127
Mies van der Rohe, L., 127, 213, 225, 253
Miki, Tokuchika, 190
Mill, J. S., 165, 285, 289
Millon, H., 273
Milton, John, 13
Minkowski, H., 52
Mishima, Yukio (Kimitake Hiroaka), 288
Mitchell, A. G., 282
Mitford, Nancy, 288
Mondrian, P., 179
Montague, Richard, 285
Moore, G. E., 275
Morris, C. W., 159, 284
Morris, William, 16
Mozart, W. A., 14, 15
Mumford, Lewis, 268
Munro, T., 266
Murray, Peter, 279

Nagel, T., 289
Negroponte, N., 271
Neri, St Philip, 120
Nervi, Pier Luigi, 271
Norberg-Schulz, C., 54, 272

Ogden, R. M., 266
O'Gorman, J. F., 272
Okakura, Teshin, 288
Osborne, H., 292

Paley, F. A., 287
Palladio, A., 65, 88, 90, 93, 96, 169, 171–2, 176, 225, 274, 289
Panofsky, E., 58, 124, 272–3, 275
Pascal, B., 54
Pasti, Matteo da, 273
Payne, E. F. J., 267, 279
Pehnt, W., 286
Peirce, C. S., 266
Perret, A., 56, 214
Peruzzi, B., 87, 91, 161
Pevsner, Sir Nicholas, 55, 193–4, 268, 272, 286
Pfister, O., 133
Pindar, 6
Plato, 59, 113, 157, 248, 273, 279
Plekhanov, G., 281
Poelzig, H., 191, 286
Pole, David, x
Popper, Sir Karl, 53, 272
Porden, W., 211
Porta, G. della, 186
Portoghesi, P., 283, 289
Pound, Ezra, 153
Prak, N. L., 279, 283
Price, V., 280
Pugin, A. W. N., 10, 17, 69, 106, 120, 174, 250, 252, 267, 275, 279
Pythagoras, 59, 62, 273

Quine, W. van O., 266
Quinton, A. M., 285
Quinton, M., 285

Rainaldi, C., 69, 275
Raphael, 181–2
Rasmussen, S. E., 278, 291
Rauch, G., 227
Ricardo, David, 151
Richards, I. A., 18
Riegl, Alois, 272
Robertson, H., 274
Rodchenko, A., 269
Romano, Giulio, 91, 161
Rorty, A. O., 289
Rothschild, V. K., x
Rotondi, P., 281
Rowe, Colin, 273
Ruskin, John, 4, 15, 17, 23, 41, 58, 72, 105, 109, 124, 125, 132, 146, 165, 173, 220, 222, 268, 269, 272, 278, 279, 281, 285, 287, 289, 291
Russell, Bertrand (Earl Russell), 287
Rykwert, J., 268

Sansovino, J., 65
Sartre, J.-P., 76, 78, 276
Saussure, F. de, 161–2, 284
Scheider, B., 284
Schelling, F., 84
Schiller, F., 265, 281, 292
Schinkel, K. F., 42, 125
Schoenberg, A., 14, 153, 283, 286
Scholfield, P. H., 274
Schopenhauer, A., 5, 11, 127, 132, 265, 267, 279
Schubert, F., 39
Scott, Geoffrey, 107–9, 278, 279, 291
Scott, Sir George Gilbert, 99, 173
Sedlmayer, H., ix, 272, 275, 286
Segal, Hannah, 143–4, 280
Serlio, S., 4, 36, 60, 66, 275, 279
Shakespeare, W., 15, 176, 180, 247–8, 289
Shaw, Norman, 167–8
Sibley, F. N., 278, 289
Simon, K., 272
Simson, O. von, 274, 275, 283, 292
Sixtus V, 243
Smith, Adam, 151
Smith, C., 276
Smythson, A., 290
Smythson, P., 290
Sparling, K., 288
Spinoza, B., 250, 289
Steiner, Rudolf, 189, 286
Stepanova, U., 269
Stevenson, C. L., 284
Stokes, Adrian, 144–50, 156, 219, 221, 251, 265, 272, 279, 280–1, 287, 291
Strachey, J., 280
Stravinsky, Igor, 16, 223, 287
Strawson, Sir Peter, 266, 276, 277, 284
Suger, Abbot of St, Denis, 15, 74
Sullivan, L. H., 10, 38, 267, 272
Summerson, Sir John, 17, 74, 84, 268, 275, 276, 278, 283, 291
Swanson, J. W., 276

Tafuri, Manfredo, 282
Tarski, A., 284, 285
Taut, B., 268, 269
Tavassila la Greca, B., 275, 287
Temanza, T., 274

Thomason, R. H., 285
Thornley, D. G., 269
Tovey, Sir Donald, 15

Vasari, G., 58–9, 273
Vasquez, F. M., 208
Venturi, R., 227
Verrochio, 99
Vignola, G. B. da, 4, 176
Viollet-le-Duc, E.-E., 10, 154, 173–4, 267, 271, 279
Virgil, 186
Vitale, S., 267
Vitruvius, 4, 16, 58, 61, 92, 196, 202, 227, 251, 273, 274, 275, 277, 286, 288
Volkelt, W., 265–6
Voysey, C. F. A., 29, 161

Waelder, R., 280
Wagner, R., 13, 72
Warnock, Mary, 276
Watkin, David, x, 55, 272, 289, 292
Webb, P., 163
Wegerner, P. 191
Weill, Kurt, 286
Weisbach, Werner, 279
Wiggins, D., 271
Wilkinson, E. M., 287
Wilkinson, M., 281
Williams, B. A. O., 275, 278
Williams, R., 281
Willoughby, C. A., 281
Wimsatt, W. K., 273
Wittgenstein, L., 30, 76, 147, 276, 277, 278, 279, 280, 281, 286, 292
Wittkower, R., 267, 273, 274, 275, 277, 278, 288, 291
Wolff, Hugo, 38
Wölfflin, H., 43, 53, 156–7, 198, 217, 250, 251, 272, 274, 283, 292
Wollheim, R., 272, 280, 283, 285, 286, 292
Worringer, W., 221, 272, 287, 292
Wotton, Sir Henry, 18, 58, 268, 273
Wren, Sir Christopher, 97, 116, 214, 216
Wright, Frank Lloyd, 71
Wright, L. von, 277
Wundt, W., 265
Wyatt, L. W., 211

Zevi, B., 43, 44, 272
Zucker, P., 280

INDEX OF SUBJECTS

Figures in *italics* refer to plate numbers

aesthetic attitude, 18–19, 206, 287
aesthetic education, 34–5, 176, 243f
aesthetic judgement, 103–4;
  sensuous element in, 113–14
aesthetics: nature of, 1, 5f, 24f, 34f;
  distinction from architectural theory, 4–5
alienation, 35, 156, 222, 245
ambiguity in architecture, 87f, 200
appearance, 34f, 63f, 96f, 107f, 125–30, 154–5, 199–200, 225f
appropriate, concept of, 24, 33f, 69–70, 103, 133, 176, 198, 201f, 209f, 225f, 240
architectural theory, distinct from aesthetics, 4–5
architecture as science, 28f
art: abstract, 5, 179ff; autonomy of, 17; decorative, 1x, 8, 222f, 228; distinction from craft, 6–7, 267; distinction between public and private, 13f, 249f; forms of, 4–5; modern concept of, 1–19
art nouveau, 130, 267
association of ideas, 138–43, 174, 186, 196, 197–8
attention: relation, to aesthetic judgement, 73, 112, 130, 143, 147, 185–6, 198, to pleasure, 112, to imagery, 77–8; imaginative, 94, ch. 3

baroque: concrete, 219; Edwardian, 167f; Spanish, 207; ships, 125–7; conception of space, 56; criticism of Renaissance ideas of proportion, 65; general, 88, 116, 122–4
base/superstructure, 151f, 282
Bauhaus, the, 56, 119, 132, 138, 227
beauty, 141, 153, 161; common to the arts, 4; 'dependent b', 9–10, 267; definition of, 209, 226, 233–5; distinction from ornament, 101, 125
birdsong, 80f, 95
breasts, 144, 146, 147
building, distinct from architecture, 23

Cartesian theory of mind, 58, 78–9, 244f, 250, 273
carving, 45, 219f, 272
causes: distinct from objects, 112–13, 139–43; distinct from reasons, 110–11, 198f; relation to meaning, 159
Christianity, 73, 146
Churrigueresque, 207
Cistercian style, 154
class, 151–2

classicism, 226–7, 232, 253–6
clothes, 33, 222, 240–1, 271
composition, in painting, 182
consistency in aesthetic judgement, 116–17, 119f, 130
constructivism, 25–6, 38, 153, 155, 156, 269–70
convention, 159, 202, 228; *see also* rules
corners, 23, 223–6
correctness in experience, 92, 103, 107, 109, 119, 133, 201f
Counter-Reformation, 120
criticism, 17, 42–3, 56–7, 69, 107f, 120f, 130, 137, 139f, 198f, 205, 225f, 241–3

demystification, 150–1, 152
design, 23
design theory, 25f, 228, 269
desires, 32, 245–6; sexual, 157, 247–8
detail, significance of, 67–8, 172–3, 203, 205, 206–36

Ecclesiastical buildings:
Abbeys:
Abbey Church, Grussau, 128, *49*
Abbey Church Ottobeuren, 129
Westminster Abbey, 175
Cathedrals:
Amiens, 84, *24*
Coventry, 99
Ely, Lady Chapel, 45
Lincoln, 2, 54, 119
Nôtre Dame de Chartres, 67, 99, 102, 204
Nôtre Dame de Paris, 44, 101, *10*
Peterborough, 174, *58*
Rouen, 184, 220–1
S. Maria dei Fiori, Florence, 13, 223;
– campanile, 104–5
– Baptistery, 97
St Paul's, London, 42, 44, 66, 69, 116, 216
St Peter's, Rome, 43, 44, 69, 223, *9*
– piazza, 10, 69, 96, 101
Westminster Cathedral, 54
Churches:
Karlskirche, Vienna, 190, *66*
Nôtre Dame du Haut, Ronchamp, 11
Pazzi Chapel, S. Croce, Florence, 154–5, 223–4, *83*
Il Redentore, Venice, 96, 169, *55*
St Anne, Limehouse, 116, *39*
S. Annenkirche, Annaberg, 139, *52*
S. Apollinare Nuovo, Ravenna, 91, *29*
St Bride's, London, 10, 116, *38*
S. Carlo alle Quattro Fontane (S. Carlino), Rome, 11, 48, 200, 216, 217, *15*, *71*, *78–81*
S. Caterina dei Funari, Rome, 185, *64*
S. Coloma de Cervelló, Chapel of Colonia Güell, 7, *1*
S. Costanza, Rome, 92
St Denis, abbey church, 15, 74
St Eustache, Paris, 12, 163, *3*
S. Francesco, Rimini, 47, 50, 150, *12*
S. Giorgio Maggiore, Venice, 225, *84*
S. Giorgio in Velabro, Rome, 91
S. Giovanni in Oleo, Rome, 209, *73*
S. Giustina, Padua, 18
S. Ivo, Rome, 47f., *13*, *14*
S. Lorenzo, Florence, 92; old sacristy, 64; new sacristy, 187, 192–3, *65*, *68*, *69*
S. Maria Annunziata, Florence, 50
S. Maria in Campitelli, Rome, 254, *90*
S. Maria dei Carceri, Prato, 224
S. Maria della Consolazione, Todi, 223
St Mary, Finedon, 41, *6*
S. Maria delle Grazie, Milan, 60
S. Maria Novella, Florence, 40, *5*
S. Maria della Pace, Rome, 96
S. Maria del Popolo, Rome, 69
S. Maria della Salute, Venice, 107–9, *35*
S. Maria della Vittoria, Cornaro Chapel, Rome, 193–5, *70*
St Mary le Strand, London, 224
St Mary Woolnoth, London, 233, *88*
S. Ouen, Rouen, 165
St Pancras, London, 14
S. Paolo fuori le Mura, Rome, 109, 119, *36*
S. Pietro in Montorio, Rome, Tempietto, 172, 209, 214, *77*
S. Sophia, Constantinople, 223
S. Spirito, Florence, 44, 90–2, 102, *11*
Ste. Sulpice, Paris, 68
Trinità dei Monti, Rome, 69
Others:
Charterhouse, Granada, 207, *72*
Oratory of St Philip Neri, Rome, 120–2, 204, *40–4*
Vatican Palace, 69
empathy (*einfüllung*), 266
empiricism, 111, 138, 245
ends/means, 6–7, 30f, 203, 227–8, 230
Enlightenment, the, 26, 75
ensemble, 11–12, 69
entasis, 142
essential properties 38–40, 47f, 55, 70
experience 1, 3, 71, 74f, 204; aesthetic, 75f; of architecture, 84f, and *passim*: relation to thought, 74f, to taste 106f; unconscious, 149
expression, 5, 7f., 13f, 41, 54, 162, 179, 187–205
expressionism, 6–8, 189–91, 286

façades, 253–4
faculties, 1, 75, 106
fantasy, 144, 202, 205, 252–3
function, 2, 107, 165–6, 167, 240, 241; virtual, 125f
functionalism, 3, 6–7, 38–43, 97–8, 106–7, 249, 267; as critical doctrine, 124–30

Gesamtkunstwerk, 211
Gestalt psychology, 86
Golden Section, 17, 61f
Gothic revival, 16, 116, 125, 138, 152, 154
grammar, nature of, 163f

happiness, 31, 240, 244–5
harmony, 59f
historical determinism, 55, 154
'historicism': Pevsner's usage, 272; Popper's usage, 54, 55, 272

iconography, 150, 190
idealism, 5, 138, 247–53, 265, 275
ideology, 151f
imagination, 32; theory of, 75ff; in architectural experience, 87f
incompatible counterparts, 81
individualism, 248–50
intention: in art, 57–8, 160, 204; in language, 159f
intentional fallacy, 58, 273
intentionality (direction upon an object), 3, 70, 73, 112–13, 139–40, 266–7
internal relations, 73, 112–13, 138, 275
international style, 226 *see also* modern movement
introspection, 77–8

jealousy, 3

Kunstgeschichte, 17, 52–7, 120, 150
Kunstwollen, 17, 57–8

language: nature of, 158–78; analogy with architecture, 167f, 174–8, 207–8, 283
Leninism, 155, 270
linguistics, 150

mannerism, 88, 171–2; and ambiguity, 91
manners, 228–30, 288
Marxism, 24, 36, 150–7, 158–9, 162, 245, 281–2
mathematics: in relation to architectural beauty, 58f, 273; in relation to the theory of design, 23f
meaning, 158f, 202; natural versus non-natural, 159, 165, 167
means, *see* ends
mediaevalism, 10, 16
menues, structure of, 162–3
metaphor, 83
modelling, 45, 219f
modernism, 13f, 173
modern movement, 13, 211–14, 219
modulor, 61f
monasticism, 109
moralism, 17, 290
morality, 236–56
moral judgement, 115–16, 119, 204, 205, 229–32, 238
mouldings, 127–8, 134, 207, 204, 220–1, 253

needs (versus desires, and versus values), 31, 112–13
neo-classicism, 11, 106, 234; in music, 16
neo-Platonism, 59f, 65, 73, 234, 273–4
niches, 214f

objectivity in aesthetics, 115, 130–4, 137–8, 209, 236, 237–56
Orders, the, 61, 65, 72, 92–3, 163, 231; theory of, 161, 172, 184
ornament, 10, 67–8, 98, 101, 125, 172–3, 222; distinguished from representation, 184–5

pattern, 97
perception, 74f; literal *v.* imaginative, 78, 86–7, 103, 221
perspective, 65–6
phenomenology, 78–9, 83, 267, 276
philosophy, nature of, 1–19, 266
place, sense of, 10f
pleasure: aesthetic, 71f, 111f; intellectual, 74f, 112f; sensuous, 32, 71–2, 111, 113, 115, 147; sexual, 72, 73, 112
politics and architecture, 15, 268
practical reason, 1, 30f, 114, 118–19, 198f, 205, 207, 225f, 230f, 238–56, 265; distinguished from theoretical reason, 30f, 240f
privileged access, 139–43
proportion, 58–70, 210–11, 233–5, 274
psychoanalysis, 143–50, 156
psychology: in criticism 138–57; of art, 265–6; distinguished from philosophy, 1f, 75, 84

rationality (see also practical reason): 25f, 72f, 90, 96, 104f, 117–18, 132, 239–56
Reason, 25, 32, 134

reference, 166, 179–80, 187, 285, 286
Renaissance, 24, 38, 53, 36, 58ff, 92, 154, 214
representation, 5, 179–87; distinguished from imitation, 180, 182–3; from resemblance, 181–2
Revolution; French, 25, Russian, 25, Industrial, 35, 152
rococo, 128f
romanesque, 109, 154
rules: in architecture, 167, 171–3, 227, 238; in art, 160f, 238

Scholasticism, 70
sculpture: distinguished from architecture, 7–9; architectural effect of, 45, 99–100, 184–5
Secular buildings:
- Ashmolean Museum, Oxford, 176, *59*
- Baker House, Harvard, 219
- Battersea Power Station, London, 34
- Barbican, London, 10, 213
- Bon Marché, Paris, 56–7, *16*
- Brasilia, Brasil, 211
- Ca d'Oro, Venice, 67, *23*
- Cancelleria, Rome, 62–3
- Carlton House Terrace, London, 40
- Casa Mila, Barcelona, 217
- Centre Pompidou, Paris, 40, 41
- Chandigarh, India, 211
- Chelsea Water Pump, 34
- Doge's Palace, Venice, 58, 209
- Downing College, Cambridge, 211, *74*, *75*
- Ducal Palace, Urbino, 145–9, *53*
- Einstein Tower, Potsdam, 104–5, 217
- Elephant and Castle Complex, London, 162
- Farnsworth House, Plano, Ill., 253
- German Pavilion, Barcelona Exhibition, 213
- Heathrow Air Terminal, London, 42
- Helblinghaus, Innsbrück, 129
- Horlicks Factory, Slough, 152
- Lansdowne Crescent, Bath, 219
- Laurentian Library, Florence, 14, 172
- Lenin Mausoleum, Moscow, 191
- Library of St Marks, Venice, 65, *21*
- Old Schools, Cambridge, 72
- Palazzo Chiericati, Vicenza, 93, *32*
- Palazzo dei Conservatori, Rome, 163
- Palazzo Grimani, Venice, 173
- Palazzo Massimi, Rome, 87–8, 90, *26*
- Palazzo Medici, Florence, 127, *46*
- Palazzo Pisani-Moreta, Venice, 85–6, *25*
- Palazzo Pitti, Florence, 97
- Palazzo Rucellai, Florence, 93, 94
- Palazzo Valmarana, Vicenza, 171–2, 175, *56*, *57*
- Palazzo Venezia, Rome, 127, *47*
- Palazzo Zuccari, Rome, 183, *61*
- Panthéon, Paris, 65–6, 69, *22*
- Pantheon, Rome, 50, 216, 220
- Parthenon, Athens, 142, 153, 221
- Piccadilly Hotel, London, 167–8, 172, *54*
- Piazza del Campidoglio, Rome, 97, *33*
- Piazza del Popolo, Rome, 69
- Piazza S. Marco, Venice, 11
- Quetzalpapolotl's Palace, Mexico, 62
- Quirinal Hill, Rome, 232, *87*
- RAC Club, London, 42, 165
- Round House Theatre, London, 40
- St Katherine's Docks, London, 139, 153, *51*
- St Pancras's Station, London, 173
- Seagram Building, New York, 214, 225, *85*
- Spanish Steps, Rome, 69
- Statione Termini, Rome, 44
- Sydney Opera House, Sydney, 11, 184, 220
- Taj Mahal, Agra, 54, 191
- Theatre of Marcellus, Rome, 93, *31*
- Tower of Peace, Hiroshima, 190
- Treasury of Atreus, Mycenae, 44
- Trinity College Library, Cambridge, 97
- Unité d'Habitation, Marseilles, 161
- Victor-Emmanuel Monument, Rome, 191
- Villa Cornaro, Piombino d'Este, 88, *27*
- Villa Savoie, Poissy, 54
- Wax Laboratories, Racine, Wisconsin, 71
- Westbourne Park Villas, London, 231, *86*
- Wolverhampton Brewery, 211

selfconsciousness, 78f, 133, 148, 245–7
self-knowledge, 156, 240, 244–56
semantic theory of art, 160, 202
semiology, 160, 161f, 176–7, 187, 284
semiotics, 160
space, 43–52; musical, 81–2
space-time, 51–2, 54
spirit of the age (*Zeitgeist*), 13, 52f
streets, 242–3, 249–50, 254
structuralism, 160, 162
style, 15–16, 33f, 55–6, 174–7, 201f, 222–4, 226f
superstructure, *see* base
syntax: in architecture, 160f, 162, 174; relation to semantics, 164–5, 166, 174, 177; distinct from style, 174–6

taste, 3, 104–34, 201f
tea ceremony, 228–9, 288
technique, 12–13
truth: relation, to meaning, 164, to objectivity, 237–8, to reason, 240, to representation, 180

unconscious, the, 144–50, 162
understanding: relation to experience, 101; representational art, 180
unity, 11, 98–102, 173–5
utilitarianism, 111, 244–5, 246

value, 6–7, 31f, 114–16, 239f, 246; aesthetic, 34, 113, 146; moral, 238ff
vernacular, 16–17, 128, 214, 230f
Vitruvian categories, 58f

wine, 115–16, 120, 227

LIBRARY OF CONGRESS CATALOGING IN PUBLICATION DATA

Scruton, Roger.
The aesthetics of architecture.

(Princeton essays on the arts; 8)
Bibliography: p.
Includes indexes.
1. Architecture. I. Title.
NA2500.S43 720'.1 79-84026
ISBN 0-691-03948-8
ISBN 0-691-00322-X pbk.